Some Political & Social Ideas of
ENGLISH DISSENT

Some Political & Social Ideas of
ENGLISH DISSENT
1763–1800

BY

ANTHONY LINCOLN

1971

OCTAGON BOOKS
New York

Originally published in 1938

Reprinted 1971

*by special arrangement with the Financial Board, The Old Schools,
University of Cambridge*

OCTAGON BOOKS

A DIVISION OF FARRAR, STRAUS & GIROUX, INC.

19 Union Square West

New York, N. Y. 10003

LIBRARY OF CONGRESS CATALOG CARD NUMBER: 72-120642

ISBN 0-374-95012-1

Printed in U.S.A. by
NOBLE OFFSET PRINTERS, INC.
NEW YORK 3, N. Y.

For

NEWTON BRANCH

Contents

Foreword

I desire to thank the Master and Fellows of my college, Magdalene, for giving me the opportunity of writing this book; the Adjudicators of the Prince Consort Prize for the facilities for revision which they have afforded me; and the Trustees of the Dr Williams' Trust for their kind permission to utilize certain manuscripts in their possession. In addition I wish particularly to express my gratitude to Dr Ernest Barker for the help and encouragement which I have received from him.

A. H. L.

September 1937

Chapter I

INTRODUCTION

SOME *Political and Social Ideas of English Dissent* is designed partly as a study of a phase in the history of English opinion in the eighteenth century, and partly as an essay upon the evolution of certain political ideas in England. As a study in opinion, it endeavours to assess the reactions of a large and peculiarly situated group of men and women to the many revolutions, political and intellectual, which marked the momentous years between 1763 and 1800. These years seemed replete with promise to that great concourse of the unprivileged in whose van stood the English Protestant Dissenters, united in their belief that the time of deliverance from religious bondage and political exile was at last upon them. In the course of examining the nature of, and justification for, this optimism, some attempt has been made to survey the unmapped valley of change lying between the Great Rebellion and the French Revolution, from its progress through which English Dissent emerged so altered in character and creed.

As an essay on the history of certain political theories, this book endeavours to trace the significant process of evolution by which Christian liberties became merged into 'natural' liberties and the particular privileges claimed in virtue of Christian conscience and Christian

salvation came to be transformed into the rights belonging to all men. As an outcome of this transference
from a religious on to a juridical plane, political theory
among the English Dissenters resolved itself into an
elaboration of two articles in the code of the Rights of
Man and Citizen: the right to freedom of conscience
without civil detriment and the right to the political
carrière ouverte aux talents. But if the attainment of these
two rights was the practical sum of their philosophy,
there was no uniformity among their protagonists. The
two leading dissenting thinkers, Richard Price and
Joseph Priestley, differed radically on the cardinal questions which divided the philosophers of their times.
Despite this diversity, however, a study of dissenting
literature of this period demonstrates the existence in
England of an indigenous and mature school of natural-
right politics, to which the French Revolution and its
ideology came as a confirmation rather than an inspiration.

But it is not easy to confine universalist principles
within the bounds of a nation, and the strenuous attempt
during the years 1772–90 to materialize dissenting political theory by the legislative achievement of the two
primary rights, an attempt which might be called
England's unsuccessful Revolution, was a first intimation
of a coming contest between Church and State; a contest
which was to blend the history of the nineteenth century
in Europe into a synthesis of the red and the black. That
that contest never developed so acute a form in England
was not for want of effort on the part of the dissenting
publicists.

But while in the sober language of enlightened reason the dissenting philosophers sought to achieve the complete secularization of politics in England, they worked in an intellectual and spiritual atmosphere no less intense and catastrophic in its sort than that which had fired their forefathers in the seventeenth century. For the English Dissenters, as for many others, the closing years of the eighteenth century were impassioned with expectation. "As I am a believer in Revelation", wrote the dissenting attorney Nash in his Reply to the *Reflections on the French Revolution*, "I, of course, live in the hope of better things; a millennium (not a fifth monarchy, Sir, of enthusiasts and fanatics), but a new heaven and a new earth in which dwelleth righteousness; or, to drop the eastern figure and use a more philosophic language, a state of equal liberty and equal justice for all men." Few who cherished that hope lived to see its realization. Indeed, the friends of freedom were destined to experience an intellectual disillusionment of a poignancy rarely equalled in history. Perhaps, for this reason, they may command the sympathy of those of us who, living in times which Richard Price would certainly have considered as of consummate political unrighteousness, still strive to remain faithful to the principles of European liberalism.

Chapter II

THE DISSENTING INTEREST

It hath often been doomed to Death and yet it still survives.
EDMUND CALAMY

They are all Whigs, enemies to arbitrary power, and firmly
attached to those principles of civil and religious liberty, which
produced the Glorious Revolution and the Hanoverian Succession.
RICHARD PRICE

THE HISTORY of English Protestant Dissent in
the eighteenth century is the history of a losing
battle against tradition. Just as the Roman
Catholics during a century and a half after 1688 suffered
as victims of a formula; that formula of 'Popery and
arbitrary power' which crystallized the theory and
apology of the Glorious Revolution; a formula which
the reformers of the Revolution Society, a hundred
years later,[1] had not yet unlearned, similarly in the century of Hume and Gibbon, the Protestant Dissenters
were remembered and condemned as sectaries and king-
killers. Their every activity, however consonant with the
intellectual fashion and tastes of their times, was rigidly

[1] Cf. Preamble to the Declaration of the Revolutionary Society, 4
November 1789: "this society, sensible of the important advantages
arising to this country by its deliverance from Popery and Arbitrary
power...." *Correspondence of the Revolution Society*, London, 1792.
A more picturesque form is "Romish superstition and French
Government", 13 Will. III, c. 3. 1.

scrutinized and interpreted in the light of the past, and in an age remarkable for its vivid interest in political forms and political practice, their most timid speculations were denied the indulgence of contemporary culture, and marked down as incantations over the spirit of the old Puritanism and their authors labelled as Commonwealth's men,[1] descendants of a congenitally perverse race whom no degree of discipline could chasten. Nor was this prejudice against them unlettered. Joseph Priestley in 1767 might complain of the ignorance of most people, even educated people,[2] about dissenting principles; but it was well-documented misinterpretation rather than ignorance. No profession of *candour* on the Dissenters' part seemed able to embarrass their critics' appeal to history. In its essence, perhaps, the prejudice against them was religious, and remained religious at the core, although a hundred lesser dislikes, bred from differences of living and thinking, formed around that core until nothing save an even surface of political hatred and distrust remained visible. This process of accretion, however, remained for a long time unseen and all but unsensed. During the first half of the century old feuds rested, while by dint of patient experiment the Hanoverian dynasty came to terms with the Anglican

[1] Another technical term, a favourite in Molesworth's day; cf. Preface to *Franco-Gallia*, 1721, part of the Whig apocrypha.

[2] *View of the Principles and Conduct of Protestant Dissenters*, 1767, 338: the whole trouble is that public prejudice has been falsely moulded by the single fact of the fall of Church and Monarchy under Charles I, *ibid.* 357–61. Modern Dissenters have nothing in common with their forefathers; so Towers, *Letters to Samuel Johnson*, 1775, 227.

Church. But once the Alliance was certain beyond all disturbance the days of tranquillity were at an end, and the old cry was heard again, growing sharper and more audible with the increasing gravity of each political crisis, as the great changes of the second fifty years accelerated and intensified the rhythm of events.

That cry was the appeal to history; to the execution of Charles and to the disestablishment of the Church by those whose descendants were now welcoming the French Revolution and clamouring against the Test Act:

> History thy page unfold;
> Did not their sires of old
> Murder the King?[1]

The same enthusiasm for history and its lessons inspired the pamphleteers:[2] *A Scourge for the Dissenters* of 1790 instances their black record in the past as an estimate of their probable future conduct: "Look at the last century", urges another, which provides a documented

---

[1] *Old Mother Church.* Cf.

> "Sedition is their creed;
> Feigned sheep but wolves indeed,
> How can we trust?
> Gunpowder Priestley would,
> Deluge the throne with blood,
> And lay the great and good
> Low in the dust. etc."

[2] *A Scourge for the Dissenters or Nonconformity Unmasked, by an Ecclesiastic,* 1790: *Look at the Last Century or the Dissenters weighed in their own Scales,* London, 1790: the author says "their ideas of liberty went full as far as any in the present day: they contended for their natural rights, the just rights and prerogatives of man—and what do the Dissenters more?"

survey of the attitude of seventeenth-century Dissent to liberty and toleration, and an assurance that time has wrought little change; sectaries are still as they ever were: "overthrowing all, being *vertiginosi spiritus*, whirligig spirits."[1] More redolent of the gutter, but of even more pungent conviction, were the publications of the government pensioner Shebbeare, who saw in his opponents "the spawn of those who were uniformly rebels to the best of Kings".[2] Gilbert Wakefield's 'constitutional layman' describes them as "a set of puritanical republican rebels—sworn enemies to our King, our bishops our clergy and the whole Church".[3] "The descendants of the Puritans", says a writer in the *Anti-Jacobin*, "are still found among us in great numbers; they retain the same principles which in England and America have produced so much disturbance; they have come, by their offspring and their seminaries, to transmit those principles to their posterity; and they have, with few exceptions, admired, extolled, even encouraged and promoted, to the utmost of their power, the French Revolution, because it was founded upon their prin-

[1] *Gangraena*, Epistle Dedicatory.

[2] *Answer to quaeries...in a letter to Dr Shebbeare*. He speaks of "the infernal altar of Presbyterian Perfidy in whose religion regicides alone are saints"; cf. his spiritual predecessor Jeffries, C.J., to the jury in the trial of Rev. Thomas Rosewell for high treason Oct.–Nov. 1684: "from these seminaries of sedition and faction, these conventicles and the clubs and cabals of discontented, irregular people, disaffected to the laws both of Church and State, was the great mischief and confusion that was brought upon us, and which at length brought us into the distraction of the late times."

[3] Gilbert Wakefield, *Cursory Reflections*. 1790, 20.

ciples."[1] These examples need not be multiplied in order
to emphasize their significance: their language is the
language of those studious and unshakable in the judgments of history. The testimony of history was reinforced
by the prevailing belief in the existence of fixed and
unchanging principles: A man is most intimately known
by his creed and the springs of action are uniform; what
a Dissenter was capable of doing yesterday affords a
measure of his activities to-day and a fair forecast of his
conduct to-morrow.

The Dissenters themselves, conscious of this heritage,
were divided in their loyalties. In their defensive publications it was their constant purpose to appear as the
makers of the Glorious Revolution, as pure Whigs in
Church and State, ruling in apostolic succession after
Sidney and Locke. This presentation of themselves, if a
little strained and inclining to intellectual discomfort, was
more credible than the tortured analogies of their opponents. But on the whole the Dissenters would gladly
have dispensed with political history. Modest heroes of
Britain's day of freedom, they were willing to forget the
slaughtered saints and the debt due to them from a grate-
ful nation. "They think that they should let the dead bury
their dead and trouble themselves about nothing but
their interest as citizens of heaven."[2] Between them and
their forefathers, they would contend, there was nothing
but a common religious bond. But it was precisely this
generous abnegation that their opponents would not

[1] *Anti-Jacobin*, 1799, II, 87.
[2] *View of the Principles*, 1767, 356.

allow them to make. History held the field and time and again the Dissenters were forced back to unsuccessful interpretation. The more they disguised themselves as the men of '88, the more surely they were recognized as the men of '49. At decisive moments, too, ancient loyalty would often oust prudence, and the proud memory of their past would be given to the world from their own lips. "We are generally zealous friends to liberty civil and religious", wrote Samuel Palmer, "and we think we understand it better than our forefathers did."[1] Uttered in the face of public opinion, these declarations were not without a certain impetuous nobility, when it is remembered that each fresh profession furnished a new text for a treasury pamphleteer, marshalled another vote against the repeal of the Test Acts. "To spread the knowledge of human rights, to extend the blessings of justice and liberty and promote peace on earth and goodwill among men...are the principles of the derided religion of the Protestant Dissenters",[2] wrote a champion of the Revolution Society in 1792, but they were unarmed prophets and the walls of Jericho were deaf to their summons. Each fresh assault against established institutions left the attackers less co-ordinated, more individualistic and impotent than before.

Victims of a sort of political original sin, they retained the mentality of revolt, and although many sank indistinguishably into the ordinary life and accepted standards

[1] *Vindication of the Modern Dissenters*, 1790.
[2] *Vindication of the Revolution Society...against Mr Burke*, 1792, 57; cf. Hazlitt: "the old Dissenters indeed, I look upon as the nursing fathers of our liberties."

of the country, there always remained some few who questioned, and though unanswered, were not disheartened. These embodied what Edmund Burke, in another connection, called the protestantism of the Protestant religion. Their protest, it is true, would not have excited much sympathy among their ancestors of the previous century. Their clarion was cast in a different mould with a far more modern ring to it, while, up to 1763, save for brief interludes, there was none of the excitement of the Civil War, and no imminent millennium dominating and complicating the ways of everyday living.

But one great principle which they had inherited was still fresh in their hearts, and lay at the centre of all that the Dissenters thought and wrote, linking them spiritually with the storms and stress of the seventeenth century. That principle was the natural right to freedom of conscience, which has, perhaps, played a more stimulating part in the development of political thought in England than all the rest of the rights of man and citizen put together. This was not only a principle implicit in human nature, a right innate in the heart of every man, constituting the essence of personality and freedom; it had also the quality of a Divine command, doubly enforced by the God of Nature and the God of Revelation; expressed in an inner voice which must be made articulate. It was an appeal away from all earthly sovereignties, something like Locke's 'Appeal to Heaven'. It implied that there were certain issues so fundamental, that no municipal laws or conventions, no social or conventional machinery, could compass or even approach them, but which could be resolved only in the reason and conscience of the individual: an inner sanctuary into which all commands of priests and magistrates penetrated only as idle, meaningless echoes. The right itself was inalienable, a property of which a man could not dispossess himself even if he would.[1] It was a positive duty as well as a negative right; not only are there certain specific matters in which a man must reply solely according to his conscience; but a man must also follow the directions of conscience; must step out boldly no matter whither he be led. In time this spiritual duty transcended its religious character and began to embrace the sphere of secular learning, and to translate itself into a duty, such as we find in the writings of Joseph Priestley, of ceaseless intellectual investigation in metaphysics, science and politics no less than in theology. As a dynamic force this duty could hardly remain unfulfilled in an age impassioned by an intense intellectual activity; as the accepted tenet of a distinct social group its sociological implications could hardly be disguised. Even enemies were impressed by this driving force.[2] Inspired by belief in this right, and stimulated by the consciousness of this duty, the intellectual elements among the Dissenters combined as individuals and as a social

[1] Locke, *Letters on Toleration*, ed. 1813, III, 11. The idea is in Fownes, Robinson, Priestley, etc.

[2] E.g. "truly it is an amazing consideration what power and influence this Enthusiastick Cant has had in all the civil wars and disturbances of Europe and particularly in our own Kingdom." Henry Sacheverell, *Nature and Mischief of Prejudice and Partiality*, 1703, 14.

group to place, as it were, a mark of interrogation against all that was accepted as axiomatic and authoritative by contemporaries, above all against political axioms relating to the sovereignty of Parliament and the province of the State.

Enjoying a unique education and socially and politically distinguished from the great bulk of the community, the Nonconformists constituted a separate group, the Dissenting Interest, which coalesced with the other 'interests', landed, commercial, monied and labouring,[1] to stabilize the political and social balance of England in the eighteenth century. These 'interests' defied close definition; perhaps they represented nothing so much as psychological entities visible in society, to capture and conciliate which was the aim of the political parties; a sort of cross-section of public opinion influencing party politics obliquely and indirectly. Thus, without suspicion of inconsistency, a man could remain firm in his Interest, and, at the same time, indulge in all the fashionable and conventional denunciation of the 'rags', 'demons' and 'frenzies' of party. "I profess myself", wrote Thomas Belsham, "not the man of a party but the servant of the Dissenting Interest."[2] This disavowal of faction, however, did not prevent the formation of groups within the Interest itself; and faithful to the spirit of the age, the city-dwelling Dissenter tended to

[1] Arthur Young's enumeration.
[2] Williams, *Life*, 307. Letter to Richards, February 1786; cf. Hall: "Parties are founded on principles, factions on men." *Freedom of the Press*, 114-15.

despise his country brethren.[1] Unlike its limits, the personnel of the Interest is pretty easy to define: it was drawn almost exclusively from the middle ranks of society. "The main body of Dissenters", wrote John White, "are mostly found in cities and great towns, among the trading part of the people", while their ministers were "chiefly of the middle rank of men, having neither poverty nor riches."[2] That was in 1746, but by 1763 the wealth of the Dissenters was on the increase. They had caught the changing economic tide and prospered, although riches combined with fashion and indifference to diminish their numbers. "Sober industry and an assiduous pursuit of their temporal affairs was considered as becoming their profession... in consequence of this bankruptcy in a Dissenter was then almost unknown."[3] The social dimensions of the

[1] Wakefield, *Life*, 1792, 212. "The city Dissenters, puffed up with a most plentiful portion of the wind of self-sufficiency, affected to despise their brethren in the country...as mere ignoramuses."

[2] J. White, D.D., *Letter to a Gentleman Dissenting*, 1746, 91; cf. "the members of their body seldom are above the middle class of society and their ministers are plain men, who could not figure among the gay and great." Bogue and Bennett, IV, 322.

[3] Bogue and Bennett, II, 174. Cf. White, *op. cit.* 10: "If I had a son brought up in any trade and had no consideration either for him or myself of another world, I should be ready to say to him at setting up—*my son, get Money, and, in order to do that, be a Dissenter.*" A correspondent in the *Gentleman's Magazine*, 1791, says dissenting property is considerable and "chiefly vested in commercial stock or the machinery of manufactories", 1791, II, 924 *et. seq.* Cf. George Walker, *Dissenter's Plea*, 1790, 41–2: "The poor house, the work house, and the prison receive few dissenters. And can there on earth be a higher encomium of a religion than that it produces few criminals and few Paupers?"

Interest were clear; it did not seek to embrace those in the highest places, who were in danger of being tainted by atheism, nor did it stoop to conquer the lowest classes so easily swayed by Methodism and enthusiasm. It is true that we occasionally hear of 'tradesmen and mechanics' in the congregation, but their numbers were probably slight and they themselves of the top rank of their profession. Thus, a preacher in 1782 defended the constitution of the Ordination ceremony on the grounds that "it tends to prevent unlearned, conceited, pragmatical persons and mechanics of the lowest station, from intruding into societies under the character of Gospel ministers".[1] Solid status, calmly enjoyed, avoiding the frivolities of fashion and the depravity of poverty —this was the social pattern.

But if in substance it was a prospering Interest, numerically it was declining. It is not easy to estimate the numbers of the English Dissenters in the eighteenth century. Their propagandists, while celebrating the increase of churches, forgot how their congregations were dwindling before the call of the world or of Methodism. Presbyterianism was certainly dying of old age, heresy and disrepute; Independency remained level and the Baptists tended to increase. To these latter denominations Presbyterianism seemed like a dead carcass to

---

[1] *Ordination Questions of Rev. M. Pope to Rev. H. Worthington*, 1782, 41. Kippis said in his sermon: "to be a Dissenter does not exclude a man of character from appearing with credit and esteem in any department of life, in any company, in any assembly." *Ibid.* 34. The social ban was declining but so was faith and the Dissenting Interest, 30, 34.

which all the obscene birds of bygone heresy—Arian, Socinian, Unitarian—gladly flew from their retreats in the west country, and the numbers of the 'orthodox' suffered in proportion.[1] Many Dissenters themselves, like Andrew Kippis, felt that the interest was in decline: it was failing before the growth of indifference and contemporary licence. But this was by no means a universal judgment. The shrewd Christopher Wyvill, an independent witness, wrote in 1792: "the Dissenters have long been a growing body: and they are now increasing, perhaps with greater rapidity than in any former period";[2] and Samuel Johnson, a less sympathetic observer, shared his opinion. In 1715 and 1716 Daniel Neal, the historian, estimated the total number of dissenting congregations in each county of England and Wales at 1107, of which 247 were Baptist but the vast majority Presbyterian.[3] Two thousand ministers, it will be recalled, had been ejected under the reaction in the previous century. The Dissenters in London, according to Neal, numbered 30,000.[4] Joseph Towers in 1775 thought that there were "upwards of 1100 congregations in England", while Robinson in 1776 placed the number at 1400 congrega-

[1] A correspondent, *Anti-Jacobin*, 1798, says, "it is well known that they [Orthodox Dissenters] have decreased in number, most having become latitudinarians in so extended a sense as to differ little from Socinians or Deists", ii, 447. Johnson considered little of their religion remained save hostility to establishments. Towers' *Letters*, 187.

[2] *Defence of Price*, 44.

[3] Bogue and Bennett, ii, 97–9.

[4] Besant, *London in the Eighteenth Century*.

tions for England and Wales in the three denominations.[1] In 1808 Bogue and Bennett accepted a total of 2002 congregations; 270 Presbyterian, 1024 Independent and 708 Baptist.[2] In the matter of distribution Middlesex and Yorkshire had the greatest number of meeting-houses and Westmorland the least. But in 1808 Bogue and Bennett complained that a congregation of 500 persons was almost unknown. Within this large social group were to be found every shape of creed, every loyalty and every sedition, with often no principle of cohesion save a common name and common grievances.[3] When men tried to harness it to the dynamic processes set in motion by the French Revolution, they found how slight was the bond that linked its members, how strong and multitudinous the ties that bound them to the greater community of the nation.

Thus in politics, as in all things, the Dissenters remained an Interest and never narrowed into a party.

[1] *Lectures on Nonconformity*, 247. Towers, *Letters*, 187. Robinson as President of London Assembly gave the figures; cf. Rev. Joseph Thompson, at the annual meeting of the Baptist Easter Association, May 1776, states there are 1243 Protestant dissenting congregations in England and Wales of the three denominations, 444 of which were Baptists. Flower, *Life of Robinson, Miscellaneous Works*, ed. 1806, I, lxvi.

[2] IV, 328. Independents increasing; Presbyterians decreasing.

[3] Cf. Wakefield, 1792: "The Dissenters are a very numerous, heterogeneous and unconnected body," *Memoirs*, I, 339; and Priestley, *View of the Principles*, etc. 1767, 254. He says Dissenters "are so widely distinct from one another in sentiment, views, and situation that it is almost impossible for them to act in concert in anything". Preface, *Works*, XXII, 335. Again, *Familiar Letters*, 1790, XIX, 142: they have "nothing but a desire of equal liberty" to keep them together.

"As Dissenters", wrote Priestley, "we have no peculiar principles of government at all."[1] This is one of the central facts which emerge from the history of their opinions in the eighteenth century: a fact which their writings and their activities consistently illustrated. Such unity of feeling as existed was founded more on sentiment than principle: Dissenters tended to meet on a certain common political ground, inclining towards the liberal side, but a ground in which no uniformity of political creed was enforced. But if dissenting opinion lacked uniformity; if they were not in a rigid sense politically principled, they were by far the most politically minded people of their times, in that they daily encountered obstacles which could only be justified or condemned in political terms. Thus their everyday life rendered their political speculations at least vaguely practical. "Modern nonconformity", wrote Robert Robinson, "naturally leads us to study government; Sidney, Locke, Montesquieu, Beccaria teach the notions which we hold of government. All think the people the origin of power, the administrative responsible trustees, and the enjoyment of life, liberty and property the right of all mankind."[2] But there was little consistency in either articles of creed or canon of interpretation. Perhaps the truth was that theological differences ran so high as to preclude any hope of political uniformity; at

[1] *View of the Principles*, 1767, 254.
[2] *Lectures on Nonconformity*, Lecture XI. "We differ, as others do, concerning the best mode of government but no one has ever attempted to subvert that which is established or even wishes to do so and all contribute cheerfully to support it." *Ibid.*

all events Joseph Priestley in his writings seems never to tire of insisting that Dissenters *quâ* dissenters have no political principles; nothing of that solidarity in sedition which their enemies would attribute to them. All they have in common, he contends, is a certain attitude to the Crown produced from historical experience.[1] Their claims, when they voice them, are the claims, not of religionists, but of men living in society. This insistence, that there was no political philosophy peculiar to persons of dissenting complexion, was a manifestation, perhaps not wholly conscious or deliberate, of a deep desire and a restless process which is visible in dissenting society throughout the second half of the eighteenth century; the attempt of Protestant Dissent entirely to secularize its relation to the larger community: to shift the basis of that relationship from religious on to political ground: to be recognized not as sectaries but as citizens. In the eager pursuit of this desire their old ideal of the rule of the Saints soon receded imperceptibly behind them, as they pressed on towards the attainment of another ideal which aimed at the domination of popular sovereignty emerging during the interregnum of the philosophers. Thus the ancient clash of rights between the congregation as a whole and the godly within the congregation died away and was heard no more.

It was this process of secularization, this *croisade laïque*,

---

[1] See *View of the Principles*, *op. cit.* A Dissenter informed the Rev. Mr Clayton in 1791 that "Dissenters when they understand their principles can have no party attachments separate from the interests of truth and virtue". *Gentleman's Magazine*, 1791, ii, 847.

frustrated though it was, which fundamentally distinguished the political activity of the Dissenters of the eighteenth century from that of their forefathers of the seventeenth; it was a crusade with a different object, a different faith and a different terrain. Their forefathers had attempted to translate religious convictions into political facts and to make a unity by identification; their descendants bent their strength to a resolute effort to separate the two: an effort in which opponents, impervious to the march of contemporary history, saw only a retracing of the past. But misinterpreted and hindered though it was, this fundamental change of purpose wielded a great influence in the final secularization of politics. It was a powerful force behind the avalanche which buried the dead age of chivalry and prevented its great mourner, Edmund Burke, from moulding the nineteenth century in England. It was foremost among those erosive processes which made the rough way smooth for Bentham.

Because we reject the Church of England, it does not follow that we are disaffected to the State of England: that was the sum of Priestley's controversial position. In religion the Dissenters were as divided as in politics, but in religion the common ground was wider and clearer. "We agree in nothing but this," wrote Priestley, "that we equally reject all human authority in matters of religion." "The religious opinions of Dissenters", said Robert Hall, "are so various that there is, perhaps, no point in which they are agreed, except in asserting the rights of conscience against all human control and

authority."[1] Rejection of human authority, the natural
right of determination according to conscience, power
in the congregation and not in a hierarchy, toleration
and, above all, freedom of criticism, constituted the
common creed of English Dissent.[2] But while accepted
as something quite distinct from the State, it was felt
that religion had a social bearing upon politics: that it
was a sanction, not a rejection of the rights of human
nature. "Christianity is not a negation of the privileges
of man but an institution for his improvement."[3] This is
the attitude of Robert Hall. Liberty is a uniform principle
in all spheres. The nature of freedom should be an
object of study among Christians, because it is through

[1] *Freedom of the Press*, 142. Priestley, *Familiar Letters*, 155. He
says: "What just now distinguishes us the most is that some of us
are Trinitarians, some Arians and others Unitarians", *ibid*.
Priestley was a Socinian and when Hall was asked if he was among
the Socinians he said: "Me amongst you Sir—me amongst you?
Why I should deserve to be tied to the tail of the great red dragon
and whipped round the nethermost regions to all eternity." Morris,
Recollections, 57. One did not need to be a Socinian to be a Whig.

[2] *Familiar Letters*, 198; cf. Rev. M. Pope, *Ordination Questions*,
1782, 47:

Q. What think you of the Principles of the Protestant Dissenters.

A. Let me select only these two—the right of Private Judgment
and the sole authority of Christ in his Church.

For criticism, cf. Bogue and Bennett, 1, 366: "I do not love a
Church of Glass which cannot bear the touch of a man's finger
without danger and without fear, which dreads the winds of
heaven to blow upon her and is afraid that the beams of the sun
will scorch her face and make her beauty fade...." For human
authority see *View of the Principles*, 1767, 341. Priestley objects to
the Church of Scotland as strongly as to that of England, 350.

[3] Hall, *Christianity Consistent with the Love of Freedom*, 1791, 9.

a just appreciation of it alone that liberty of conscience and elasticity of enquiry, so essential to the truly Christian life, can be enjoyed. Religious freedom is one of the prerogatives of a free state, and on this account Hall would have dissenting ministers "well skilled in freedom", because all politics have a simple and a complex aspect—according to whether they are measured by principle or by expediency, and while a just appreciation of the second entails the statesman's training, the first can readily be evaluated by all.[1] A minister should be educated to discourse reasonably on politics, not because such a secular training is implicit in his religious office, but on account of his position in the congregation, since dissenting ministers are "the natural guardians in some measure of our liberties and rights".[2] Robert Hall more than once repeats that dissenting religion is one thing and dissenting politics another; thus, despite its keenness, the zeal of the Unitarians for freedom "cannot be imputed to any alliance between their religious and political opinions but to the conduct natural to a minority".[3]

In practical as in theoretical politics, the same diversity characterized the Dissenting Interest. Dissenters could always be found who approved of the American War; who petitioned Parliament against the extension of Toleration; who supported Pitt and joined the volunteers during the French Revolution. If we find Richard Price, Joseph Priestley, Robert Hall and Robert Robinson on

[1] Hall, *op. cit.* 23.   [2] *Ibid.* 23.
[3] *Ibid.* 16, 17; "if any party were ever free from the least tincture of enthusiasm it is the Unitarian", 46.

the one side, there were the Rev. Edward Pickard, the Rev. John Martin, the Rev. John Clayton and the Rev. David Rivers on the other. "There are not wanting among us persons who are ready upon all occasions to oppose those principles on which the very existence of our dissent is founded."[1] But as a whole, the years 1763–1800 witnessed a remarkable gravitation in the party politics of Dissent: an alienation from the House of Hanover and their ancient loyalties which grew progressively more complete. The covenant of 1714 was broken or—more truly—was slowly forgotten by both parties. "I am sorry", wrote Belsham in 1769, "that so many Dissenters should show such a spirit of discontent and bitterness under the best and most gentle of governments, which is so tender to liberties in general and theirs in particular."[2] But by 1769 the estrangement was unquestionable. For nearly sixty years after the Revolution of 1688 the Throne could look for its firmest friends among the Protestant Nonconformists. They in turn looked upon the Protestant Succession as something peculiarly their own: a blessing enjoyed by their sacrifice. "To the records of that period and subsequent records, Dissenters appeal with high satisfaction."[3] At

[1] Hall, *op. cit.* 6. The Rev. John Clayton, a dissenting minister, in a famous political sermon of 1791 inveighed against the loyalty of his fellow Dissenters as "born to vex the state". Another famous sermon was that of the Rev. John Martin in London, who was appointed Almoner of the *Regium donum*. Morris, *Recollections*, 103, 107.

[2] Williams, *Life*, 219; in a letter to his son Thomas, October 1769.

[3] *Protestant Dissenters Magazine*, March 1794, 103, "Remarks on he present unpopularity of Dissenters".

the end of Queen Anne's reign it seemed that the Schism Bill would disturb this mellowing alliance, but the timely accession of George I ensured another half-century of co-operation. The Dissenters were a Hanoverian body-guard. They bombarded the Throne with lengthy but fervid declarations of loyalty and esteem. The memory of Sir Thomas Abney and their loyal activities in the crisis of 1715 they never tired of recalling.[1] But the rebellion of 1745 told the proudest story in dissenting loyalty. We hear of meeting-houses being burnt, of Dissenters persecuted by Jacobites, of Philip Doddridge helping Lord Halifax to raise the Northamptonshire Regiment.[2] The sermons of the time tell their own story. The nonconformist Samuel Roberts preached upon "the love of our country" in the crisis of 1745. It is interesting to compare the fervid loyalty of his address with Price's famous sermon of the same title some years later. "Let not this fair land of liberty", he prays, "be overrun with desperate Ruffians, Popish miscreants and inhuman mur-derers."[3] The rebellion brought George II a popularity among Dissenters which he never forfeited; for them he was the King who would have no persecution for con-

[1] Cf. their advocate-general Toulmin in the *Gentleman's Magazine*, January 1793, I, 4.

[2] Bogue and Bennett, III, 176.

[3] Samuel Roberts, *Love of our Country and Zeal for its interest Recommended*, Sermon at Salisbury 6 October 1745, 15: "the mad sons of violence and plunder led by a patched up hero: a base pretender", 10. He says: "Amidst the many kind and generous affections which the kind and benevolent author of our being has implanted in our constitution, that of the love of our country is certainly one of the noblest and most amiable", 7.

science sake while he reigned. Samuel Chandler was proud "to receive the good King's bounty".[1] Isaac Watts would have children informed "of the great and invaluable privilege of being born in Great Britain and of living under so excellent a government, enjoying a religious liberty unknown elsewhere".[2] Samuel Chandler's funeral sermon of 1760 is an elaborate parallel of the dead king and David; like Price in a later age he cried, reviewing the great reign that had just ended, "this is indeed the Lord's doing and it is wonderful in our eyes".[3] The death of George II closed a definite period in the relations between the Dissenters and the State: the days of calm were done. "With him", wrote a pamphleteer of 1766, "died the remembrance of the merits of those who had struggled for the preservation of a constitution which had cast them off as citizens and of an established Church which persecutes them."

For a time the Dissenters shared liberally in the widespread enthusiasm with which the new reign was greeted,[4] but the spirit of opposition was already stirring which first became articulate in the case of Wilkes, which grew ardent during the American War and which was confirmed in hostility by failure to repeal the intolerant acts. It was usual among contemporaries to date this

[1] I.e. The *Regium donum*.

[2] Essay, *Encouragement of Charity Schools, Works*, II, 420.

[3] London, 1760, 39. He was "an utter enemy to all methods of persecution for conscience sake", 33. Chandler was a F.R.S.

[4] Hollis wrote of the new king in his Diary on 25 October 1760: "may his pattern be that of Alfred, as historicated by the incomparable John Milton." *Life*, I, 98.

alienation from the American War, and it is certain that with the outbreak of hostilities the breach had attained definite shape. The Dissenters were charged with interfering violently and incautiously in the war; even with provoking it.[1] We hear of their ministers hastening across the Atlantic to stir up trouble while the Dissenters themselves sat at home, drinking their favourite toasts of "success to the Americans" and "General Washington".[2] The cultural and religious bond with the rebels was close. "The Dissenters in general adopted the cause of the Americans and repudiated the measures of the Ministry as impolitic and unjust...a constant and extensive intercourse was kept up between them: mutual assistance was given in whatever related to the advancement of the cause of religion and they considered themselves as members of the same body."[3] Up to the first year of the war there was no stronger friend to the House of Hanover, no bitterer opponent of American independence than John Aikin. Then came a change which he places in 1778: "From this period he became a strenuous supporter of the cause of civil liberty in what-

[1] *Protestant Dissenters Magazine*, 1794, I, 103: "Present Unpopularity of the Dissenters."

[2] *Anti-Jacobin*, I, 629.

[3] Bogue and Bennett, IV, 153. In a Fast Sermon 13 December 1776 before the University of Oxford Myles Cooper declared: "If anything can still be more unnatural and audacious it is that these degenerate insurgents have had their fomentors and abettors in the very heart of this kingdom: who, forgetful for awhile of themselves and their country, not only appeared publicly and exaltingly in our streets and in our markets but too many of them, even in our pulpits—in our Senate—in our most secret and most solemn councils." Oxford, 1767, 11.

ever quarter of the world her banner was displayed."[1] "The American War", wrote Southey, "made the Dissenters feel once more a political party in the state. New England was more the country of their hearts than the England wherein they were born and bred."[2] But the process had begun earlier. The Dissenters shared liberally in the country's hatred of 'Parchment and Butism', and in the general feeling that the detested minister was a secret power for evil. The articulate disaffection, as Priestley noticed, emerged with the Wilkes agitation. "Round the standard of 'Wilkes and Liberty' the nonconformists flocked in crowds....A Dissenter and a Wilkite were synonymous terms."[3] The unsuccessful attempts to modify or repeal the intolerant laws pointed and polished their opposition. Failure of this sort in 1772 and 1773 was the prelude: then two years later came the disastrous and fratricidal war. The return of peace brought a renewed possibility of alliance between the Crown and the Dissenters, but this opportunity was let slip, and their failure in 1787 to secure the repeal of the Test Acts added the bitterness of recent discontent to the tumultuous emotions aroused by the Revolution in

[1] *Memoirs*, 46.

[2] *Essays*, 1832. "Popular Disaffection", 1817, 73: "and when the flag of republicanism was hoisted, it awakened hopes which were lying dormant and brought forth their old opinions with increased strength."

[3] *Anti-Jacobin*, I, 629. The writer attributes Wilkes's politics to dissenting parents. Priestley says: "the break came in the present reign at the time of the Middlesex Election." *View of the Principles*, I, 767, XXII, 354–6. Before that there had been the Schism and Assize Bills.

France. This change between 1768–78 is the central fact of dissenting politics in this period, and as such, attracted the hostile notice of many contemporaries. It became fashionable to contrast the loyalty of Doddridge's day with the sedition of Priestley's.[1] The 'regium donum' which Chandler had been proud to receive grew in unpopularity. It was felt to be a primary cause of dissenting disunity: "It hath been an Achan's wedge in their camp", said a newspaper in 1774, and the Government pamphleteer Shebbeare attributed their disaffection to the diminution of the royal bounty.[2] But the cause lay far deeper in that imperceptible process by which sympathies unconsciously became antipathies, when men still trod the old paths but no longer came upon familiar places. William Belsham was nearest the truth when he felt that the unpopularity of the Dissenters

---

[1] Cf. *Gentleman's Magazine*, 1790, ii, 740; 1791, i, where Doddridge's behaviour is compared with "the party spirit, the fierce and haughty sense of liberty in political matters, which, however foreign to the character of a Christian minister, agitates so large a portion of the present Protestant Dissenting Ministers", 128.

[2] *London Magazine*, 1774. Shebbeare, *Answers to Queries*, 177. In the 'nineties the office of Almoner of the *Regium donum* controlled about £1700; *Gentleman's Magazine*. The *Regium donum* played an unedifying but important part in the attempt of 1772–3; Robert Bisset placed the change in dissenting political loyalty between 1772 and 1790: the differences in the former period being over worship and discipline; in the second much more political and connected with disestablishment. *Life of Burke*, 1800, i, 268. In a letter to Bisset a correspondent says: "in 1772 there were among the Dissenters no *known* principles inimical to our establishment. Before 1787 principles unfavourable to the constitution of our state had been published by their leading men" headed by Priestley's *First Principles. Anti-Jacobin*, i, 590.

arose not from individual acts, but from a shifting of the political strata. The zeal of the Dissenters for the Throne, he wrote, remained unchanged, but once the Church began to bid against Dissent for regal favour it was clear which side would lose.[1] Ousted from their ancient worship the Dissenters sought other idols: the rights of man and the sovereignty of the people. For a while they hesitated between the English parties, their old loyalty spasmodically reasserting itself. Their opposition to Fox's India Bill was solid; Fox himself felt the weight of it, and in the election of 1784 the momentary favour of the Dissenters was transferred to Pitt.[2] But the failure to repeal the Test Act in 1787 soon changed the balance once again, and after the renewed defeat of 1789 the issue seemed for ever clear. "Mr Fox", wrote Priestley, "must I think recover his popularity with the Dissenters and Mr Pitt must certainly lose ground with them."[3] But to be a Foxite in the years after 1789 was political

[1] William Belsham, *History of Great Britain*, ed. 1805, v, 21 *et seq*. He says: "Rest, rest, immortal spirits of Locke, Hoadly and Somers! Seek not to know by what improvements on your exploded principles the house of Brunswick now governs the Empire of Britain", 26.

[2] *Defence of the Revolution Society*, 44. Wyvil, *Defence of Price*, 73–4. Price shared in their sentiments on this occasion. *Ibid*. Fox noted it in his repeal speech of 1790.

[3] Letter to Lindsey, May 1789. *Memoirs*, I, pt. II, 25. Towers and Hall had a low opinion of Pitt that never grew any higher. Wakefield wrote to Wilberforce: "You stand impeached at the bar of Religion Reason and Humanity for that high crime and misdemeanour—a long and uniform and ardent support, in your political capacity, of William Pitt." *Letters to Wilberforce*, London, 1797, 39.

death, and the consummation of unpopularity. The highly developed technique of association and agitation, which the Dissenters had employed against the Test Act, added an exaggerated fear of their efficiency as revolutionaries to the already rapidly accumulating causes for distrusting and disliking them.[1]

It is not easy to exaggerate their unpopularity:[2] it was the theme of every pamphlet, the story of every newspaper. Even learned works, such as John Gillies's edition of Aristotle, could not resist the temptation to attack them. But outstanding in political and social unpopularity was a group of men styling themselves the 'Rational Dissenters'; men who might well be regarded as the consummate products of the education in the

---

[1] Hall writes: "The prejudice entertained against us is not the work of a day but the accumulation of ages, flowing from the fixed antipathy of a numerous and powerful order of men, distributed to all classes of society", but "till the Test business was agitated, however, we were not aware of our labouring under such a weight of prejudice." *Freedom of the Press*, 149–50. Aikin, after the failure of repeal in 1790, gave as a reason the warmth with which Dissenters had embraced the French Revolution and general reform. *Letters*, I, 420. A reviewer (Nov. 1789) speaks of "their hearty disposition to introduce that anarchy into their own country". *Gentleman's Magazine*, 1789, II, 10, 22.

[2] "No system of government is calculated to rule and satisfy the Dissenters. The turbulence of their principles would embroil a democracy and convert it into an anarchy." *Gentleman's Magazine*, 1790, I, 246. Another writer says their exclusion from all political life "is an axiom in politics". *Ibid.* 249. Horsley used the same expression in the same sentiment. The *Address to the People of England* issued by the committee of Protestant Dissenters after the failure of 1790 regrets "the violent spirit that has been raised against us". This document is printed in the *New Annual Register*, 1790.

most liberal of the dissenting academies, and who embodied in themselves and illustrated in their activities all that was most intellectualist, sceptical and symptomatic in their times. Their distinguishing sign was the exercise of the natural right of freedom of enquiry, and a frequent characteristic was theological heresy, Arian, Socinian and Unitarian.[1] Equally disliked by Churchmen and orthodox Dissenters, they formed a cultural unit remote from and above the Nonconformist community, and the history of significant dissenting opinion in the years 1763–1800 is the history of the Rational Dissenters. Perhaps England never witnessed so prominent a minority. In politics, in literature, in theology, in all they were marked men, and if it seemed usually with the mark of the beast, their prominence was in proportion to their unpopularity. Priestley and Wakefield shared with Godwin and Paine the honour of being the four chief bogies of the *Anti-Jacobin*. Priestley, Price and Robinson were quoted by indignant orators in Parliament: and every government poet strove to immortalize their damnation.[2] In spite of this, men like Lindsey, Towers, Kippis, Belsham, and the rest, represented much

[1] *Anti-Jacobin*, I, 362: "In no age did Socinianism prevail more in England than among the Dissenters during the last thirty years. The chiefs of that sect considered it incumbent on them to manifest their political as well as their religious nonconformity." As an example of the abuse of the word, this writer numbers among them the Arian Price and poor Mrs Macaulay. They paved, he says, the way for Paine.

[2] E.g. "Let our vot'ries then follow the glorious advice,
In the Gunpowder Legacy left us by Price,
Inflammable matter to place grain by grain
And blow up the State with the torch of Tom Paine."
A Jacobin Council.

that was most admirable in English thought and life. "These," wrote Wakefield of the Rational Dissenters, "take them all together, are, in one word, the most respectable set of men I know: genuine lovers of truth, liberty and science."[1] It was with these men that John Clayton and the orthodox quarrelled so violently.[2] Intellectually Rational Dissent expounded the liberal views which accompanied the decay of Presbyterianism, and when the Church and State mobs shouted destruction to Presbyterians and Jacobins they were nearer the truth than they knew.[3]

As enquirers they were fortunate in their times. The years following 1763, when the greatest peace in English history left this country at the head of Europe, were quickened by intellectual restlessness and speculation of every kind:

> Teeming with metaphysics old and new
> Unheard and untried systems burst to view.[4]

"On more accounts than one", wrote Priestley in 1770, "the present time seems to be peculiarly seasonable for the discussion of everything relating to civil and religious liberty"; and to this freedom in speculation was added

[1] Wakefield, *Short Strictures*, 6.
[2] Clayton in his sermon said: "I affirm we greatly disapprove of the theological and political sentiments of those who (by a patent of their own creation) style themselves *rational dissenters*." This was the attitude of the Rev. David Rivers. The Bishop of London was gratified to learn from Hall that the "rational dissenters were a tiny minority". *Recollections*, 107.
[3] 'Presbyterian' like 'Socinian' was a technical term used quite indiscriminately, e.g. *Gentleman's Magazine*, 1793, II, 808.
[4] T. J. Mathias, *Pursuits of Literature*.

the intellectual incentive of great events abroad.[1] In no sphere was interest more eager than in the scientific sphere of 'natural philosophy', from whose alliance with metaphysics and politics so many utopias were predicted and so much optimism generated. This is no place to tell the history of dissenting scientific thought, but it is an honourable history. Predominant in the Royal Society they found and shared the trove of wonder which rewards the fortunate pioneer. Friendships arising from common study were enduring; Richard Price was a Fellow of the Royal Society and his close friends included Benjamin Franklin, Joseph Priestley, Thomas Percival and many of his fellow academicians. These men sought in science something profounder than a social diversion, and their researches in physics and chemistry, and into the slowly yielding mystery of electricity, lent a patience tempered by an eager sense of being upon the brink of imminent discovery to their work in other fields.[2]

[1] *Letter to the Author of Reviews*, 1770, XXII, 402. Gibbon noticed in 1780 how "country meetings, and committees of correspondence announced the public discontent". *Memoirs*, 207.

[2]   "What various scenes all wonderful arise
                From the pursuit of electricity."
Benjamin Martin, *Young Gentlemen and Lady's Philosophy*, 1759, I, XI.
   The Dissenters were peculiarly sensible to it: a poet in the *Academical Repertory* writes:
                "Discovery fearless darts her rays
                Through the thick gloom of error's maze,
                Aided by Truth her cause maintains
                And frees the soul from servile chains."
                D. W. L. North. MSS. 10 September 1785.
   So Jerningham, *Enthusiasm*, 1789:
                "Now Science hears a voice unknown before,
                Haste pilot, pilot quit the drowsy shore."

But it was peculiarly the study of political philosophy which arrested and retained their vagrant interest. "It is a mark of the social and public spirit of this nation", wrote an essayist in 1782, "that there is scarcely a member of it who does not bestow a very considerable portion of his time and thoughts in studying its political welfare, its interest and its honour."[1] The storm of controversy which broke over the American dispute blew back the sacred veil of 1688, and men began to search behind the altar: to reread and revalue the politics and theology of the preceding century. With the reformers Locke remained the holy of holies or, as Tucker called him, "idol of the levellers of England",[2] but he had close rivals in Harrington and Sidney: Milton and Marchmont Needham. Publishing extracts from their works was among the activities of the Society for Constitutional Information. The reading of a man like Thomas Spence is quite remarkable.[3] Nor was the process confined to the liberal side: the accepted values of a century had been challenged, and to interpret the settlement of 1688 the government pamphleteer had also to go back to the years before. Many old ghosts, Cavalier and Puritan, were raised; even the pale shadow of Filmer lay along the page of

[1] Knox, *Essays*, ed. 1782: "On the influence of Politics." So Hall, *Freedom of the Press*, 159.

[2] *Four Letters*, 1783, 110. He speaks of "Mr Harrington whose authority jointly with that of the great Sidney and Locke has been urged both in prose and verse against the poor Dean of Gloucester", 87.

[3] He had read the American Joel Barlow, Volney, Ogilvie, Paine, Locke, Pufendorf, and Harrington. Rudkin, *Thomas Spence*, 19.

controversy, and 'Filmerian' furnished Burke's opponents with an adjective.[1] There was an eager pursuit of French and other foreign ways of thinking, but while English thought was unusually sensitive to continental influence, it was never completely dominated; even the celebrated 'French principles',[2] which appear as a technical term in the State trials of the 'nineties, were largely English ideas clothed in a Parisian model, and represented English grievances and English ambitions slightly caricatured by the French technique in their presentation. From Edmund Burke to Peter Pindar all was politics, and in the same measure that reiterated debate doubled conviction, so did the apparent deficiency of things as they were, grow clearer to those who would have had things as they might be. Every indication seemed to witness the inevitability of change—and the old régime in Europe, shaken by crisis yet still tenacious; a Europe which revealed a Joseph II like nothing so much as a belated shepherd hastening after his flock in the gathering storm; an old régime of powerful kings and profound

---

[1] Cf. "The obsolete politics of Sir Robert Filmer, that Trumpeter of despotism under the reign of the second Charles, now flame in the van of our patriots." Correspondent in *Gentleman's Magazine*, 1791. Wyvill calls Burke "our Modern Filmer". *Defence of Price*. It was mostly second-hand knowledge *via* Locke's first *Essay*.

[2] In her unfinished novel *Wrongs of Women* (which Godwin published posthumously) about the sufferings of Marian aged "six and twenty" Mary Wollstonecraft's Judge, summing up on good masculine grounds in the divorce case, says that we do "not want French principles in public or private life". He is an obvious caricature of Braxfield.

philosophers, were seen only in the wealth of their bygone opportunities and the poverty of their past achievements.

But nowhere was the temper of the times more brilliantly illustrated than in the life of Thomas Hollis, "a character of remarkable singularity and by no means calculated for general imitation", whose curious biography was written by Francis Blackburne in 1780. Though never professedly a Dissenter, he was a friend of Dissenters, a Whig, a supporter of America and of civil and religious liberty all the world over. Adoration of Milton and service as his disciple was graven on his "truly patriotic and cosmo-political heart". By new editions, by reprints, by medals, by portraits, by gifts of money or books with the cap of liberty embossed upon them, he strove to make English language and thought the universal instrument of establishing freedom and of stamping out Popery. He inserted in the newspapers curious advertisements of wholesome advice to rulers and ruled. Universities, both foreign and American, benefited from his liberality—Harvard to the extent of £4865 together with many books. He brought out new editions of Locke, Needham, Neville and Sidney; it was the appearance of this latter reprint which earned him the epithet 'republican'. His own faith was summarized for him in Molesworth's Preface to *Franco-Gallia*; Buchanan's *De jure regni apud Scotos* was a favourite book. In his private orisons he could tabulate personal confessions of political faith such as were found, after his death, among his papers:

Locke, A. Sidney, Neville, Harrington it is apprehended, well understood, form the circle of government,

Reason, practice, adoption, plan of government.

Thomas Hollis throws a revealing light upon the history
of English political thought in the eighteenth century;
while such men lived, Priestley and Price would not
want for readers and adherents.[1]

In this sympathetic atmosphere the political activities
of the Dissenters were as notable as they were considerable. They fought the offensive battle: the Established
Church the defensive. Methodism was a semi-neutral
common ground, although in State as in Church the
Methodists tended to be the conservatives of the cen-
tury.[2] The Dissenters fought for their ideals in the press;
in their clubs and associations and in the law courts.
They were great pamphleteers. Among the thirty-eight
'replies' elicited by Burke's *Reflections on the French
Revolution*, were those of Joseph Priestley, Richard Price,
Joseph Towers, David Williams, the dissenting attorney
Nash, and an anonymous member of the Revolution
Society, while George Rous, Capel Lofft, Mary Wollstone-

[1] Archdeacon Blackburne, *Memoir of Thomas Hollis*, 1780, I,
III–IV, 119, 125, 135, 152, 188, 216, 295, 306, 475, 496, 501, II,
551.

[2] "The conduct of the Methodists for fifty years past, has
completely wiped out this aspersion [of disloyalty] and I understand
that during the present revival of political contentions, they have
even excluded from their community any persons who wrote and
spoke against the measures of government." *Anti-Jacobin*, II, 218.
They were ardently ministerial in the American War. E.g.
Wesley.

craft and Mrs Macaulay replied in defence of the Dissenters. Their hold on public opinion was remarkable. "They have almost appropriated to themselves the direction of every periodical work", wrote a pamphleteer in 1790. "It so happened", wrote Southey in 1817, "that our literary journals were almost wholly in the hands of Dissenters, and more particularly those Dissenters who prided themselves upon the freedom of their opinion."[1] The Dissenters themselves admitted the charge although not always gladly.[2] Important among these periodicals was the *Monthly Review* which scandalized Southey by its leniency towards Godwin's *Political Justice*.[3] Many of these reviews were "devoted almost wholly to Socinianism and infidelity". The *Critical Review* answered to this description, and so did the *Analytical* until it met its death at the hands of the *Anti-Jacobin*, which was consistently directed against these three reviews and their publisher Phillips. In addition the Rational Dissenters could boast of one famous newspaper, Benjamin Flower's *Cambridge Intelligencer*, which the *Anti-Jacobin* considered "the most infamous paper that ever disgraced the press";[4] the paper that consoled Priestley in his American

[1] Southey, *Essays*, 76–80. *Observations on the Conduct of Protestant Dissenters*, 1790, 5. Bogue and Bennett, IV, 388. It was felt a matter of general concern that the *Biographia Britannica* was in their hands.

[2] "The press has always been more under the influence of Dissenters than many would expect or would wish to believe." Bogue and Bennett, IV, 500.

[3] The *Monthly Review* was edited by John Aikin after 1796. *Memoirs*, 187–8.

[4] I, 130.

exile and Fysche Palmer at Botany Bay. It published the early poems of Coleridge, and its editor more than once in a stormy career clashed with the authorities. Newspapers were used for propagandist purposes; thus the manifestos of the dissenting committees were published in the *Gentleman's Magazine* and the *New Annual Register*. "We print and publish many pamphlets", wrote Priestley in 1790, "as well as insert the Resolutions of our meetings in the public papers, in order to give our countrymen the information which we see they want concerning our situation and the reasons for our application to Parliament."[1] A pamphleteer of the same year complained: "we cannot take up a newspaper in a coffee house without perceiving advertisements announcing the meetings of the Nonconformists in various parts of the kingdom, and publishing the various unanimous resolutions of these respectable and loyal members of society."[2] It was this newspaper notoriety that led Burke to denounce the Harlow Synod and the Unitarian Society. Robert Robinson translated the Paris Revolution Magazine from the original French.[3]

A pamphleteer of 1790 divided 'reformers' into two classes, civil and religious, with a third 'compounded of both' which consisted of the Dissenters. "Even the solemn offices of devotion", he writes, "are polluted with their unhallowed strains; and the assemblies of the saints profaned by the secular language of coffee-house

[1] *Familiar Letters*, 1790, XIX, 141.
[2] *A Scourge for the Dissenters*, 1790, 44.
[3] Dyer, *Life*, 427.

politicians."[1] In the political life of London and the country the Dissenters played a prominent and organized part, particularly as members of the advanced clubs. Burke attacked the Society for Constitutional Information and the Revolution Society in the *Reflections*, calling the second a 'Club of Dissenters'—a false generalization, since it contained some members of the Established Church and a number of Whigs like Lord Stanhope.[2] But Dissenters were certainly prominent in its councils. The ministers Price, Kippis, Rees, Morgan and Pickbourn—all Rev. Drs—Thomas Brand Hollis, Henry Beaufoy, John Ingram, John Towgood and others were members.[3] It was their three Resolutions, adopted as fundamentals by other sister societies, around which Price built the famous sermon which provoked Burke's *Reflections on the French Revolution*.[4] The activities were

[1] *Observations . . .*, 1790, 3. On 6 July 1790, 600 persons celebrated the Revolution together in London. Towers wrote: "I took some pains to promote this meeting in London, and attended it with a high degree of pleasure as I have always wished for the establishment of liberty in France and been desirous of promoting every public testimony of the same sentiments among my countrymen." *Thoughts on a New Parliament*, 1790, 84-5.

[2] *Proceedings of the Revolution Society*, 1789, 6. Towers, *Thoughts on a New Parliament*, 78. Among the distinguished laymen were the Dukes of Norfolk, Richmond, Leeds and Manchester, *ibid. Vindication of the Revolution Society*, 1792, 39.

[3] *Proceedings of the Revolution Society*, 10.

[4] The three declaratory principles of the Society moved 4 November 1788 at the London Tavern were: (1) all civil and political authority derived from the people; (2) abuse of power justifies resistance; (3) right of private judgment, liberty of conscience, trial by jury, freedom of press and election "ought ever to be held sacred and inviolable", *Proceedings of the Revolution*

varied and not always restrained; at their dinners forty-one toasts were drunk for the cause of liberty. The members were addressed at the London Tavern on 20 September 1790 by Messieurs Français and Bourgon of the Friends of the Constitution at Nantes, amid mutual satisfaction.[1] Similar societies existed all over the country. Robert Robinson founded the Cambridge Constitutional Society, which distinguished itself in the County Association Movement in favour of parliamentary reform. It was modelled on the London Constitutional Society upon the formation of which Capel Lofft sent Robinson a model of its procedure for adoption. "They wound up and confirmed my sermons", wrote Robinson to a friend, "by good revolutional songs." From this society one of the first petitions against the slave trade was sent to Parliament. It adopted the fundamental principles of the Revolution Society in its meeting at the Black Bull on 4 January 1790.[2] The Revolution

Society, 14. The Rev. Dr Rees, the Rev. Mr Worthington, the Rev. Mr Jervis were members: so was William Smith, a well-known Unitarian, M.P. for Norwich and champion of the Dissenters in the Commons, Clayden, 375.

[1] Bourgon said: "Divinité de Westminster, et nous aussi, nous t'élèverons des temples." *Correspondence Revolution Society*, 67. Towers, *Thoughts on a New Parliament*, 88.

[2] *Correspondence*. Dyer, *Life*. They corresponded with the Friends of the Constitution at Nantes, *Correspondence*, 70. The members were chiefly townsmen and Dissenters. Earlier in 1783, they had declared their principles and resolutions, e.g. (1) "that in our opinion every individual of Mankind is born with a natural right to Life, Liberty and Property"; (2) society formed for security of these rights; (3) "that the consent of the people is the true origin and happiness the only worthy end of civil govern-

Society corresponded with the societies of Norwich and Manchester.[1] Thomas Rogers belonged to the 'Friends of the People'. Joseph Towers adhered to the Revolution Society and the Society for Constitutional Information, the propagandist activities of which included printing and distributing extracts from Sidney, Locke, Trenchard, Somers and many others. As a result of his energy as a member of the Constitutional Society, this deep student of constitutional history underwent examination before the Privy Council.[2] Richard Price and Thomas Rogers were members of the Society for Con-

---

ment"; (4) "that there is in all states impliedly, and in the British State expressly, a mutual contract between the governors and the governed"; (5) need of reform in Parliamentary Representation; (6) English Constitutional Government "the most perfect theory of government in the world." Wyvill, *Defence of Price*, 107. Dyer says of Robinson: "in politics he felt an ardour that bordered upon enthusiasm: with subjects connected with government few men of his time were more conversant, none possessed more variety or greater originality of ideas." *Life*, 121. Robinson was a great admirer of the American Constitution and in 1784 entertained at Chesterton the American General Reed and an envoy from the States "listening", he wrote in a letter, "to the honied accents of their tongues, distilling with all the richest and most fragrant sounds of liberty, property, law, commerce, religion and a future state of perfect and everlasting felicity". *Ibid.* 250.

[1] *Correspondence*, 145.
[2] Clayden, 276. Wyvill says the great majority of the Constitutional Society were Dissenters. *Defence of Price*, 99. Among its members were Lord Liverpool, D. Adams, Joel Barlow and J. Frost. Arthur Young, *Example of France*, 1793. Towers, *Thoughts on a New Parliament*, Appendix. Lindsey, *Funeral Sermon for Towers*, 1799, 36. The Constitutional Society felt that parliamentary reform and annual parliaments "is no romantic object but worthy of a free people to demand". Wyvill, *Defence of Price*, 104.

stitutional Information (founded 1780), while George Tierney, Thomas and Samuel Rogers, John Towgood, Alexander Kippis, Joseph Towers and J. T. Rutt belonged to the Society of Friends of the People.[1]

Meeting in the big coffee-houses of London, the Dissenters were closely connected with civic politics and the Whig corporation of Alderman Sawbridge's day. Price dedicated his *Additional Observations of* 1777 to the Lord Mayor, Aldermen, and Commons of London: he received the freedom of the city in a gold box. Behind the great clubs was a network of smaller societies. In 1795 the *Anti-Jacobin* roused the nation against book clubs and debating clubs. Dissenters were prominent in both. The Royston Book Club enjoyed a more than local reputation. Robert Robinson patronized it. Crabb Robinson in 1796 heard a debate there: "Is private affection inconsistent with universal benevolence?"[2] To the book societies the *Anti-Jacobin* coupled the debating societies—especially the Westminster Forum, where in 1797 Crabb Robinson spoke on the French Revolution.[3] Attached to the Daventry Academy was the Northampton Literary Society, who held their first meeting 11

[1] Crabb Robinson, *Diary*, 35.

[2] *Anti-Jacobin*, 1, 475. A writer (520) considered that in the political lectures, the speeches from Palace Yard, Chalk Farm and the Whig Club there was much that Aristotle would have put in his seventh book of *Politics*. William Frend left "a vast number of books upon the Heads of Houses and others in Cambridge at the time of the Slave Trade and Test Act agitations". *Proceedings Against Frend*, 1793. But Thomas Belsham disapproved of book clubs as distracting from study. Williams, *Life*, 397.

[3] Crabb Robinson, *Diary*, 40.

November 1779; in 1785 the members admitted Samuel Palmer. In January 1780 the society in session voted England in the wrong over American taxation: in April of the same year 3 votes were cast for the State of Nature against 9 "for civilization". On another occasion it condemned Lycurgus's Institutions on grounds of education and decorum, and voted Alfred a greater man than Charlemagne by 11 votes to 1.[1] The titles of Academical 'Orations' in the *Academical Repository* ranged from Capital Punishment and Annual Parliaments to the extent of Legislative Authority, the Slave Trade and the Advantages of Studying Modern History.[2] Thomas Percival joined the Manchester Literary and Philosophic Society, being himself a member of the American Philosophical Society of Philadelphia.[3] David Williams founded clubs of every kind and originated the Royal Literary Fund.[4] These social contracts held implicit within them the possibility of association for sterner and more public ends.

Political and social association was enlivened by the political sermon. If the Church of England had the first word on 30 January the Dissenters had the last on

[1] *MSS. Minute Book of the Northampton Literary Society*, D. W. L. North. MSS. 7.
[2] *The Academical Repository*. North. MSS. 10. In September 1785 there was a debate upon the right to representation in which the speaker for the affirmative said "that men come into the world in a state of freedom, that it was the gift of God and that they could not forfeit but by insanity or guilt", 73. The motion was carried by 19 votes to 8.
[3] Percival, *Works*, 1, lxvii, lxxxii.
[4] Lucas, *David Williams*, 4.

4–5 November.[1] Joseph Towers replied to Dr Nowell's famous absolutist sermon preached before the Commons in 1772, and when it was expunged from the *Journals* of the House Robert Robinson wrote: "I shared your pleasure in Dr Nowell's disgrace. May every Goliah be so slain."[2] Robinson himself preached on "Questions concerning liberty and religious moderation" to crowded audiences in the fashionable parts of London and in the village barns around Cambridge.[3] National fast days were particularly the occasion of such discourses. It was these sermons that Burke condemned in the *Reflections*, while Fox himself admitted in 1790, that he would rather have heard Price's 'love of our country' "from the House than the pulpit."[4] "For myself," wrote Robert Hall in his defensive open letter to Simeon, "all who have heard me are witnesses that I never introduced a political topic into the pulpit on any occasion; nor have I any doubt the other dissenting ministers in this town can make the same declaration with equal sin-

---

[1] "My predecessor Dr Price, as well as myself and many other Dissenters, always observed the days appointed for public fasts in the course of the American War, though by no means adopted the language of the prayers published by authority for the use of the clergy on those occasions." Priestley, *Fast Sermon*, 1793, xv, 495.

[2] *Letters. Works*, iv, 305.

[3] Dyer, 268, *Barn and Village Sermons*. Dyer admits "by some they may perhaps be reckoned too political". The Baptist ceremony of public Baptism was accompanied by "a short discourse on the blessings of civil and religious liberty". Robinson, *History of Baptism*, 1790, 543, for one such at Whittlesford near Cambridge.

[4] Hansard, 1790, xxviii, 387 *et seq.*

cerity."[1] He had succeeded Robinson as Baptist Minister in Cambridge in 1791. Jeremiah Joyce and Winter-botham could hardly have made such a claim. Dissenting influence extended into municipal government. Thomas Percival's statistical measures for public health reform were influential in Manchester, where he lived. The Rev. George Walker, F.R.S., was political guide and coun-sellor to the town and corporation of Nottingham—the corporation which Gilbert Wakefield harangued in 1789.[2]

But civic politics had their terrors, and they produced one of the most interesting legal cases of the century: the case of Allan Evans. This case has a queer dis-creditable history, but its importance as furnishing an interpretation of the Toleration Act was considerable. In its broad dimensions the issue concerned the extent and influence of the Act of Toleration and the question whether it abolished the crime of, as well as the penalties upon, the profession of Nonconformity. In 1748 the Corporation of London made a by-law inflicting heavy financial penalties upon those who, being nominated by the Lord Mayor, declined to stand for election to civic office, and then proceeded to nominate Dissenters, thus forcing upon them the alternative of suffering under the

---

[1] *Cambridge Intelligencer*, 8 August 1795. Dyer noticed the liberal political sentiments of English and American Baptists and especially the Welsh. Dyer, 303.

[2] Aikin, *Memoirs*, 411. The Nottingham Petition for recognizing American Independence impressed Burke. Walker was "a deep thinker on political subjects". Wakefield, *Address to the Inhabitants of Nottingham*, 1789. Percival, *Memoirs*.

by-law or the Test Act, because to plead Nonconformity against the by-law would be to plead a crime. The City gained £15,000 in fines in this discreditable fashion. Allan Evans, a Dissenter, when fined for this 'offence', refused to pay, and was brought before the Sheriff's Court in September 1757: both here and in his appeal to the Court of Meetings in 1757 he lost his case. He appealed to the Court of Judges Delegate [Willer, C.J.; Palmer, C.B.; Foster, J.; Bathurst, J.; Wilmott, J.], who unanimously reversed the judgment of the previous courts. In a notable speech Mr Justice Foster asserted that the Toleration Act "doth in my opinion declare the public worship among Protestant Dissenters to be warranted by Law and entitled to public protection". The Corporation appealed to the Lords, where, on 4 February 1767, Lord Mansfield made one of the great speeches of his career and carried the day for English Dissent. Nonconformity, he contended, was certainly not a crime. He passed from law to philosophy in the course of his opinion: "There is nothing, certainly, more unreasonable, more inconsistent with the rights of human nature, more contrary to the spirit and precepts of the Christian religion, more iniquitous and unjust, more impolitic than Persecution."[1] From that day no Dissenter spoke ill of Lord Mansfield.[2]

Legally recognized; given, as it were, a sort of negative

[1] See Appendix to Furneaux's *Letters to Blackstone*, 215, 248. Furneaux had a phenomenal memory and his version of the case, taken down after the hearing, was submitted to Mansfield who authorized it for publication as his actual speech.

[2] Belsham, *Memoirs of Lindsey*, 262.

ground against which the political activity of English Dissenters became clearer, more definite, more purposeful and—for their opponents—more menacing. It was the theme of every pamphleteer, "how much the Presbyterians in general and particularly the seditious writers amongst them, contributed to promote the rebellion in America".[1] Their design to involve the nation a second time in bloodshed seemed apparent in their seditious writings and audacious conduct on every occasion.[2] It became customary to attribute the Gordon Riots to their leadership.[3] The American contest was thought to have done some service to the country in that it revealed the Dissenters in their true guise. The *Anti-Jacobin* considered that it was Richard Price's *Essay on Civil Liberty* that "contributed very much to the spreading among the Dissenters (the Socinians at least) of those democratical principles to which Socinians are so prone", a contagion which seemed to increase with the success of the rebels in America.[4] Why, asked a pamphleteer in 1793, do the Dissenters attempt to deny their activities in circulating Paine and promoting the American Rebellion, when these activities were once their boast?[5] That there were loyal Dissenters in plenty—men who went elsewhere than to Paine and Priestley for their politics and religion —no one denied, but the failure of such men of goodwill

[1] Anthony Stokes, *Desultory Observations*, 1792, 66.   [2] *Ibid.* 57.
[3] *Scourge for the Dissenters*, 22: "the many fires kindled in the metropolis by sectarists, the agents of their brethren and abettors, the Americans, on the other side of the water." The Gordon Riots were due to them. *Look at the Last Century*..., 125.   [4] Vol. I, 115–5.
[5] *Letter from John Bull to...Thomas Bull*, 1793, 8.

publicly to dissociate themselves from this ill company was widely condemned.[1] In cumulative addition to the writings of Price and Priestley, Mauduit, Toulmin and John Erskine, there were their practical exertions. Dissenters acted as colonial agents; Price, Priestley and Dr Wren, a dissenting minister in Portsmouth, worked for the relief of American prisoners.[2] Their fast-day sermons were all for the rebels and none for the Government. Samuel Rogers remembered how his father told his children the causes of the Rebellion, demonstrating that the English were in the wrong. He wore mourning for the victims of Lexington.[3]

The French Revolution told a similar story, but longer and more intense in character: That "France is taking the lead and England should follow her example", was the watchword of the Revolution Society. In 1778, too, all had been sweet reasonableness, but eleven years later the philosophers were in closer spiritual harmony with the men of God and the sober language of enlightenment was shot with a vivid strain of apocalyptic inspiration. For the Revolution Society the French Revolution "seemed like an inspiration from Heaven".[4] For Richard

[1] *Anti-Jacobin*, 1, 716. Dr Hunter was a loyal Presbyterian. *Letter from John Bull...*, 8, 10.

[2] *Northumberland Letters*, 167. Rev. Newcome Cappe preached many sermons against the "unjust American War". Ward, *Funeral Sermon*, 47.   [3] Clayden, 33.

[4] *Correspondence*, 20: "I recollect too that it was while I was with H. R. Crabb [his uncle, a dissenting minister] that the French Revolution broke out, that everyone rejoiced in it as an event of great importance and that Popery and absolute government were both to be destroyed." Crabb Robinson, 13. He, too, was in youth a Jacobin.

Price it was the column of light that heralded salvation; in its fresh brilliance the veterans of freedom could lay down their arms in the conviction of victory. "They considered it was the handmaid of pure religion."[1] Gilbert Wakefield felt the war against the Revolution was 'impious': Pitt was a Sabbath-breaker and a murderer; opposing a Government designed to glorify God in the happiness of the people. "Paine, Holcroft and Godwin", wrote Robert Bisset, "had established three great banks of anarchy (there might be much greater capitalists than did now avow themselves) whose notes inferior dealers took and circulated for current cash",[2] and at this bank the Dissenters were established customers. "Your country", wrote Percival to Madame Necker in 1789, "now presents the most interesting and august scene ever exhibited on the theatre of the world: and I hope no clouds will arise to obscure the brightness of the prospect which is before you." "The French Revolution has always appeared to me, and does still appear, the most splendid event recorded in the annals of history."[3] Like Edmund Burke, the Dissenters felt that they were living in one of those rare epochs, when

[1] Bogue and Bennett, IV, 194. "When therefore they looked around and saw a combination against the cause of liberty, they viewed it with unutterable horror, as a conspiracy against the Lord and his anointed." *Ibid.* 201. It was the principles of religious liberty that chiefly attracted them, 189. The Rational Dissenters in particular were strong opponents to the government's defence fund. *Anti-Jacobin*, I, 136. Horsley preferred the emigrant French clergy, Papists though they were, to the English Dissenters.

[2] Bisset, *Life of Burke*, II, 397.

[3] Hall, *Freedom of the Press*, 172. Percival, *Memoirs*, clxi.

history momentarily loses its natural uniformity, and responds directly and catastrophically to the will of God. They greeted the Revolution, says the *Anti-Jacobin*, "with an enthusiasm bordering upon frenzy".[1] They were prominent in the London Corresponding Society. Thomas Hardy belonged to a dissenting club and Thelwall's lectures were considerably attended by Dissenters. They bought and circulated Paine's *Rights of Man*. Jeremiah Joyce was a sought-after preacher on his release from Newgate; William Frend, expelled from Cambridge for his liberalism, was a friend of the Dissenters, with an extensive connection among them. Like Crabb Robinson they read Holcroft's and Godwin's novels. Priestley, like Paine, belonged to the Friends of the Constitution at Bordeaux.[2] Citizen Stone, a pupil at Hackney Academy, stood in the pillory for his seditious behaviour. Helen Maria Williams, the republican poetess, was a Dissenter. David Williams visited Paris in 1792, enrolled as a French citizen and shared the adventures of Paine, Christie and Mary Wollstonecraft. The Dissenters could hardly fail to recognize themselves in the *Anti-Jacobin's* receipt for a perfect Jacobin.[3] They welcomed the Revolution at banquets in which enthusiasm supplied

[1] *Anti-Jacobin*, 1, 629.

[2] *Correspondence of the Revolution Society*, 217. Priestley did not belong to the Revolution Society or to that for Constitutional Information.

[3] 'The prescription is compendious; take a lad of lively parts and half educate him at a grammar school, so as that he may have some little smattering of the learned languages; when removed from thence, place him under the tuition of a thorough-paced Dissenter, who may imbue his yet ductile mind with all the

the place of sobriety. They did not realize that the thing which seemed so familiar to their hopes was, in reality, utterly alien to much of their thought and many of their ideals. Nor did contemporaries realize it. The Dissenters were felt to be a foreign group in the nation, whose ways were not as other men's and whose minds were formed only to perceive the obverse side of a question: "what to us is rebellion to them is the sovereignty of the people: and what to us is an attempt to restore the constitution, to them is rebellion, the only sort of rebellion now remaining in the world: where we see massacre, they see deliverance; what we call anarchy they call government; and what is misery in our eyes is enjoyment in theirs."[1] Aliens among their fellow countrymen, it was labour lost to form associations and offer guarantees of con-

dangerous doctrines and practices so plentifully dispersed in the multifarious writings of Dr Priestley: then remove him to London, and initiate him in debating societies, spouting clubs, etc. Next let there be procured for him in some noted conventicle, an appointment, if not as a preacher, yet as a probationer where he may be regularly trained to pay his court to multitudes and, being very occasionally touched with the sweet soothings of popular fame, learn not only to love it beyond all other gratifications but learn also by what arts it is most easily acquired. Thus qualified for any service that even Jacobinism requires, he may confidently look up to the patronage of any editor of a popular newspaper or any popular publisher, whether he be wanted to pen newspaper paragraphs, write essays in the *Monthly Magazine*, reviews in the *Analytical*." 1, 617.

[1] *Letter from John Bull...*, 1793, 9. *Look at the Last Century...*, 1790, says: "with what pleasure they contemplated the anarchy and confusion of France", 120–1. The abuse was as violent, said Hall, "as if attachment to the King were to be measured by hatred to the Dissenters." *Freedom of the Press*, 138.

sistent loyalty; to found a periodical designed to sway a public opinion irrevocably predetermined.[1]

Their political isolation was reflected in and coloured the social life of the Rational Dissenters. They became a sort of cultural *imperium in imperio*: closely connected with each other and forming a separate chapter of English life, in which appeared all aspects of contemporary thought so adapted as to fit inside its limits. But while retaining their unity in this fashion, they shared— indeed they led—another process that was affecting the whole dissenting interest; a process of reconciliation with the world. In Priestley's youth the Sabbath was strictly celebrated: no meat was dressed: no journey undertaken. But Priestley noticed a change which, in

[1] The avowed object of the *Protestant Dissenters Magazine* which first appeared in 1794 was to be a channel of communication between Dissenters and to show them to be good and loyal subjects: "to enforce those precepts of our holy religion 'fear God and honour the King'." It was orthodox in tone: hostile to Priestley and Wakefield. A correspondent in the *Gentleman's Magazine* (Dec. 1792, II, 1020) tells how a large congregation of Dissenters in the London district met under Edward Jeffries and issued a public declaration of their loyalty to England's Constitution. Their example was followed by many other large bodies of Dissenters "and particularly by a respectable meeting at the Library in Red-Cross St.". Price received threats of assassination, Morgan, 94. In his *Defence of the Established Church*, 1786, Rev. William Jones had said: "the Dissenters are, generally, zealous republicans; and, in their hostile designs against our ecclesiastical establishment, they can never be cordial friends to the aristocratical and monarchical parts of our constitution." Cf. "I am convinced a New Testament Christian will be a peaceful and useful member of civil society under any government." Correspondent in *Dissenters Magazine*, 5 February 1794.

his maturer years, was going on around him.[1] Much that had been still was: English Dissent, for example, had yet to reconcile itself to the theatre.[2] But Priestley observed in 1770 "a new species of Dissenter that I was sensible had been for some time springing up among us...who have as little of the spirit as they have of the external appearance of the old Puritans"—young gentlemen of the type produced by William Enfield's Academy, whose guiding star was 'politeness'—a flabby indifference in which Priestley saw the decay of 'just zeal'.[3] Nor was this wholly the distortion natural to a mature man remembering his own past. Samuel Palmer complained of late dining and resulting absence from afternoon service of the rich Dissenters.[4] A correspondent in 1794 speaks of a growing ignorance among orthodox dissenting youth of the doctrines of Christianity, and Bogue and Bennett dated this process of degeneration from

[1] Priestley, *Memoirs*, vol. I, pt. I, 17. *Letter to the Author of Remains*, 1770, XXII, 400. Crabb Robinson writes: "I have a faint impression of having learned a catechism in which there was this: 'Dear Child, can you tell me what you are? *A.* I am a child of wrath like unto others'." *Diary*, 5.

[2] The spirit of Prynne was not laid: the theatre was regarded as a national sin. We hear of a young dissenting minister dismissed for attending one and for quoting Shakespeare in his sermons. Priestley, *Letters*, 434. Wakefield once went to Drury Lane but thought little of Mrs Siddons. *Memoir*, II, 62. Even this taboo was breaking down: "to crown all they at length entered the doors of the theatre...". Bogue and Bennett, III, 387.

[3] Priestley, *View of the Principles*, 1767, 378. Dissenters are less well read in the grounds of their nonconformity, 375. Aikin says of Enfield: "candour was interwoven in his very constitution." *Memoirs*, 307.

[4] Sermon, August 1794. *Dissenters Magazine*, I, 363.

the lectures of Philip Doddridge, which concentrated more upon intellect than faith.[1] The truth was that Dissent was becoming more fashionable in tone, as the brilliant gatherings in Lindsey's Unitarian Chapel testi-fied. "They must have Universities near the capital", complained a reviewer in 1789, "and houses at the west end of the town: and they must mix if they can with the genteel world; and all this at the moment they contend that the Kingdom of their master is not of this world."[2] They paid extreme court to the great Whig aristocracy: and as tutors, clients, advisers and chaplains they saw much of the great and rather less of the good. These London ministers, prominent as they were in the society of the capital, did not impress Robert Robinson: "Well", he wrote, "the carnality of the whole disgusts me, and blessed be God *Robinson* can ramble with impunity, though in their esteem a kind of outlaw, a wild savage."

But internal unity remained whether it manifested itself in literary, theological or scientific friendships. The Rational Dissenters were universally self-revealing People.[3] Their funeral sermons were small biographies

[1] *Dissenters Magazine*, 34. Bogue and Bennett, iii, 480. Priestley thought these lectures "exceedingly favourable to Free Enquiry". *Memoirs*, i, 24. The trouble was the young Dissenters were learning what a preacher of 1776 called "that dissipated and voluptuous abuse of time and fortune called the Art of Living".

[2] *Gentleman's Magazine*, July 1789, ii, 59.

[3] And great journal keepers. Dyer thought a diary "as a kind of check to the waywardness of passion or any frivolity of character and as a register of the most important transactions of life, presents nothing either vain or enthusiastic". *Life of Robinson*, 29.

which usually contained the promise of a larger work. They lived their lives together and wrote their story for posterity. Priestley corresponded with Richard Price, Theophilus Lindsey, whose great friend he was, Christopher Wyvill, and many others. Wyvill himself, though not a Dissenter, corresponded with Lindsey, William Burgh, Towers, Disney and Thomas Walker. Priestley knew the Aikins well: they were related to the Belshams. Percival corresponded with Dr Beattie, the Bishop of Llandaff, Robertson, Paley and Madame Necker as well as with Priestley and many prominent Dissenters. The friendships of Price were remarkable for number and diversity.[1] Crabb Robinson knew George Dyer the friend and biographer of Robert Robinson; Robinson in his turn was a friend of Wakefield, William Frend and other Cambridge notables—among them Lindsey's friend, the unfortunate Fysche Palmer (one of those destined, to use an attractive contemporary euphemism, to make the voyage to the Antipodes). Mary Wollstonecraft was a close friend of Price's at Newington Green, and shared this friendship with Dr James Fordyce, himself the friend of Price and Kippis. As 'Pierce Delver', Hollis corresponded with Lindsey and Priestley. Benjamin Franklin had many close friends among the Rational Dissenters. The list might be extended indefinitely. Jebb and Burgh were well known

---

[1] Among them were Franklin, Jefferson, Priestley, John Adams, Hume, Smith, Kippis, Condorcet, Necker, Turgot, Paine, Howard, Towers, Erskine, Lyttelton, Shelburne, Stanhope. Thomas, *Price*, 155.

figures in dissenting circles: so was Stanhope.[1] "I dined yesterday", wrote Lindsey in 1775, "with Drs Price, Franklin, Priestley and Mr Quincey: no bad company you will say. We began and ended with the Americans."[2] It was at the request of Fothergill and Franklin that Priestley published his pamphlet on the American War in 1774. Franklin, Price, Kippis and John Lee were members of the Whig Club meeting in the London Coffee-house. It was through John Lee that Priestley met Burke, and we are given a picture of Burke, arm in arm with Priestley, forcing his way into the Privy Council to hear the interrogation of Franklin and his insulting treatment by Wedderburn.[3] Wakefield corresponded with Fox upon Lucretius and similar classical studies from Dorchester Jail—'gentle litigation' he called their arguments, which made soothing reading in the bitter years after 1796.[4] In the *Cambridge Intelligencer* which Benjamin Flower edited weekly after 20 July 1793, there were quotations and articles from Mrs Barbauld, George Dyer, J. T. Rutt, Christopher Wyvill, Mary Wollstonecraft and a full record of dissenting

[1] James Burgh's famous *Political Disquisitions* was a favourite hand-book in dissenting politics while Whig Dr Jebb knew it as he knew his Bible: see *D.N.B.* It is well worth reading as a contemporary analysis of the state of representation.

[2] Rogers met Paine at William Morgan's home and drank there to "the Republics of the world". Morgan was a F.R.S., a writer on finance, a Dissenter and Price's biographer. In Rogers' Diary for 1792: "Dined at Tuffin's with Cooper, Tooke, Dr Priestley, Dr Crawford, etc. Politics". Clayden, 246, 261.

[3] Priestley, *Letters to Monthly Magazine*, *Works*, Appendix, 396.

[4] Wakefield, *Letters to Fox*, ed. 1813, 90.

activities and misfortunes. This paper became a sort of nation-wide congregational magazine for the Rational Dissenters. But their name extended beyond England. Kippis and Priestley were urged to accompany Captain Cook.[1] Price was invited to take the control of America's State finance—a distinction he refused as coming too late in life.[2] Howard interested Joseph II in matters of prison reform.[3] With the French revolutionaries a stronger connection was formed. "Nos cœurs ont tressaillés aux idées consolantes de Price et de Sheridan", the Friends of the Constitution of Montpellier told the Revolution Society.[4] Price corresponded with Rabaut-Saint-Étienne, and the Duc de la Rochefoucauld. On his death the French Constitutional Societies wore mourning for a week.[5] A little later, the Birmingham riots brought letters of consolation to Priestley from every part of the intellectual world.[6]

The price of this cosmopolitan political connection was

[1] Priestley, *Memoirs*, 79.

[2] Morgan, *Price*, 80.

[3] Aikin, *Howard*, 135. Percival thought Howard's humility arose from preoccupation with Calvinistic original sin, not modesty. *Memoirs*, correspondence, 1785. He advised Aikin to submit his scheme for exterminating small-pox to Catherine of Russia, *ibid*.

[4] *Correspondence*, 42. The Friends of the Constitution at Vire wrote: "dans toutes les parties de la France, les noms de Milord Stanhope, du Docteur Price, de R. Sheridan et de tous les membres de la Société de Londres ont été répétés avec attendrissement", 85.

[5] *Ibid*. 19.

[6] He received messages of condolence from Condorcet for the Academy of Science, the Jacobin Club, the Revolution Society, the Society of Rennes, the Unitarian Society, the United Irishmen and the Republican natives of Great Britain in Ireland and America. *Memoirs*, II, 127–251.

that the Rational Dissenters were considered, politically speaking, Shelburnite pamphleteers: part of the 'republican malady' that afflicted him.[1] The generalization was false, but it was at Shelburne's house they could find all that was fresh in opinion from all over Europe.[2] "He professed", wrote Robinson to Lindsey in 1771, after a visit of Shelburne's to Price's house, "a warm regard to the Dissenters as friends of liberty etc., and promised, if ever he came into power, to exert himself in supporting their rights and placing them on the same footing as other Protestant subjects."[3] Price's friendship with Shelburne began some time before his first political writings.[4] Priestley became Shelburne's librarian and pensioner in 1772, and their friendship lasted seven years and was less happy.

But it was in the quiet places of retirement, in Newington Green and Hackney where Price spent his life: at Stoke Newington where Samuel Rogers grew up that the best side of dissenting life was to be seen. There were to be found dispassionate politics, cordial

[1] Tucker, *Familiar Letters*, 1783, 40.
[2] "I was seven years in the family of the Marquis of Lansdowne, which was altogether a political house, where I daily saw, and conversed with, the first politicians, not only of England but from all parts of Europe." Priestley, *Northumberland Letters*, xxv, 124. In Paris Priestley met Turgot, Necker, Brissot and Pétion. Percival, a member of the Royal Society of Paris, dedicated the third volume of his scientific essays to Lansdowne. *Memoirs*, lxvii.
[3] Rutt's note, *Memoirs*, 175.
[4] Morgan, 32. Priestley wrote to Price in 1772 of Shelburne: "I conceive him to be for ability and integrity together, the very first character in the Kingdom." *Memoirs*, letters, 175.

disagreement; all that *esprit de salon* which grew to maturity at Warrington, and attained culmination and disaster in the Academy at Hackney. In the short years of peace after 1783 and in such refuges as these, the Dissenters enjoyed a peace and an intellectual freedom which lived on as the memory of a Golden Age into the troubled years of the French War. "What a proud pre-eminence", wrote Thomas Belsham in his Diary of 1805, "to have enjoyed the intimacy of Price, of Priestley and of Lindsey."[1]

But if discord never penetrated into these retreats, religious difference split and split again the whole body of English Dissent. "The terms heterodox, heretic, deist, infidel", wrote William Frend, "are scattered abroad with great rapidity in dissenting communities, and under pretext of consulting the good of his soul, a narrow-minded congregation will frequently deprive an individual of all his earthly comfort."[2] This intolerance was doubly serious in that the minister was entirely dependent on the congregation for his usually inade-quate wage.[3] Thomas Belsham, Robert Hall, David Williams and many others were obliged on this account

---

[1] Williams, *Life*, 558.

[2] *Peace and Union*, 1793, 57.

[3] The maximum to be hoped for was £100, the average £40, a year. A correspondent in the *Dissenters Magazine* says "£70 or £80 is thought a capital sum", 503, I. Priestley speaks of ministers as starving. A correspondent in the *Dissenters Magazine*, March 1795, writes: "I know there are hospitals in abundance for the sick, and the insane, for old men and old women, for orphans and prostitutes but is there an hospital or decent retreat for old, infirm, ministers?" II, 119.

to quit one church and one congregation for another. For the first half of our period the cry of the heresy hunters was Arianism—Arianism that sprang from an Arminian root and spread over Devonshire, Lancashire, Cheshire, Warwickshire and many other counties. In the second half the favourite epithet was 'Socinian', which was used in a free way to cover a number of things from the system of Faustus Socinus to sympathy with the politics of Paine. On the whole it meant the denial of the doctrine of Atonement together with a freedom of scriptural interpretation. It was a common ground for attack both on the part of the orthodox Church and of orthodox Dissent. In Priestley's Warrington days it was hardly known and, although Priestley did much to propagate it, Socinians remained a minority. "A Socinian", wrote Thomas Belsham to Kenrick in 1790, "is still a sort of monster in the world."[1] The unpopularity which this creed brought Priestley is almost unbelievable: we have to go to Paine and Godwin for anything to equal it, and even then he probably came in for the largest share of vituperation. That his unpopularity was even greater with Dissenters than with Anglicans is the constant theme of his writings and letters. He abstained in 1790 from the agitation for repeal of the Test Act so as not to prejudice it by his name. After the Birmingham riots the indignation that this new Servetus aroused among the Calvinists of the day had far-reaching repercussions. Indeed, religious differences were so intimate and bitter that by a supreme

[1] Williams, *Life*, 426–7.

inconsistency the Dissenters, at the very time they were petitioning against the Test and Corporation Acts, were imposing private test acts in their academies in which "free enquiry had become an idol, which they bowed down to worship". This process of exclusion, together with the reaction in England after 1790, completed the downfall of the Rational Dissenters. Price died in 1791: Robinson in 1790. The year 1795 was a serious year of mortality for the leaders of dissenting thought: Stennett, Kippis, Harris, Romaine, Beddowes, Clark, Toller and Flaxman. In the funeral sermon which John Evans preached for the first three there is a note of falling off in the ministry: a suggestion that the giants are dead and only the pygmies remain: "help Lord, for the Godly man ceaseth: for the faithful fail among the children of men."[1]

But while they lived the Rational Dissenters endeavoured to model their conduct on principles of intellectual honesty. The key-word of their writings, the text of their apology, the sum of their ideology was 'candour'. "Candour", wrote John Aikin, "is in some measure the opposite of bigotry; for its essence consists in a disposition to form a fair and impartial judgment on questions and actions."[2] Aikin's *Letters* were published

[1] John Evans, *Funeral Sermon*, 18 October 1795, 10.
[2] *Letters*, I, 91. "On Prejudice, Bigotry, Candour, and Liberality." Cf.

> "Candour (alas!) is always frank and young;
> Whene'er she speaks, she looks with steadfast eyes
> And what she says is said without disguise."
>
> (Poem of 1798.)

in 1796; his second volume was written in the times that tried men's souls after 1794, and the long shadow of the dying century creeps over his pages. In politics the rule of 'Candour' demanded unfettered enquiry—"to think with freedom, to speak and write with boldness, to suffer in a good cause with patience, to begin to act with caution but to proceed with vigour"—this for Priestley was the whole duty of political man.[1] In religion it exacted complete toleration—an ideal that Priestley upheld in his writing and his conduct.[2] In all spheres its sovereignty enforced the exercise of reason and individual judgment on the right conferred and the duty exacted by education. "When learning or abilities are employed in the cause of despotism", wrote Towers, "they are entitled only to the contempt and detestation of mankind."[3] To 'Candour' Methodism was 'enthusiastical cant'. Neither morality nor religion would suffer from honest enquirers. "An intimate connection", wrote Wakefield, "subsists between letters and morality, between sensibility and taste, between an informed mind and a virtuous heart." His own motto was 'truth and freedom'. He read Godwin's *Political Justice* with pleasure and improvement: "I differ perhaps on many points, but

[1] *Letters*, *Works*, XXII, 455.

[2] "One day, I remember, I dined in company with an eminent popish priest: the evening I spent with philosophers, determined unbelievers: the next morning I breakfasted, at his own request, with a most jealously orthodox clergyman, Mr Toplady; and the rest of the day I spent with Mr Jebb, Mr Lindsey and some others, men in all respects after my own heart", 1790, *Memoirs*.

[3] Towers, *Letter to Nowell*, *Works*, II, 211.

I confess that I love such men, and wish ardently that they were not almost, but altogether, such as I am."[1] Rationalism would never lead to Atheism: "We can go without danger, wherever investigation can carry us." "The uncorrupted religion of Jesus will approve itself to the understanding of every impartial and reasonable man."[2]

"This false candour", wrote two hostile critics, "was the crying sin of Presbyterian Dissenters in the early part of George III's reign."[3] In the closing years of the century it allied itself with 'sensibility', but only rational sensibility. There is a romantic strain purely English in some dissenting authors of this period, for already Romance was walking in the gardens of England. The personal character and literary qualities of Robert Robinson reveal this blend of candour and sensibility into a humane rationalism; a balance not outweighed by the emotions but setting them off harmoniously against the promptings of intellect.[4] But at this very time they would have been better advised, had they foreseen what

[1] *Letters to Wilberforce*, 64–5. It is only fair to add that his great opponent, Watson of Llandaff, wrote to Percival in May 1791: "I have read both Dr Priestley's and Mr Paine's answers to Mr Burke and admire them both' —not bad for a prelate. *Memoirs*, clxix.

[2] Towers, *Genuine Doctrine of Christianity*, II, 334. Hall's famous sermon on "Modern Infidelity" was attacked by Anthony Robinson and Godwin, *Recollections*, 145. Robinson, *Liberality of Sentiment*, 1784, 215–17.

[3] Bogue and Bennett, IV, 373.

[4] Dyer says: "His manners were unvarnished by the frivolities of a polite education: his heart uninflated by the tumour of false greatness", *Life*, 5. Dyer himself was a romantic, a disciple of 'pure simple nature'.

was to come, to harden their hearts and steel their minds. The Rational Dissenters were destined to witness the impetuous back-rush of intolerance; the passions released by the French Revolution; mob violence and ministerial apostasy; wholesale desertion and reviling of principles once felt and avowed to be so sacred; the revelation that all the cherished enlightenment of the age was no more than a thin dust overlaying hatreds as barren and fierce as those of the seventeenth century; the heart-breaking repudiation of the philosophers' alliance.[1] In this reeling chaos the one abiding reality seemed to be the hypocrisy of those in power with their lip service to the fact and the heritage of 1688. "They persecute freedom", wrote Robert Hall in an impassioned sentence, "and adorn its sepulchre." But the agony of this disillusionment was too sharp to be endured and was succeeded by numbness and inarticulation. "It is nevertheless apparent", Paine had written in the intoxicating freshness of 1792, "that Spring is here", but it was Bentham who had gone on planting and tending undeceived.

[1] In his appeal to the Court of Delegates, July 1793, Frend said: "I have not called it an enlightened age, nor shall I easily be induced to call it so, while such a cabal and such judges can be found to exist in it." *Proceedings*, 233.

Chapter III

EDUCATION AND POLITICS

"THE DISSENTERS", wrote a correspondent to the *Gentleman's Magazine* in 1791, "are levellers by principle and education."[1] The influence of Protestant Nonconformity upon English education, at the time when education had sunk to almost its lowest point, has only of late years received adequate recognition.[2] For nearly a century and a half, from the Restoration in 1660 to their decline at the end of the eighteenth century, their academies gave the best and most practical instruction for youth to be found in Britain, outside, that is, the colleges and universities of Scotland. Nor were the Dissenters only practitioners of education; they were also its most consistent and ablest theorists, and if, in their first capacity, their work has now been recorded, their activities in the region of theory—the writings of men like Philip Furneaux, Joseph Priestley and David Williams—have yet to be fully recognized. Unendowed and unfriended, dissenting education had only its merits as a system, aided by a certain loyalty, already overtaxed

[1] 1791, 1, 556.
[2] Mr H. M'Clauchlan's *English Education under the Test Acts*, 1931, is a most able and exhaustive study to the valuable bibliography of which I am much indebted. He has completed the work begun by Miss Parker in 1914.

to support dissenting ministers, upon which to exist; and, when the decay at last set in, it was rather because that loyalty was alienated than by reason of neglect or bad service. In addition to consolidating their cultural unity at home, their system kept in close touch with the development of knowledge and thought abroad, with the result that much which was neglected at Cambridge, and which never reached Oxford, had a sympathetic reception in the dissenting academies.

"They who know the Dissenters will acknowledge that none appear more sensible of the importance of good education or less sparing in their endeavour to procure it for their children."[1] Three elements combined to determine the Dissenters' attitude to education: a natural right, a psychological theory, and a religious precept, with a result that their culture came to rest upon the double foundation of the Word of God and the *Essay Concerning Human Understanding*. By nature it was thought a child had a right to receive education; by nature the parent had a right to give it to him and to decide the content of it. For the parent this was one of those fundamental rights of which the State had no cognisance. "If any trust", wrote Priestley, "can be said to be of God and as such ought not to be relinquished at the command of man, it is that which we have of the education of our children."[2] "It is", wrote Kippis, "quite the greatest trust that can possibly be put

---

[1] John Aikin, *Life of Howard*, 1792, 11.
[2] *First Principles of Government*, 1771, 48–9.

into the hand of man."[1] Education should be a sphere for the exercise of private right and private enterprise: "Education is a branch of Civil liberty which ought by no means to be surrendered into the hands of the magistrate,"[2] or God's bounty in the progressive revelation of truth may be interrupted. Yet while they remained hostile to all forms of state control, the Dissenters annexed limitations to their individualism by giving to education a predominatingly social character. Education was held to be designed, not to produce occasional prodigies, but fashion good citizens, acceptable members of the congregation, skilled in the deportment of human society. "Children", wrote Furneaux, "should be carefully trained up in the knowledge and practice of the social duties", an ideal which could easily become, as it did in Priestley's hands, purely utilitarian,[3] designed to develope in the pupil not a brilliant character, but a useful one, and in this way to endow its possessor with the only real source of happiness.

Underlying this ideal was a psychological creed, derived from the school of sensation and experience; a creed to which all subscribed, some with such ardent faith that to attain to a millennium in human affairs by

---

[1] *Example of Jesus...Recommended*, Sermon for Southwark Charity School, 1 January 1780, 20; cf. Furneaux, *Sermon on the Importance of Education* for the same school, 20. "Education is a personal trust, lodged in a parent, and which cannot be delegated to another but in case of absolute necessity."

[2] Priestley, *First Principles of Government*, 54.

[3] Furneaux, *op. cit.* 12. Priestley, *Miscellaneous Observations Relating to Education, Works*, xxv, 1785, 5–6.

means of education seemed a simple and rational aspiration. In a child's mind resides the *tabula rasa* described by Locke; taken in its unformed state, all the principles of a good life, true notions of virtue, mental flexibility, candour, benevolence, the love of God and knowledge of His laws could be written indelibly upon it. All depended upon time and care. All knowledge comes from experience, but education is experience anticipated and "there is no arguing against experience".[1] It is never too early to form character and principle, never too late to acquire wisdom. Education was regarded as a seal: if the wax was clear and warm, a uniform and definite impression could be left. Thus the design of dissenting education was to simplify knowledge into first principles, in order that a child's first conceptions might be moulded decisively.

But beyond the life of the world lay the life of the spirit, and education should also be instruction for salvation. Obedience to the Divine precept, "train up a child in the way he should go, and when he is old, he will not depart from it", was the recurrent theme of dissenting education, the text of sermons, the sum of hope.[2] True learning was religion's first ally; in a world

---

[1] Furneaux, *op. cit.* 34: "When we first come into the world, our minds are a kind of blank slate that will admit of anything being drawn upon them; of rough materials that may be moulded into almost any form", 21. There is "a desire and thirst of knowledge and instruction which is natural to the mind of man", 31; cf. Watts, "We are born ignorant of every good and useful thing", etc. *Discourse on Education of Children and Youth, Works,* v, 360.

[2] Furneaux, *op. cit.*; Watts, *Discourse,* v, 359.

full of evidence of God's purpose, everything should yield a lesson in His supreme power and goodness. "God and religion may be better known, and clearer ideas may be obtained from the amazing wisdom of our Creator, and of the glories of the life to come, as well as the things of this life, by the rational learning and the knowledge of nature that is now so much in vogue."[1]

To these domestic activities must be added the foreign connections of dissenting culture with Holland, America and Scotland. It is difficult to estimate the total, still more the individual, influence upon dissenting thought of these three civilizations, but it is perhaps near the truth to say that during the seventeenth century and for the first twenty years of the eighteenth, Dutch influence was undoubtedly predominant. At the close of that period the academies drew nearer to Scotland and America, as the events of the American War of Independence were to illustrate. But Holland had been first in the field, the Holland which so profoundly influenced Locke, and, though the connection weakened during the eighteenth century, it was never wholly in abeyance. It was a not infrequent practice for a student to proceed from an academy to a Dutch university; Nathaniel Taylor did so in the seventeenth century, while Charles

---

[1] Watts, *Discourse*, 380; cf. Milton, *Of Education*, "the end then, of learning is to regain the mind of our first parents by regaining to know God aright, and out of that knowledge to love Him, to imitate Him, to be like Him, as we may the nearest by possessing our souls of true virtue, which, being united to the heavenly grace of faith, makes up the highest perfection." *Works*, Amsterdam, 1708, ii, 845.

Mery de Veil, D.D., wandered from Metz to France, France to Holland and Holland to England in the train of his doctrinal fluctuations.[1] Samuel Jones, tutor at Tewkesbury Academy, who taught both the future Archbishop Secker, and the grandfather of William Godwin, was educated at Leyden.[2] Jeremiah Hunt, too, studied at Leyden, and Daniel Neal, the dissenting historian, at Utrecht, while John Kerr, Tutor at Highgate, was Doctor of Medicine of Leyden. We hear of Philip Doddridge receiving Dutch pupils.[3] As the eighteenth century wore on Dissenters went more often to Scotland to obtain their degrees, but in 1765, when a difference arose at a Scottish university between the medical students and their professors, the students, among whom was Thomas Percival, did not hesitate to migrate to Leyden.[4] This university also gave John Aikin his degree. Holland was John Howard's 'great school' in sociology to which he never tired of returning; a familiar process in the development of English social philosophy. For many, too, the land of glorious William had a patriotic as well as a cultural appeal.[5]

But the English Dissenters were more closely tied in culture and tradition to the American colonists than any

[1] Bogue and Bennett, ii, 188 *et seq.*
[2] Kegan Paul, *Godwin*, 1876, i, 3.
[3] Milner, *Life of Watts*, 1834, 91. Bogue and Bennett, ii, 67. Parker, *Academies*, 92.
[4] Thomas Percival, *Works*, 1807, i, xvii.
[5] Aikin, *Life of Howard*, 73. Aikin wrote in 1784 from Delft: "the statue of William, the great Assertor of Liberty, excited in me sentiments of the profoundest veneration." Lucy Aikin, *Life of J. Aikin*, ed. 1820, i, 70. Priestley disliked Holland.

other community overseas. The chain between the
English academies and the American universities was
slender but unbroken. Morton, tutor of the second
academy at Newington Green, emigrated to New England in 1685, where he eventually became Vice-President
of Harvard. Theophilus Gale, divinity tutor of Newington Green (d. 1678), left his library to Harvard, but
retained the philosophical books for his own students.[1]
Isaac Chauncy, tutor of Hoxton (d. 1712), had graduated
in Harvard, of which his father was President. He
educated Richard Price.[2] Isaac Watts's American correspondence is illuminating. "Your catechisms", says one
correspondent of November 1745, "are taught among us
and have learned to speak Indian." His sermons, his
own gift, were read every Sabbath evening in the Hall of
Yale College with whose rector, Elisha Williams (1726–
39), he corresponded. "All which, and indeed, every
piece that drops from your golden pen, meet with joyful
acceptance in general from those who see them here in
New England, as well as those at home."[3] At a later
date Priestley's lectures in history and general philosophy
were studied in American colleges.[4] These cultural relations were not without value when, later in the century,
English Dissenters acted as colonial agents and swelled
the agitation against the project for an American episco-

[1] Parker, 62. Bogue and Bennett, II, 49.
[2] M'Clauchlan, *English Education*, 119.
[3] Thomas Gibbons, *Memoirs of Rev. Isaac Watts*, 1780, 439, 445.
Letter from Z. Boylston, Boston, 1732, 449.
[4] *Familiar Letters*, 214.

pate and the Quebec Act. "Shall I go to war", asks a pamphleteer of 1769, "with my American Brethren?"

In Holland, dissenting learning had made contact with the maturity of the great European school of natural jurisprudence, the school of Grotius, Pufendorf and Jean Barbeyrac. With America it had ties of religion and tradition and for the Dissenters the colonies afforded an object lesson in religious liberty. It was in Scotland that English Dissent found its last and most important intellectual alliance; a Scotland moving swiftly and surely down the midstream of European culture; the Scotland of Beattie, Hutcheson, Hume, Smith, MacKenzie, Robertson and Macintosh.[1] Dissenting youths studied in the Scottish universities, and from this source distinguished leaders of the Dissenting Interest received their doctorates. Price and Priestley were given Scottish doctorates. In an earlier generation, James Guyse (1680–1751) was Doctor of Divinity of Aberdeen. James Fordyce (d. 1796) was a Doctor of Divinity of Glasgow; Nathaniel Lardner (d. 1762) a Doctor of Divinity of Marischal College. Thomas Percival studied at Edinburgh where he enjoyed the friendship of Hume, Robertson and Macintosh. He obtained the Doctorate of Law of that University for Joseph Priestley, the Rev. Nicholas Clayton and the Rev. William Enfield.[2] At the close of the century, the practice of receiving such degrees had become so common as to be disreputable;

[1] All these were friends and correspondents with leading Dissenters.
[2] Bogue and Bennett, IV, 425. Percival, *Memoirs*, 1807, XVII.

when Robert Robinson was offered a Doctorate of
Divinity from Edinburgh he considered that "so many
egregious dunces have been made D.Ds both in English
as well as Scotch and American Universities, that he
declined the compliment".[1]

One thing was notable; the absence of any markedly
French influence. It is true we hear of two French
students at David Bogue's Academy at Gosport, but
their presence was exceptional.[2] French was widely
taught in the academies with varying success; the accent
seems to have been usually poor; and there was occasionally a French tutor at the academies, for example at
Warrington, but Isaac Watts thought attainment of the
language was labour lost, seeing that all the most
valuable works were obtainable in English translations.[3]
In later life, however, Dissenters were occasionally deep
students of French thought; Robert Robinson and John
Aikin are examples, but the majority were little affected
by it.

As centres of culture, the academies exhibited considerable variety of type, size, curriculum and stability.[4]
In origin, an unexpected result of the Restoration
Settlement, when the so-called 'Clarendon Code' ejected
two thousand dissenting ministers, and savagely re-
pressed under the Conventicle and Five Mile Acts, their
existence was precarious until the Revolution of 1688

[1] Dyer, *Life of Robinson*, 1796, 199.
[2] Bogue and Bennett, IV, 280.
[3] Watts, *Discourse*, 378.
[4] Cf. Priestley, *Discourse* of 4 December 1791.

came to mark the beginning of their greatness. Bogue and Bennett, in a division widely accepted, place the second and most brilliant period of their history in the years which culminated in the death of Philip Doddridge, who personified the remarkable mid-century flowering of what had been a casual and haphazard sowing.[1] By that time the permanent features of these institutions had hardened to uniformity, and the brilliance of their tutors and the latitude and fearlessness of enquiry which prevailed in them, foreshadowed the reasons why they must fall into decay, should they ever become alienated from the great body of their supporters. Institutionally they generally professed Presbyterianism and Independency, but their pupils were drawn without distinction from among both Dissenters and Churchmen. It was not until the reign of George III that the Baptists began to take interest in education. Their solitary academy at Bristol could number Robert Hall among its tutors, and the Bristol Education Society of the Baptist Denomination financed students in the northern universities. With their aid Hall studied at King's College, Aberdeen. Robert Robinson hoped to found a dissenting college at Cambridge, for which he and Capel Lofft drew up the plans, but little came of it.[2] In organization, these

[1] Vol. III. Among the seventeenth-century pioneers were two Magdalene men: Spademan (d. 1708) and Tallants (of Shrewsbury Academy), Fellow and Vice-President, author of a universal history. Bogue and Bennett, I.

[2] Morris, *Biographical Recollections*, 37, 46, 51. Dyer, *Life of Robinson*, 189. He wrote to Daniel Turner: "we want a College for law and physic and for gentlemen of independent fortunes", 190; Bogue and Bennett, IV, 293.

institutions were a blend of educational establishment and congregation, the 'family', as it was called, following Milton's advice in being "both school and university".[1] The period of residence varied from three to five years; the method of instruction was lecturing. Isaac Watts has left us his picture of the perfect tutor.[2] Many of the most distinguished men of the century received their education in this way. Secker, subsequently the villain of the scheme for an American episcopate, Henry Beaufoy, William Smith, M.P. for Norwich, and Malthus were educated at dissenting academies, while to Alexander Kippis and the Hoxton Academy belonged the distinction of instructing William Godwin.[3]

"Thus", wrote Priestley challenging the established order, "while your Universities resemble pools of stagnant water, secured by dams and mounds and offensive to the neighbourhood, ours are like rivers which, taking their natural course fertilize a whole country."[4] It was in the novelty and width of their curriculum that the academies could claim to be unique. That curriculum merits particular study in three aspects: the instruction which it gave in history, in philosophy and in the science of politics. Throughout the eighteenth century the

[1] *Op. cit.* 847.

[2] "He should also have much candour of soul, to pass a gentle censure on their impertinencies and to pity them in their mistakes and use every mild and engaging method for insinuating knowledge into those who are willing and diligent in seeking truth, as well as reclaiming those who are wandering into error." *Improvement of the Mind, Works,* v, pt. 1, 322.

[3] M'Clauchlan, *English Education,* 44. Kegan Paul, *Godwin,* 5.

[4] *Letter to Pitt,* 1787, 128.

Dissenters continued to pursue the semi-medieval ideal of universal science; a quest in which they were strengthened by their belief in the unity of knowledge.[1] But if their educational system surveyed many fields, it had but one centre, one single essence: the knowledge of God as manifested in the world. A study of Philip Doddridge's *Memoirs* reveals a man whose primary interest lies in theology, alleviated by a sprinkling of *belles-lettres*. Similarly at his academy the chief object of his pupils' attention and study, during the three years of their course, was his system of divinity.[2] This theological predominance persisted long after 1763. "With us", wrote Priestley in 1790, "everything is made subservient to the study of theology." "Every other branch of knowledge should be valued in proportion as it bears upon theology and illustrates the sacred scriptures."[3] It was Doddridge who inaugurated the change from Latin to English as the language of the academies—a far-reaching reform which exercised great influence over the classical studies of the pupils, and in later years became

[1] "Every man who pretends to the character of a scholar, should attain some general and superficial idea of most or all the sciences: for there is a certain connexion among the various parts of human knowledge, so that some notions borrowed from any one science may assist our acquaintance with any other...." Watts, *Improvement of the Mind, Works*, v, pt. 1, 302.

[2] Job Orton, *Memoirs*, 1766, 92.

[3] Bogue and Bennett, III, 271: to theology "classical learning, the belles lettres, mathematical science and the whole encyclopaedia of human knowledge, bear scarcely the proportion of the glow worm to the sun", 265; also IV, 304. *Familiar Letters*, 274, e.g. "Proper Objects of Education": "I hesitate not to assert, as a Christian, that religion is the first natural object of Education", 14.

one of the more prominent private battle-grounds with
Joseph Priestley on the defensive and men like Gilbert
Wakefield and William Enfield in the attack. "If",
wrote Edward Tatham in 1794, "instead of wasting
their time in breeding civil mutiny and fermenting
dissentions in the state, if these superficial and ostensible
but industrious men could make Greek grammar the
subject of their labours, the nation might be more free
from faction for fifteen years to come."[1]

Isaac Watts enumerated the "ornaments and accom-
plishments of life" proper for young persons as "grammar, logic, geometry, geography, astronomy, natural
philosophy, history and poetry",[2] but it was in the field
of natural philosophy, despite the prevailing dearth of
'philosophical apparatus', that the academies chiefly
distinguished themselves. Priestley at Warrington
Academy taught classics and Hebrew, modern languages,
grammar and rhetoric, logic, history, politics and law.
Outstanding emphasis was laid upon mathematics,
natural science and 'pneumatology'. History and pneumatology deserve special attention. In his writings,
Priestley more than once claims for himself the credit

[1] *Chart and Scale of Truth*; Wakefield's censure must be approached
with caution: thus when he says that in history "every student of
moderate faculties is competent to be his own instructor", it is
probably just a sneer at Priestley and Hackney College. *Memoir*, 1,
358. He speaks of digesting the *Encyclopaedia* in three years—
"away with such trumpery from the earth", 358. His criticisms
gave a handle to anti-dissenting opponents. Cf. Priestley, *Miscellaneous Observations*, 24.
[2] Gibbons, *Memoirs of Rev. Isaac Watts*, 1780, 181. Watts was
educated at Thomas Rowe's Academy in London, 20.

of introducing the study of history into the academies. This is certainly an exaggerated claim, however much he may have done to popularize its study and present it as something deeper than a polite relaxation popularized by Bolingbroke. History was taught at Kibworth under the Rev. John Jennings in 1728, and Philip Doddridge sometimes descended from divinity to "history natural and civil" and "particularly the history of nonconformity and the principles on which a separation from the Church of England is founded", as presented by Calamy and in harmony with Locke.[1] "History", wrote Watts, "is a necessary study in the supreme place for gentlemen who deal in politics. The government of nations and the distressing and desolating events which have in all ages attended the mistakes of politicians, should be ever present in their minds to warn them to avoid the like conduct." He would have history studied in conjunction with 'philological knowledge'; a sort of vocabulary of customs, manners and laws, designed to facilitate translation of the often cryptic lessons of the past.[2] That such lessons existed was undoubted: "the knowledge of history ancient and modern, sacred and common, is the best substitute in the place of experience."[3] The lives of the persecuted dead are the inspiration of living martyrs, and this early introduction to the story of their great wrongs could not fail to affect the temper of English Dissent. In the instance of men like

---

[1] Orton, *Memoirs*, 96. Priestley, *Memoirs*, I, pt. I, 51.
[2] Watts, *Improvement of the Mind*, *Works*, v, pt. I, 304, 314.
[3] *Ordination Charge* of Rev. Hugh Worthington, 1782.

Robinson and Towers, it can be seen how intimately woven into their intellectual texture English history had become. History, too, was capable of transcending the limits of sect or country and embracing all humanity: "that to a human being", wrote Aikin in 1796, "no study can be more important than that of the character and fortune of mankind, may be almost assumed as a self-evident proposition." The study and knowledge of man is the proper object of history and biography.[1]

The textbooks for historical studies were largely foreign in origin, until Priestley produced a work specially designed for Dissenters. Pufendorf's *Introduction to the Study of Europe* was in constant use; it was to be found, together with his other works, in the Bristol, Sheriffhales and many other academies.[2] Warrington students in addition read his *History of Sweden*. Out of the 670 books in the library of Warrington Academy, 82 related to history and kindred subjects. In the library of the Caermarthen Academy was Hotman's *Franco-Gallia*, Pufendorf's *Introduction* and Voltaire's *Louis XIV*.[3] The Swiss Turrettin was another popular author.[4] "For civil history", writes Doddridge, "we read Pufendorf's *Introduction to the History of Europe* with Crull's continuation and his *History of Asia, Africa and America*...for French we read *Telemachus*."[5] Priestley's

<hr/>

[1] Aikin, *Letters from a Father to his Son*, 1796, 217, 234.
[2] M'Clauchlan, *English Education*, 302.
[3] Parker, 159, for Warrington. *MSS. Catalogue of Books in Presbyterian Coll. Caermarthen.* Dr Williams' Library, *Records of Nonconformity*, 15. [4] M'Clauchlan, *English Education*, 302.
[5] *Correspondence and Diary of Philip Doddridge*, ed. 1829–31, II, 465.

lectures became a textbook in the Northampton and Hackney Academies.[1] The historian Rapin was widely read; Rollin filled Godwin with "the greatest transport".[2] More modern historians fared worse: Hume, "the infidel historian", found few admirers, although Dissenters were always willing to quote his view that England owed her liberty to the Puritans. But on the whole they agreed with Joseph Towers that his *History* was not a book for young people, "especially with regard to their conception of the rights of men and of citizens". It was felt, however, that while a man should choose his authors with care, he ought to gain the best from all. "The acquirements of a Grotius and a Montesquieu, a Jones and a Gibbon", wrote Aikin, "cannot be viewed without high admiration or the use they made of them, without liberal applause."[3]

But since the history of nations was conceived as the history of individuals, it was felt that it could only be understood by a thorough knowledge of human nature.[4] Accordingly, the past was interpreted in the light of

[1] *Familiar Letters, op. cit.*

[2] Kegan Paul, *Godwin*, I, 12.

[3] Aikin, *Letters*, Bogue and Bennett, I, xxvi. Towers, *Observations on Hume*, 421–2. Blackburne wrote in his life of Hollis: "Eachard, Hume, Smollett and others of their turn, write their histories upon the principle of tyranny for the use of Kings.... Wilson, Osborne, Coke, Rapin, Mrs Macaulay, Harris, etc. write for the use of the people." I, 210.

[4] "Societies being composed of individuals, the history of the former consists of the actions of the latter", Aikin, *op. cit.*, 223. He could not help noticing, however, "the silent and unobserved manner in which some of these great personages steal out of the world".

'pneumatology', a wide term stretching from the study of the simple mechanism of the human brain to the knowledge of ethical and metaphysical systems. "The study of human nature and of human laws and govern-ment is another most important and distinct object of attention in a course of liberal education."[1] "That which is of most importance for all learned men to be ac-quainted with", wrote Watts, "is the law of nature, or the knowledge of right and wrong among mankind, whether it be transacted between single persons or communities, so far as common reason or the light of nature dictate and direct." For this reason Watts thought that the third chapter of Pufendorf's *De jure naturae* was well worthy of "the study of every man of learning, particularly lawyers and divines together with other treatises on the same theme".[2] In this, as in every sphere, the bible of dissenting educational faith was the *Essay Concerning Human Understanding*.[3] Of almost equal

[1] Priestley, *Miscellaneous Observations*, 1785, 20. It is an essential to all political knowledge.

[2] Watts, *Improvement of the Mind, Works*, v, pt. 1, 308.

[3] Locke was the secular prophet of English Dissent which adored him in prose and verse. Towers and William Belsham write in his defence. For Percival he was "one of the most distinguished ornaments of the human species". Watts wrote:

"Locke has a soul
Wide as the sea,
Calm as the night,
Bright as the day:
There might his vast ideas play
Nor feel a thought confused."

Cf. Doddridge, Letter to Mr Clark 1721—the greatest part of the logic taught at Kibworth is built upon Locke.

popularity with Locke were Pufendorf, Le Clerc and Grotius. "Our ethics", wrote Doddridge, "are drawn up by Mr Jennings and collected chiefly from Pufendorf and Grotius and we are referred to both of them under almost every section."[1] Ethics were a part of pneumatology, and Philip Doddridge delivered many lectures on the subject: it was widely interpreted, and Aikin included as 'pneumatology' political philosophy and economy. It was at Warrington that Thomas Percival contracted his deep love of ethical studies. In an earlier generation Samuel Palmer at his academy was taught Suarez, Baronius and "the moral works of the great Pufendorf".[2] Grotius on *The Truth of Religion* was a standard work; Doddridge found it a plain, easy, practical book: a plentiful source of spiritual comfort. He recommended it to his pupils in their studies, together with the works of Erasmus, Locke, Baronius, Le Clerc and others.[3] It is the fact that such subjects were fundamentals of a wide system of education that is significant. The obverse side of all this cosmopolitan learning was the danger of overstocking young minds and producing a mental surfeit, a danger to which

[1] *Correspondence and Diary of P. Doddridge*, I, 42; II, 462 *et seq.* Jennings was tutor at Kibworth, where Doddridge was educated. "Our ethics were a part of pneumatology." *Ibid.*

[2] Bogue and Bennett, II, 81. Morris, *Recollections of Hall*. Edward Percival, *Memoirs of Thomas Percival*, 1807, VIII. He was a pupil of the Rev. John Seddon.

[3] *Correspondence and Diary*, II, 481; IV, 490. For ethics and history he recommended Pufendorf, *De officio hominis et civis* and *Introductio ad historiam*.

Wakefield was sensible. "With respect to metaphysics, morals, history and politics", he wrote, "young men in these institutions are choked with such infusions, to a degree that makes even the strongest stomach regurgitate under the operation."[1] Be that as it may, instruction in psychology and history was certainly an incitement to political theorizing.

It is the political implications of these academies which we have chiefly to study. Throughout the century, from the days of Sacheverell to those of the anti-Jacobins, they incurred the political odium cast upon their tutors and sponsors. In the seventeenth century Robert South attributed all the evils, religious, moral and political, of his day to "the exorbitant license of men's education" which they received in "conventicle, frantic academies, in defiance of the Universities". He urged the great men of his time "utterly to suppress and extinguish those private, blind conventicling schools and academies of grammar and philosophy, set up and taught secretly by fanatics, here and there all the kingdom over", whose sole design was "to derive, propagate and immortalize the principles and practices of 'forty-one' to posterity... schism and sedition for every faction and rebellion *in saecula saeculorum*: which I am sure no honest English

---

[1] Wakefield, *Memoirs*, I, 1792, 355. Such subjects are begun too young. Education for the ministry is "prodigiously absurd" and fixed lectures "the mere popery of education", "a digestion of the whole *Encyclopaedia* in three years the very quintessence of empiricism", 366. Mind and attention suffer in such multiplicity of pursuits. Where better can the student find "such flowers of sentiment favourable to civil liberty" than in classical history? 361.

heart will ever say 'Amen' to". There would be no hope for England until "these lurking subterranean nests of disloyalty and schism be utterly broken up and dismantled".[1] Sacheverell in 1704 urged the destruction of "these illegal seminaries that are planted up and down the several parts of the kingdom, as 'twere so many schismatical Universities set up in opposition against the established church...for the education of youths in all the Poysonous corrupt maxims of Republicanism which in our constitution have and must for ever end in anarchy and confusion". They are "academical conventicles", "schools and nurseries of rebellion".[2] Samuel Wesley, in his controversy with Palmer, objected to the use of such authors as Milton in the academies, while Job Orton, by writing his *Life of Doddridge*, hoped to remove "some prejudices, if such remain, against these seminaries as if they were nurseries of Schism, Enthusiasm and Faction".[3] He did not succeed in his design, for thirty years later an academy was considered the best training place for the complete Jacobin, and the two

[1] Robert South, Sermon on *Virtuous Education of Youth the Way to a Happy Old Age*, 1685, *Works*, ed. 1723, III, 381, 410-11. The dedication of Lord Clarendon's history to the Queen asks: "What can be the meaning of these several seminaries and, as it were, universities, set up in divers parts of the kingdom, by more than ordinary industry, contrary to law, supported by large contributions, where the youth is bred up in principles directly contrary to monarchical and episcopal government?" Milner, *Life of Watts*, 79.

[2] *Nature and Mischief of Prejudice and Partiality*, Sermon 1703-4, 23-4.

[3] M'Clauchlan, *English Education*, 79. Orton, *Memoirs of Doddridge*, Preface, iv.

institutes of Warrington and Hackney were regarded as something very close to political clubs for republicans.

An examination of 'politics' as it was taught in the academies will show the extent to which this label was justified. The tradition of political teaching as part of a polite education is as old as the academical idea itself, stretching back to the Renaissance and beyond. The Dissenters had no claim to originality in this respect. Thus, Milton numbered the study of politics among the pursuits necessary in places of instruction.[1] The Dissenters could only claim what was perhaps the largest share of a common practice, and an interest of a very practical kind in such instruction. It was the manner rather than the matter which was potentially important, and though there was no consistency of practice, this strain of political theorizing never ceased in the academies of the eighteenth century, but rather increased in the measure that the academies themselves flourished. Defoe at Newington Green learned "politics as a science", and the Newington Green Academy was associated with Morton, the author of a famous political work called *Eutaxia*. In 1791 Priestley describes the academies as places "where youth are taught the most liberal principles both in religion and politics"; while in the middle period Watts' attachment "to the republican cause of

---

[1] Among the subjects taught "must be the study of politics, to know the beginning, end and reason of political Societies: that they [pupils] may not, in a dangerous fit of the Commonwealth, be such poor, shaken uncertain reeds, of such a tottering conscience as many of our great Counsellors have lately shown themselves, but steadfast pillars of the State. After this they are to delve into the grounds of law and legal justice." *Of Education*, 848.

freedom" was remarked on.[1] Politics was taught sometimes by itself, sometimes in conjunction with civil law
which was identified with the law of nature and nations,
and sometimes, as was Priestley's practice, in conjunction
with history. Law lectures were read at Sheriffhales;
law and politics were taught at Bristol.[2] The standard
books were Pufendorf's *Law of Nations* and *Duties of
Man*; Grotius *De jure belli* and the works of Locke.
Copies of these and other similar books were to be had
in the academies' libraries. Of Warrington's 670 books,
there were 40 dealing with politics, commerce and law
as against 85 devoted to history and Scripture.[3] The
catalogue of the Presbyterian College at Caermarthen
contained some remarkable things.[4] In addition to the
three already mentioned, Le Clerc and Cumberland were

[1] Priestley, *Proper Objects of Education*, 425. Milner, *Life of
Watts*, 669. Parker, 60. Defoe wrote of Morton's Academy:
"neither in his system of politics, government and discipline, nor
in any other exercise of that school was there anything taught or
even conveyed that was anti-monarchical or destructive to the
constitution of England." Milner, *op. cit.*, 84. This book of
Morton's *Eutaxia* "established the principles of policy exactly
correspondent to the English Constitution: asserting at once the
rights and honours of the Crown and the Liberties of the subject".
Toulmin, *Historical View*, 1814, 233.
[2] Toulmin, *Historical View*, 227. M'Clauchlan, *English Education*,
101.   [3] Parker, *Academies*, 159.
[4] *MSS. Catalogue* [D.W.L. *Records of Nonconformity*, 15]. It contained Bayle; Doddridge's lectures; Geddes the Roman Catholic's
works; Grotius, *De jure* and *De veritate*; Harrington's *Works*;
Hartley "On Man", Hobbes; Hutcheson's *The Independent Whig*;
Le Clerc; Montesquieu's *Lettres Persanes*; Locke's *Works* (several
copies of the *Human Understanding*); Lambard; Milton's *Works*;
Pufendorf, *De Officio Hominis*, *Introductio ad Historiam Europae*,
Elementa Jurisprudentiae and *Feudal Law*; *Rights and Liberty of the
People Vindicated*; Selden; Sidney; Voltaire; etc.

popular authors; these with Locke furnished the textbooks of the Taunton Academy in the opening years of
the century, and maintained their popularity till the
end.[1]

But in the last issue it depended entirely on the
personality of the tutor himself whether, to transpose
Burke, this unplumbing of the dead would furnish
material to assassinate the living, and, in the case of men
like Price, Priestley, Robert Hall, Andrew Kippis and
William Belsham the zeal of the instructor certainly
determined the character of his lectures.[2] But here
again, if we except Priestley's *Lectures*, there was little
that could be called exceptional. At the end of the
century, certainly, when public opinion finally turned
against them, the dissenting academies became more
radical. Sedition was not the prerogative of Hackney
only: John Fell of Homerton in 1797 was forced to
resign his tutorship for his political opinions.[3] But a

---

[1] Toulmin, *Historical View*, 231.

[2] Robert Hall owed "his undying passion for liberty" to his
schoolmaster at Northampton, the Rev. John Rylands, who once
said during the American dispute: "were I the American commanding officer, I would call together all my comrades and brother
officers; I would order every man to bare his arm that a portion of
blood might be extracted and mixed in one basin on the table. I
would then command everyone to draw his sword and dip the
front of it in the basin and swear by the Great Eternal never to
sheathe the consecrated blade, till he achieved the freedom of his
country. If after that anyone should turn coward or traitor, I
should feel it a duty, a pleasure and luxury, to plunge my weapon
into that man's heart." Morris, *Biographical Recollections*, 31. Hall
himself taught at the Bristol Academy.

[3] M'Clauchlan, *English Education*, 180.

truer view of the politics taught in the academies can be gained from the manuscript and printed lectures which became textbooks than from these individual scandals. Two in particular are illustrative of all: the printed lectures of Philip Doddridge and the manuscript lectures of John Horsey. Doddridge's lectures were the most famous of dissenting textbooks: Kippis edited them, and Toulmin wrote in 1791: "It is the text-book in other seminaries of the Dissenters and is now read by Mr Belsham."[1] Doddridge's successors, Ashworth and Robinson, both used it. In the course of a large body of lectures, Doddridge devotes ten of them to 'civil government'. The lectures themselves are in the old formal style, and singularly devoid of enthusiasm. They are unequal and noncommittal, contractual in theory and largely drawn from Locke. Obedience is grounded in hedonistic utilitarianism, and "virtue requires that obedience should be paid to civil rulers in those things in which the authority of God is not apprehended to contradict their commands".[2] A mixed government, such as the English, is universally considered the best.[3] In these dismal pages one can share in the fatigues of an

[1] Letter to *Gentleman's Magazine*, April 1791, I, 330. Joshua Toulmin was the general advocate of the Dissenting cause in the *Gentleman's Magazine* and in the civic politics of London.

[2] Doddridge, *Lectures*, ed. of 1763, 167. He refers to Krasinski's *Poland* and Knox's *Ceylon*, for "instances of the oppressions which have attended arbitrary governments", 166, while illustrating his arguments by historical references to the Spartan and Carthaginian Constitutions, the Saxon Witenagemot ("the original of the British Parliament") and the Spanish Cortes, 160.

[3] *Op. cit.*, 165.

unwilling audience. But if the lectures themselves are below criticism, the references he gives his pupils are highly interesting. There are extensive citations of Pufendorf's *De jure* and *De officio*, Grotius's *De jure*, Locke's *Essay on Civil Government* and Sidney's *Discourse*.[1] The lectures themselves, however, would not have disturbed the most suspicious of despots. The same is true of John Horsey's lectures on "Government and the British Constitution", delivered at the Northampton Academy. These are pretty well a repetition of Doddridge brought up to date. What is not borrowed from Locke is taken from Blackstone. Sir Robert Filmer, as in Doddridge, is once more slain: government is "a lesser evil adopted to avoid a greater", and Paley's objections to Locke's view of contract are dumbly accepted.[2] In the choice of forms of government appeal is made to a hedonistic rather than a juristic criterion: the best government is that which gives most happiness and government is a revocable trust. A perfunctory reference to Priestley gives no illusion of up-to-dateness or modernity to these drab pages. The *Lectures on the British Constitution* is simply a handbook compiled from Blackstone and Delolme, devoid of any originality and waking to life only over certain practical matters: over the iniquity of restraints upon liberty of conscience; the wretched state of prisons; the want of a regular police

[1] He cites Pufendorf 26 times; Grotius 16; Sidney 12; Locke 11; also Temple, Voltaire's *Charles XII*, Montesquieu, Priestley, *On Government*, Filmer, Hobbes, More's *Utopia*, and *Télémaque*.
[2] Dr Williams' Library, Northampton MSS. 3.

in large towns "to suppress houses of ill fame, put down the miseries of vice and debauchery, to clear the streets of vagrants, to compel the idle and disorderly persons to work and to assist the magistrate in the apprehension of thieves and felons". The style of these lectures is a trifle more humane; but even so the author's references remain far more interesting than the text.[1] These lectures are not the stuff of republicanism and levelling.

In the Warrington and Hackney Academies we have two wholly exceptional institutions. But there was nothing inconsistent in their existence; they represented a logical development of dissenting educational theory and practice: that theory which said "question all, for from questioning only comes the truth". They illustrated, too, the prominence enjoyed by the 'Rational Dissenters' in the culture of their century, and if they came at last upon evil days and passed away unregretted, it was only because those Rational Dissenters themselves and their ideals were no more. In a lesser degree this was as true of the Manchester as of the Warrington Academy: "the vigour of both", said an observer, "seemed to languish with the decay of that spirit from which they derived their origin."[2] The closing years of the century saw these institutions falling into ruin on all sides. The academies at Kendal, Taunton, Warrington, Exeter and

[1] 477, 479. References to Locke, *On Government*; Grotius, *De jure*; More's *Utopia*; Pufendorf, *De jure*; Paley, Sidney, Lyttelton, Cambray, Montesquieu, Beccaria, Priestley, *On Government*, Doddridge, Belsham's *Essays*, Blackstone, Delolme, Furneaux's *Letters*, etc.

[2] Percival, *Memoirs*, lxxxi.

Daventry all disappeared. "I am a few years passed three score",[1] wrote a Dissenter, "and have seen wonderful revolutions with regard to the Dissenting Academies", and if these changes were in part the outcome of their over-ambitious nature, it was chiefly that the academies outgrew their age and perished in intellectual solitude when the French Revolution hardened English thought and shortened English tolerance. But for twenty years after 1770 they fought the battle for unfettered enquiry and fought it in the spirit of Robert Robinson: "may the sword of the Lord", they said with him, "and of Liberty cut thro' all the host of slavery and superstition."[2] The finest talents, and greatest hopes of Rational Dissent centred in the academies of Warrington and Hackney:

> ...the seats where science loved to dwell,
> Where Liberty, her ardent spirit breathed.[3]

The story of these two academies has been told too often to require repetition. Founded in 1757, Warrington had many famous names among its tutors. John Taylor, D.D. (1757–61), gave it its peculiarly broad theological

---

[1] *Gentleman's Magazine*, May 1793, 1, 409. He says of Hackney: "they have ruined the institution by setting it out in too superb a style, inconsistent with the plainness and simplicity of the Dissenters." *Ibid.*

[2] R. Robinson, *Lectures on the Principles of Nonconformity, Works*, II, 29. A correspondent in 1789 considered this plan of lectures to contain "so much fuel of fanatical fury, as is not to be met with in so small a compass in any other performance within my knowledge". *Gentleman's Magazine*, January 1789, 19.

[3] Anna Laetitia Barbauld. For Warrington, see Parker, M'Clauchlan, and H. A. Bright, *Warrington Academy*.

tone, and John Aikin, D.D., directed the days of its glory. He was a remarkable character as all who came into contact with him asserted: "Religion", wrote Wakefield, "had brought every wayward idea and irregular passion into subjection to the law of reason and had erected her trophy in the citadel of his mind."[1] His staff included Joseph Priestley, Gilbert Wakefield, George Walker and William Enfield. His successor in the divinity tutorship was Nicholas Clayton. All these men were well known, and some notorious, in political and religious controversy. Brilliant as the teaching was, it was the humane atmosphere of Warrington that was most remarkable: "the literary offspring", wrote Thomas Percival, one of the first pupils of the academy, "cherished in its shade from the researches of Taylor to the inimitable poetry of Barbauld, have conferred on the seat of their retirement a name of more than ordinary lustre."[2] It was at Warrington that Priestley had his apprenticeship as a tutor; it was there that he delivered his lectures in history and civil policy and began the practice of dissertations and 'orations' to develop the powers of the students in theological and political controversy. Logic, "ontology and pneumatology", law, history, politics, ethics, natural and moral philosophy were taught. In the midst of all this profusion, theology suffered and Warrington was remarkable for the small number of

[1] Priestley described him as "a man who to the learning and dignity of a tutor, joined the ease of a friend and the affection of a father". *Letter to the Author of 'Remarks'*, 1770, 431.

[2] Percival, *Works*, I, xli.

ministers it produced. Such as it did were not of the orthodox persuasion; Arianism was the accepted creed of the place; Priestley had not yet turned Socinian, but that faith was represented by Seddon. At Warrington was born that indiscreet political enthusiasm which caused the downfall of Hackney. But for a few years it was a delightful centre of culture, and the members of it loved and revered it. "The year employed in academical pursuits", the Rev. John Horsey told his pupils at Northampton in 1796, "if harmony reigns in the family, constitutes, perhaps, as agreeable a period as any in the whole course of life", and of nowhere was this truer than of Warrington.[1] The tutors, their families, and the elder students all met on an equal footing of learning and politeness. The quarrelsome Gilbert Wakefield tells how much he enjoyed "that flow of reason and that peace of soul" which his colleagues provided; "especially at a weekly meeting, holden alternatively in the house of each other".[2] But the liberality was too great; disciplinary troubles, a characteristic of the academies, appeared and when, after three disastrous years, the academy was closed in 1786 the story of Hackney had already been foretold.[3]

[1] *Vacation Address*, 1796–8, Northampton Academy. Dr Williams' Library, North. MSS. 7.

[2] *Memoirs*, 1792, I, 215. His friendship with William Enfield was the brightest thing for him: he applies to it the Virgilian lines 'His amor unus erat', etc. The spell of Warrington can be found in the Aikins' writings; Lucy describes it in *Life of J. Aikin*, I, 10. See Priestley, *Memoirs*, 58: "we drank tea together every Saturday and our conversation was equally instructive and pleasing."

[3] "The dissolution of the academy at Warrington was a fatal

The Hackney Academy was founded in 1786 in order to remedy the lack of any considerable dissenting place of education in the capital, and almost from the outset it was drawn into the exciting whirl of London politics, a dangerous implication which grew deeper in the ten years of its existence. It was to be no ordinary institution, but the sum, as it were, and model of the educational experience of more than a century. "The Dissenters", declared a newspaper, "are establishing a University of their own."[1] Thomas Belsham had noted that save at Daventry there was no theological freedom left in the academies: English Dissent was beginning to impose its own private test acts. Hackney was rashly designed to remedy this growing illiberality: "It will be a Unitarian Academy", wrote Priestley to Lindsey, "do what they will."[2] The greatest hopes attended it. Perhaps it might "form in a civil capacity such a man as Hampden, or Algernon Sidney in England, a William Penn, a Franklin, or a Washington in America, or even such an illustrious character as those which are now conducting the glorious revolution in France."[3] The curriculum was to include

blow to the wide Dissenters of whom it was the guide and boast."
Bogue and Bennett, v, 284. Thomas Belsham wrote to the Rev. J. Yates, March 1786: "I know not how to think without poignant regret of the approaching desecration of those buildings, so long the seat of learning and the muses and which the venerable names of Taylor and Aikin will render dear to every friend of science and virtue as long as the Dissenting Interest shall last." Williams, *Life*, 315.   [1] *London Chronicle*, 13 July, 1787.

[2] April 1787, *Letters*, 1, pt. 11, 20. Belsham, *Memoirs of Lindsey*, 281, ed. 1812.

[3] Priestley, *Discourse on the Proper Objects of Education*; to the supporters of the New College, April 1791, *Works*, xv, 422.

"History, Civil and Ecclesiastical, the principles of Law and Government".[1] The time was felt to be propitious. A report of 1790 expressed the hope that the new institution "will concur with other events, which none of you can disregard, in disseminating those principles of civil and religious liberty that must necessarily conduce to the general improvement of Society and of mankind".[2] Priestley hoped no less: "May the sons of this institution eagerly catch and wisely direct, the beam of sacred truth and let them apply it, like Ithuriel's spear, to every object without distinction, whether of a civil or a religious nature." The invitation was accepted only too readily, but public opinion was not impressed by the new Ithuriels. Cobbett sneered at the "Hackney coach"; "Nova Cracovia" it was called and "the slaughter house of Christianity".[3] Burke described it in the Commons as a "hot bed of sedition".[4] Of those connected with the college, no less than ten members of the committee

[1] MSS. Minutes of Hackney College (left by Belsham at *D.W.L.* in 1812), 67.

[2] MSS. Minutes, 20 January 1790, 127: Harvard presented Hackney with a copy of its Library Catalogue. Cf. Priestley: "Another and most important circumstance which calls us to attend to the proper education of our youth is the new light which is now almost everywhere bursting out in favour of the civil rights of men and the great objects and uses of civil government: while so favourable a wind is abroad, let every young mind expand itself, catch the rising gale and partake of the glorious enthusiasm." *Discourse*, 434.

[3] *Gentleman's Magazine*, June 1792, I, 495; May 1793, I, 412.

[4] Cf. "There is no doubt but that their great teacher of the rights of man [Ball] decorated his discourse on this valuable text with lemmas, theorems, solutions, corollaries and all the apparatus of science, which were furnished in a great plenty and perfection

were members of the Revolution Society.[1] The connection with Priestley was particularly discrediting; "what faithful parent or guardian, who regards our constitution, can commit the education of a child to such teachers?", asked a correspondent in the *Gentleman's Magazine*.[2] Even Priestley counselled moderation to the students. But discipline was poor and zeal ran high. Jeremiah Joyce, once a foundation pupil, distinguished himself in an unfortunate capacity in the state trials of 1794. The forces of orthodoxy followed the lead of the Coward Trust and kept aloof to see the illustration of 'quem deus vult perdere'.[3] Political passion steadily increased until at last, on one mad enthusiastic day, the college entertained Tom Paine to dinner at "the most glorious republican party that the walls of the College ever contained".[4] That was the beginning of the end: no institution could continue on such lines, and in 1796 it expired lamented by many. "The giving up of the College", wrote Priestley to Belsham, "is certainly very

out of the dogmatic and polemical magazines, the old horse-army of the schoolmen, among whom the Rev. Dr Ball was bred, as can be supplied from the new Arsenal at Hackney." *Appeal*, 91, Rivington's edition.

[1] Price, Kippis, Rees, Turner, Brand, Hollis, Henry Beaufoy M.P., John Ingram, Edward Jeffries and George Jeffries. *Proceedings of the Revolution Society*, London, 1789, 10, MSS. Minutes, 1 *et seq.*

[2] *Gentleman's Magazine*, June 1791, 1, 500. Another, later in the same year, (a moderate Dissenter) says he will no longer support the Academy after Priestley's adieu to the students. Belsham's mother once wrote to him "I hope you will never take your politics from Junius or your theology from Dr Priestley."

[3] Priestley, *Dedication*, 1794, 390. *Gentleman's Magazine*, 1793, 1, 409.   [4] M'Clauchlan, *English Education*, 252–3.

mortifying to the friends of liberty." The closing of the Hackney Academy is part of the history of the English reaction to the French Revolution. As Belsham said, the spirit of the times was against the institution. It was too closely connected with Price and Priestley and their tenets to survive.[1]

"You cannot but be apprized", Priestley told his pupils at Hackney, "that many persons entertain prejudice against this College on account of the republican and, as they choose to call them, the licentious principles of government which are supposed to be taught here."[2] The New College at Hackney is an epitome of the question of how far were the political principles of English Dissent moulded by its education, and how far by contemporary culture. It is clear that in the average academy all the political freedom and sedition existed only in the imagination of opponents. The congregations themselves, bodies of men which Robinson considered "constitutionally in possession of Christian liberty",[3]

[1] Belsham, *Memoirs of Lindsey*, says: "the mania of the French Revolution, which began so well and ended so ill, pervaded all ranks of society and produced a general spirit of insubordination" (282). His intimacy with Lindsey began at Hackney, of which he draws a pleasing picture. But Wakefield defended the behaviour of the students: "never was I connected with such a set of orderly, industrious, attentive, respectful and amiable youths" (I, 374), but he is not to be trusted. Anyway his connection ended in 1791. Belsham wrote to Samuel Palmer in 1783: "young men will be young men and my spirits are sometimes too much hurt by their impudence." Williams, *Life of Belsham*, 247.

[2] *Op. cit.* 390.

[3] Dyer, *Life of Robinson*, 241. Southey noted: "this insensible but natural inclination towards democracy which arises from the principles of a popular Church Government." *Essays*, 1832, 46.

were a far more practical lesson in liberalism than the lectures of Doddridge or Horsey. Again, there was nothing exceptional in the books which were studied, or the fact that instruction in politics was given. At one period the *Essay concerning Human Understanding* may have been forbidden in Oxford, but in the second half of the century Blackstone was lecturing there, and Paley at Cambridge. Nor were there any agreed principles upon which political instruction could be based, since Dissenters had no such uniform political faith. "The Protestant Dissenters", wrote Towers, "like the members of the established Church, differ in their sentiments upon some public measures and on political subjects. As a body of men, however, they have generally and justly been considered as firm friends to the great interests of civil as well as religious liberty." More explicit than that they could not in their nature be. Their sentiments as men might be quite independent of their sentiments as churchmen.[1] All depended, in the academies, upon the character and opinions of the tutors, and if Arianism or Socinianism flourished there was likely to be revolt in the metaphysical and political sphere. "I am very sure", wrote Thomas Belsham, "that the diligent and impartial study of the scriptures which is the only plan of study which I can conscientiously recommend, will never lead to orthodoxy nor will a courageous and conscientious

[1] Towers, *Letter to Samuel Johnson*, 231. As Molesworth said: "Whiggism is not circumscribed and confined to any one or two of the religions now professed in the world but diffuses itself among them all." Preface to *Franco-Gallia*, 1721, XI.

his work above the level of the many pamphleteers, who, in dreary day to day controversy, applauded or decried the Rights of Man. Price, too, sustained the Rights of Man, but the Rights of Man as a moral agent, capable of infinite moral improvement. He strove to fix events, however pressing their topical interest, in the true historical and philosophical perspective. Thus, it might be said that, in the ultimate analysis, he saw in the American Revolution less an economic crisis, or any arresting historical process, than a vivid, widely drawn illustration of the existence and virtue of philosophical liberty. The aloofness of this universal viewpoint was not without its disadvantages; thus, at times, there emerges from his writings a political man who is but a slight shadow of a free agent moving gingerly and unconvincingly amongst solid, eternal, utterly obligatory laws and truths. But this occasional disproportion can be overlooked. Certain convictions and hopes were so intimately woven into the stuff of his being, that his restless intellectual energy had to search for some immutable foundations in time and space, upon which to erect a moral tabernacle reaching from earth to heaven. Mentally in opposition to the governing convictions of his day, his intellectual life was a long revolt against the philosophy of sensation and experience and the scepticism in which that philosophy culminated. Sympathetic study of his work, too, reveals another inspiration of which he himself was perhaps ignorant; an aesthetic conviction of the dignity of man, which was impatient of intellectual compromise and of a moral system founded on utilitarianism. His absoluteness was not, as has been suggested, that of the mathematician: it was the unyielding instinct of the artist. His *Principal Questions in Morals* was published early in his life in the 'fifties of the century, and remained his creed till his death; a creed which he defended against his friend Priestley in one of the few literally 'candid controversies' of the times. His political system is most readily to be understood as the translation of these moral convictions into a code of political conduct.

In morals he opposed the standards of absolute good and evil to the calculations of utility; similarly, in psychology, he upheld the existence of necessary truth in place of the accepted theories based upon sensation and experience. Underlying his system are visible the personal characteristics which most deeply affected him; a religious conviction of a fervour incompatible with philosophical anarchy, and an independent half-romantic disposition which was moved by the aesthetic appeal of the very word 'liberty' to revolt against the machine-men of deterministic materialism.[1] It is true that, in his writings, he did not always escape the language of the mechanist, or the mathematician; but on the whole he

[1] On the sensational system "there is neither matter, nor morality nor Deity nor any kind of external existence left. All our discoveries and boasted knowledge and the whole universe is reduced into a creature of fancy". *Review of the Principal Questions in Morals*, 1757, ed. 1757, 85. "Without Physical Liberty, man would be a machine acted upon by mechanical springs, having no principle of motion in himself or command over events and therefore incapable of all merit and demerit." *Civil Liberty*, 1776, Philadelphia Reprint, 5.

preserved himself creditably from that facility which analogy lends to argument. Formal logic he accepted, but he was not without an honest doubt of the short-comings of language as a medium into which to translate thought.[1] In this atmosphere of intellectual honesty, and stimulated by deep personal feeling, he commences his *Review* with his own theory of the nature of the human understanding.

His theory is presented as a negative criticism of Locke's. Price discovers a difficulty in determining from the *Essay concerning Human Understanding* the exact rôle played by 'sensation' and 'reflection', particularly in their relation to new ideas of every kind.[2] His doubt resolves itself into a broader question: from whence are our ideas, especially our moral ideas, derived? Are they the product of a sense or of the understanding? Price is convinced that there is a distinction between these two possible sources: sense and understanding, he asserts, are two completely different faculties of the soul, different in their province and in their nature.[3] The utmost function of sense is to obtrude upon us, inde-pendently of our wills, certain impressions which are the material, perhaps of some, but by no means of all, our

[1] *Morals*, 146. He realized, however, that criticism of this kind moves in a circle and if a man questions his faculties "at the very time and in the very act of suspecting them, he must trust them", 149. He accepted rationalism and logic as a mental condition: "what things seem to us we must take them to be, and whatever our faculties inform us we must give credit to", 158. This is his reply to Hume and Berkeley: "Because we sometimes dream, must it be doubtful whether we are ever awake?" 155.

[2] *Ibid*. 16.   [3] *Ibid*. 21.

ideas. The actual formation of an idea, he contends, is the work of an independent intellect. Sense is capable of presenting certain 'forms' such as light and colour to the mind, but only the intellect itself by its own unfettered activity can attain to universal, abstract ideas; can perceive the total nature of things of which sense can appreciate only the rough exterior.[1] Thus no impression, however vivid, of sense and no degree, however wide, of experience can endow us with such an idea as that of gravity, because the idea of gravity is an abstraction which only the intellect, the real understanding, which pursues a more perfect, short and certain way to truth than the road of experience and observations, can formulate. "As bodily sight discovers to us visible objects; so does the understanding (the eye of the mind and infinitely more penetrating) discover to us intelligible objects; and thus, in a like sense with bodily union, becomes the inlet of new ideas."[2] Single individual ideas are of two kinds: 'original' ideas which are conveyed to us immediately by the organs of sense, and 'subsequent' ideas which result from our perception of their nature and their relations. This division might be equally well presented in another way: into ideas which imply that there is nothing real outside the senses, nothing real outside the perceptive agent's own affections and sensations, and ideas which denote that there is something distinct from such affections and

---

[1] *Ibid.* 19. "Sense sees only the outside of things, reason acquaints itself with their natures."
[2] *Ibid.* 51–2.

sensations, which denote in fact their real and independent existence and truth. Our moral ideas belong to the second category: 'right' and 'wrong' are simple ideas, existing objectively and unchangingly, and capable of immediate perception in the understanding. It is true that some impressions of pleasure and pain generally attend our perceptions of virtue and vice, but such impressions are merely effects, concomitants[1] of the process of perceiving and not the perceptions themselves. Sense and true perception are in substance utterly different and remote from each other; they are as separate as matter from spirit.

This dualism extends beyond the mind and reaches into the whole realm of being. There is no doubtful marcher-land nor shared sovereignty. Matter and spirit inhabit different planes; the soul has no common ground with the body. This clear distinction has the force of necessary truth; we are irresistibly confronted with its existence whether we turn to Divine revelation for enlightenment or whether we pursue knowledge in the light of nature and reason. On the physical plane the distinction is peculiarly self-evident, since thought and reflection are independent of the modifications of matter. "Matter is something that is solid and extended and figured and moveable: Spirit is something that acts and wills and judges."[2] Again, if more proof were needed, we know that all matter is 'discerptible', that is, capable of infinite division, while the essence of spirit, of mind,

[1] *Ibid.* 19, 63.
[2] *Nature and Dignity of the Human Soul*, Sermon, 1766, 2.

These conclusions lead naturally to a more specific study of the nature of morality. "Morality", Price writes, "is a branch of necessary truth and has the same foundation with it."[1] Good and evil are absolute and unqualified; they are as isolated from each other as matter from spirit. We must distinguish clearly in our minds between morality considered in itself and what might be called social or socially-conditioned morality. Morality is unaffected by utility, and stands aloof from all considerations of apparent public benefit and extenuating circumstance. "That Morality is external and immutable" is the 'important corollary' which results from Price's theory of the understanding.[2] Just as in art there are certain forms and qualities possessing a natural aptitude to please or to offend, so in morality we are able to distinguish immediately and intuitively a good from an evil action, and the clarity of that distinction will to some degree depend upon the strength of our intellect. "Vice is of essential demerit: and virtue is in itself rewardable";[3] from the moral tribunal there is no appeal in heaven or upon earth. 'Absolute and eternal rectitude' is determinable in itself and cannot be affected by considerations of 'publick utility and inutility'. To measure virtue and vice by a hedonistic calculus is to confuse the thing itself with the cause of the thing. "Virtue and vice, from the nature of things, are the immediate and principal and most constant and intimate causes of private happiness and misery."[4] Happiness is indivisible from rectitude, and, since rectitude is itself

[1] *Morals*, 137.   [2] *Ibid.* 74.   [3] *Ibid.* 149.   [4] *Ibid.* 92.

unchanging, the happiness which accompanies it is un-
faltering and everlasting, and it is in obedience to rectitude, and in the free pursuit of goodness, that individual
and social virtue consists. Once we have discovered the
nature of virtue, we shall also have discovered the secret
of private happiness, and the characteristics and province of the ideal state.

We can distinguish, says Price, two kinds of virtue:
there is absolute or abstract virtue and there is relative
or practical virtue. The two are distinct. The first belongs
to the eternal world: its laws run unchallenged through
that immortal realm of which man, by birthright of his
soul, is a citizen. The second is the virtue of this world,
the perception of which determines both individual
conduct and the character of the state. Virtue of the first
kind, abstract virtue, is comparable with abstract reason:
"It denotes what an action is, considered independently
of the sense of the agent: or what in itself and absolutely,
it is right that such an agent, in such circumstances
should do: and what, if he judged truly, he ought to
do."[1] But Price never laid the full burden of this absolute
obligation upon the shoulders of imperfect humanity.
While convinced that a rational perception of good and
evil was the most active human motive force, the most
elastic spring of action, he was aware that the rational
faculty differs in different men in that the degree of
virtue is affected by the degree of rationality.[2] For this

[1] *Ibid.* 298.
[2] Yet reason remains the supreme guide. "Reason in man, like
the will of the community in the political world, was intended to

reason he erected a relative system of moral evaluation in the shadow of the eternal objective standard, but he remained sensible to the compromise and a nostalgia for this absolute standard pervades his work. "Rectitude, then, or virtue is a law. And it is the first and supreme law, to which all other laws owe their force, and in virtue of which alone they oblige. It is an universal law. The whole creation is ruled by it: under it men and all rational beings subsist....It is coeval with eternity: as unalterable as necessary everlasting truth: as independent as the existence of God and as sacred and awful as His nature and perfections."[1] Such a weight of sovereignty might well crush human nature beneath it. But the attainment of perfect harmony with the supreme law remains an ideal, the realization of which men are morally obliged to attempt. Such realization may be won by way of an intermediate stage: the achievement of the paramountcy of the individual conscience. But since the perception of rectitude and, consequently, the degree of virtue which we attain are limited by our individual intellectual capacity, the whole rule of right in its every aspect can be learned only by the possession of a universal and unerring knowledge such as no human mind can possess. Hence it follows that, "the Universal Law of Rectitude, though, in the abstract idea of it,

govern his whole conduct, and to be the supreme controlling power within him. The passions are subordinate powers, or an *executive force* under the direction of reason, kindly given to be, as it were, wind and tide to the vessel of life in its course through this world to future honour and felicity." *Additional Observations*, 1777, 31.

[1] *Morals*, 178-9.

always invariably the same, must be continually varying in its particular demands and obligations",[1] and it is amongst these necessary modifications that we must look for virtue of the second sort: relative or practical virtue, which determines the immediate principles of action in a virtuous agent. The characteristic of this relative virtue is that it depends for its worth upon the agent's conscious opinion of the motive underlying his actions. "What denominates an agent virtuous and entitles him to praise is his acting from a regard to goodness and right."[2] Thus a man, desiring to act virtuously, must first inform his intellect as best he can of the various ways open to him; he must then follow that road towards which his rational conscience directs him. For the individual, therefore, the capacity to act virtuously postulates a free determination of his own conscience. Accordingly, if a civil magistrate determines what a man's religious faith shall be, he robs that man of all title to virtue.

The possession of virtue, then, implies certain capacities: it also implies certain duties. Foremost amongst these stands our duty to God. Price shared with Locke and Rousseau a profound conviction of the social necessity and value of religion; a conviction most forcibly and peculiarly illustrated in his conception of national sins. From religion we derive the purest and strongest impetus to the performance of all social duties: "he that forgets God and His government, presence and

---

[1] *Ibid.* 277. "Numberless are the facts and circumstances which vary and modify the general law of right, and alter the relation of particular effects to it", 264.   [2] *Ibid.* 202.

laws, wants the main support and living root of genuine virtue, as well as the most fruitful source of tranquility and joy."[1] Another duty which obedience to the law of rectitude exacts is duty to ourselves, a duty difficult to observe but indispensable. "Private interest affords us, indeed, the fullest score for virtue",[2] but this duty lies to our true selves; it is dictated by true self-love, to which we are impelled not by an unworthy desire to gratify our lower appetites, but by a semi-aesthetic consideration: by our knowledge of the dignity which should adhere in man who was made in God's image. Translated into social terms this self-duty becomes benevolence. It is true that benevolence can be either instinctive or rational, but it is the second only, "universal, calm dispassionate benevolence", which is the duty of the virtuous. In addition there are the duties of gratitude, veracity and justice in matters of property and commerce.[3]

It is when we turn to investigate the capacities of a virtuous agent that the root of all Price's political thinking is uncovered, and it is around those capacities that the whole of his lofty moral and political system revolves. The law of rectitude is, as we have seen, a law not arising from any act of will, but arising from the nature of things, from the character of God and His universe. It is the perception of rectitude, not response to command of any kind, which is the spring of human action, and it is only when we act in conformity with our rational perception of rectitude that we act virtuously. But this

[1] *Ibid.* 241.   [2] *Ibid.* 249–51.   [3] *Ibid.* 251–3.

act of conformity must be free and self-determined. "Liberty and Freedom constitute the capacity for virtue", because no moral capacity can exist where there is not liberty and free self-determination according to individual reason and conscience. "It is truth and reason that in all cases oblige and not mere will", will which is swayed by the unworthy motive powers of pleasure and pain in themselves.[1] Simple conformity in any individual to any external will, merely because it is a will, is a form of externo-determinism which is the negation of all moral self-government. It is true that we virtuously obey the will of God, but we do so not because it is a simple will, however stupendous, but because it is the will of God and, as such, a manifestation of the Divine knowledge and goodness. All obligation is founded on reason and rectitude, and it is only when obligation is in harmony with rectitude—a perfect harmony in the instance of the law of God—that it becomes binding. For once a conjunction is effected between will and rectitude, the element of will is transmuted, and from the fusion there emerges something which is a reflection of the eternal law of goodness. We have thus heard the conclusion of the whole matter. The essential demand of Price's system is for complete moral liberty and self-destination. "Virtue supposes determination and determination supposes a determiner: and a determiner that determines not himself is a palpable contradiction."[2] To be virtuous a man must be free; morality postulates

---

[1] *Ibid.* 78.   [2] *Ibid.* 306.

liberty. The political implications of this philosophical creed are not difficult to foresee.

He displayed them at greatest length in his *Observations on the Nature of Civil Liberty*, which was given to the world in 1776 as "the sentiments of a private and unconnected man".[1] This is a curious work which, while having all the flavour of definitiveness, is curiously lacking in definition, but it was written fervently and in a cause too pressing to wait upon niceties. It requires supplementation from his other political writings and from his sermons. Yet, in a sense, all his works written subsequently to his *Review of the Principal Questions in Morals* are applications of, footnotes to, his moral theory. It is chiefly by regarding his political writings as satellites revolving around this central moral system, that their originality can be assessed, for Price himself wore with pride the label 'Lockian' liberally affixed upon him by contemporaries, and was happy to be recognized as a disciple.[2] But if he often used the phraseology of Locke he differed from him in certain cardinal aspects: in his psychological beliefs and in the purpose of his work. The *Essay on Civil Government* is an apology for an accomplished political fact, and only incidentally a political theory. Price, on the contrary, was preoccupied

---

[1] *Observations on the Nature of Civil Liberty and the Justice and Policy of the War with America*, 1776. Philadelphia reprint, Advertisement.

[2] *Ibid.* 53. "Price, Priestley, Rousseau, Paine, could justify on the principles of Locke, their own visionary doctrines, pregnant with consequences so mischievous to society and so different from what Locke himself intended." *Anti-Jacobin*, i, 396.

with the idea of a state and with its nature. His whole conception of politics was an elaboration of his primary dogma of philosophical liberty, and, if in its expression he sometimes fell into the prevailing terminology of property, it was because he felt that moral self-determination was the most precious property a man could possess. His moral convictions rendered repugnant all theories which sought to establish the State on a basis of experience or utility; to explain it and justify it in terms of historical evolution or past custom. This attitude is exemplified in his approach to the problem of the American colonies. "The question", he writes, "with all liberal enquirers ought to be, not what jurisdiction over them Precedents, Statutes and Charters give, but what reason and equity and the rights of humanity give",[1] since, unlike the rotting parchments of past expediency, reason and equity are unchanged and unchanging with the years. He relies upon arguments based on the existence of natural rights and an absolute standard of rectitude: "just government...does not infringe Liberty but establishes it; it does not take away the rights of mankind but protects and confirms them."[2] It would be contrary to the dignity of man as morally free and capable of virtue, and as being fashioned in the image of the Deity, to accept rights from so earthly a contrivance as the State. For God does not play a negative part in the temporal affairs of the world; He does not dwell remote from the world in deistical impartiality, unhearing and

[1] *Ibid.* 19–20.
[2] *Additional Observations*, 1777, 13–14.

unseeing the splendours and miseries of men's earthly sojourn. God watches over the politically-righteous in the State; they are of His party; they receive the considerable patronage of His dispensation; and it is when national sins harden the heart of a people that we begin to realize "the importance of righteous men in a Kingdom".[1] There may always be a handful of just men in Sodom to allay the vengeance of the Lord; some small minority to acknowledge the sovereignty of the unchanging Law of Right, in comparison with which ordinances dictated by earthly expediency sink to the level of paltry impotent by-laws.

Thus the State should exist to illustrate an idea: the idea of liberty, or self-determination. "Every object of the understanding has an indivisible and invariable essence: from whence arise its properties and numberless truths concerning it";[2] and it is from the essential idea of 'self-direction or self-government' that arise the four types of liberty: physical, moral, religious and civil. Physical liberty is "that principle of spontaneity or self-determination which constitutes us agents": the property which differentiates a man from a machine. Moral liberty is the power to follow at all times and in all circumstances our perception of right and wrong; it is

[1] *Fast Sermon at Hackney*, 10 February 1779, 14. "It is to them that States owe their preservation. It is on them that the very being of a society depends; and when they cease, or are reduced to a very small number, a nation necessarily sinks into ruin." Thus, in Price we find the rule of the Godly displaced by the political weight of the Righteous: the Elect have become the Patriots.

[2] *Morals*, 74–5.

the free capacity for virtue. Religious liberty consists
in the possession of the unqualified rights of private
conscience. Civil liberty is "the power of a Civil Society
or state to govern itself by its own discretion".[1] In
general terms, to be free is to be able to follow one's
own will, when that will is motivated by a conception of
rectitude; to be unfree is to be in subjection to the will of
another. In private life the free man shapes his own
destiny; in public life he is his own legislator. Since the
only true happiness arises from the pursuit of righteousness, it follows that there is in free government a value
and a dignity worthy of divinely created man. "As
moral Liberty is the prime blessing of man in his private
capacity, so is *Civil* liberty in his *public* capacity",[2] and
the value of both consists in their moral worth. At this
stage in the argument Price becomes more concrete; the
liberty which he claims is not a state of enslavement to
our passions, but a state of rational obedience to the Law
of Rectitude, the Sanction of which is our own free will.
In our private capacity, moral liberty is not freedom to
act anarchically but freedom to act virtuously: to obey
our real will. But 'real will' in Price denotes something
very different from the organic real will of the *Contrat
Social*. The real will enjoys that harmony with the
eternal Law of Right which transmutes the element of
simple will within it; a harmony which is attained less
by social co-operation than by the removal of those
obstacles which impede the moral path of the individual.

[1] *Civil Liberty*, 3–4. *Additional Observations*, 2.
[2] *Civil Liberty*, 12–13.

But for these obstacles, every individual would live and act in perfect righteousness; indeed, even in the present weakly state of reason, a man cannot act wickedly "but is conscious of a tyranny within him, overpowering his judgment and carrying him into a conduct for which he condemns and hates himself: 'the things that he would he does not, and the things that he would not, these he does'".[1] Similarly in the life of the State, Price distinguishes between 'liberty' and 'licentiousness'. The State is worthy to be called free when it follows its whole will in conformity with the Law of Rectitude; its will thus losing the character of will, and gaining the character of law. Political 'licentiousness' is "government by the will of rapacious individuals, in opposition to the will of the community, made known and declared in the laws".[2] A government which is founded on a cynical farce of representation; which attempts to deprive a man of his property without his consent and so to rob him of a part of his freedom and of his capacity for virtue; which tries to force its arbitrary will upon a separate community; that is a government guilty of political licentiousness; these are the circumstances in which government defeats its own ends, and enacts that injustice and wickedness for the mitigation of which it was created. For the right of a separate community to determine itself is absolute: a right equivalent in nature and sanctity to the self-determination of the individual.

With his completed definition of liberty Price's political philosophy was written; what remained was appli-

[1] *Additional Observations*, 8–11.   [2] *Civil Liberty*, 9–10.

banding together we are united by a common striving after righteousness. Thus, it has been the age-long task of human ingenuity to contrive "such forms of association as should be most likely to produce security, peace and comfort": to combine together in order to render circumstances more favourable for the attainment of virtue. Thus the State is at one and the same time the servant and the sanction of the master principle of self-determination. It is true that the State has inherited other minor but less commendable characteristics. Thus, to some extent, the State may be said to originate from the wickedness of men or, if not from their actual depravity, at least from their imperfections; to some extent, too, the State may fairly be termed an institution of human prudence. But in its essence it is a guardian and guarantor of human property, especially of human moral property; it conditions the life of virtue by delivering us from subjection to other wills, and leaving us free to obey our own. The State can do little to aid us in our moral lives; it can in no way dictate to our consciences and wills what is right and what wrong. The State, if it is not to become a tool of unrighteousness, must guarantee to its citizens full freedom of opinion and conscience since, to Price's mind, public liberty seems to resemble some sort of phoenix which is continually reborn in public discussion of rights from the ashes of that despotism and decay towards which all

its different forms are no more than so many modes in which they [the people] choose to direct their affairs and secure the quiet enjoyment of their rights". *Civil Liberty*, 5.

forms of government seem inevitably to decline. But as we have seen the State within these limitations exercises a negative moral function in removing obstacles to the pursuit of rectitude. In a word the State affords the citizen security for free self-destination. Just as there can be no half measures in morals and politics, so there can be no true freedom without security of rights. Security of rights indeed is a part of liberty. There is a very considerable distinction between positive and accidental freedom—as considerable as that between instinctive and rational benevolence. Only positive freedom, freedom that is, plus 'security', is morally precious, and one form of government can be estimated above another "in proportion as it gives more of this security".[1] It is in this evaluation that we come to realize the perfection of the supreme government of the Deity. This coupling of security with, and as an integral part of, liberty was a characteristic of dissenting political thought: a characteristic easily appreciable in the shadow of the unenforced but unrepealed Test and Corporation Acts. But for Price security represented this and something more; it represented security for the enjoyment of 'property' in the widest sense of the word; it was the sanction of those rights which men claim in virtue of their moral nature.

The State itself may be considered free when it obeys its righteous will, and Price identifies this will with "the will of an assembly of representatives appointed by itself

[1] *Additional Observations*, 3–4. It is not "the mere possession of liberty that denominates a community free; but that security for the possession of it which arises from such a free government", 14.

and accountable to itself".[1] Thus, it is in the will of the people willing righteousness and justice that ultimate sovereignty reposes; indeed the immediate sovereignty of the State, a sort of secondary supremacy which Price calls its 'omnipotence', is far from being limitless. Price felt that writers on government had mistakenly laid over-great stress upon the State's attribute of power. Government in its very nature is a trust; its sovereignty consists of an aggregate of particular powers vested in the State for the achievement of particular ends, and not an unlimited credit of absolutism.[2] The sovereignty of the State is limited by the Law of Rectitude; it is also limited by the State's own nature and purpose, which is to protect the people against public and private impediment to the achievement of their destiny as moral agents. Accordingly every government is responsible to the people; "for their sake government is instituted; and theirs is the only real omnipotence."[3] The will of the people commands the will of the State to realize the Law of Rectitude, and Price, eying the contemporary world of politics, contrasts the rigid imperialism of the Government of 1776 and their 'lust for dominion' with the 'humility of Christians'.[4]

As we have seen the State for Price is, in a sense, a guardian of property, but this conception, upon analysis, reveals itself to be wider than the prevailing Whig conception of the place of property in government, and to be fundamentally moral in character. Of all his varied

---

[1] *Civil Liberty*, 8–10.
[2] *Ibid.*
[3] *Ibid.*
[4] *Ibid.* 31.

property, acquired or inherited, a man's capacity for virtue is his most precious possession. In his *Review of the Principal Questions in Morals* Price gives more specific consideration to the material, as opposed to the spiritual, content of property. The result is disappointing. The application of ethical criticism to conceptions of property has produced many of the major revolutions in social thought, but the very universality of Price's definition of property renders criticism almost impossible, and the matter is dismissed all but undebated with the phrase: "such is truth, such is the nature of things."[1] For Price the term 'property' is of the widest: "the limbs, the faculties, and lives of persons are theirs, or to be reckoned amongst their properties, in much the same sense, upon the same grounds, with their external goods and acquisitions."[2] In character and origin our idea of property resembles our ideas of right and wrong in general; we recognize it intuitively as the determined relation of a particular object to a particular person, and a person's power of using his property as he will is inherent in the idea of property itself. For the origin of actual possession Price is content with a purely Lockian explanation: that with which a man mixes his labour is that man's own. Nevertheless, the affairs of property are to be regulated by 'Justice'; by what should be our prevailing regard to the unchanging and absolute Law of Right and Wrong. In issues of property, as of conduct, Price rejects all plea of extenuation based upon the

[1] *Morals*, 265.   [2] *Ibid.* 263–4.

demands of public utility; a wrong committed in a matter of property remains a wrong however much public benefit may accrue. But although at times Price seems disposed to accept certain social limitations upon the rights of private property he maintains pretty consistently that the sovereignty of the State does not fully extend to property; it stops short at its guarantees. For this reason the Declaratory Act is the most unmixed and unrighteous tyranny.[1] Price is admittedly uninspiring on the question of property, but he was carried away by the extent to which aspects of moral personality were included in his definition. The whole character of the Dissenting Interest, too, was such as to discourage heresy on this subject. It was not for them to raise a hand against the ark of society.

The State, then, is a group of individuals cohesive only in unity of purpose: the achievement of virtue. There is no suggestion of a transcendental or organic principle of unity in this community of men, and Price's conception remains uniformly atomistic; atomistic not in the sense taught by the materialists but atomistic in the sense that each individual has a separate contact with, and duty under, the Law of Rectitude. The freedom of self-determination is common to both the individual and the State, but the free will of the State is only just when it mirrors the free will of the citizens. The freedom of the State is chiefly exercised in its relation to other states. A citizen is free when "the power of commanding his

[1] "I defy anyone to express tyranny in stronger language." *Civil Liberty*, 21.

own conduct and the quiet possession of his life, person, property and good name are secured for him by his being his own legislator",[1] and the State which guarantees him this power is, for him, a free State. While it is true that amongst mankind there are innumerable inequalities of age, means, strength and ability, there is at the same time a uniform moral equality among mature men, in the sense that "no one of them is constituted by the Author of Nature the vassal or the subject of another, or has any right to give law to him, or, without his consent, to take away any part of his property or to abridge him of his liberty":[2] to deprive him, that is, of the means of attaining virtue. Men's equality in free self-destination is a most sacred right: "Mankind came with this right from the hands of their Maker":[3] and those who violate that right by private or national sin may anticipate the Divine wrath. Subjects stand in a peculiar fiduciary relationship to government; they can cashier it; can convict it of breaking the contract of trust and dispossess it of power. This sanction, however, is applied only in affairs of great moment. In everyday life the simple function of the State in the moral and political sphere, is to give "to everyone in temporals and spirituals the power of commanding his own conduct...provided he does not fall foul of others".[4] It co-ordinates and guides men's

[1] *Additional Observations*, 14.
[2] *Ibid*. 21.
[3] *Ibid*. 22. "Civil Liberty (it should be remembered) should be enjoyed as a right derived from the Author of Nature only, or it cannot be a blessing that merits this name", 4.
[4] *Ibid*. 13.

individual powers, so that the moral independence of no one is impaired.

With forms of government Price was not concerned; he was not specifically a republican. A perfect government would be one which "to our equal and perfect liberty, adds the greatest wisdom in deliberating and resolving and the greatest union, force and expedition in executing".[1] Such a mission of perfection could be equally well fulfilled by a mixed government. Indeed, the British Constitution is supposed to perform it—"I will not say with how much reason." What must always be foremost in our minds, is that man is born capable of infinite moral progress, and that it is the function of the State to furnish the chief instruments, freedom of speech and opinion, of such progress. For to increase virtue is to increase happiness, and the righteous happiness of the people is one of the ends of government. Only once does Price touch upon the actual mechanics of government and when he does so it is to discover in 'representation' the key-principle of politics and the equivalent in politics of moral freedom. He had unlimited faith in the efficiency of representation. Representation is the great discovery of modern political theory; it is compatible with infinite moral progress; it takes liberty out of the city and gives it to the world; it may even become an instrument for universal peace. To comply with the demands of free government, representation must be complete and the representatives of the State must be freely chosen, and, after choice, be free themselves,

[1] *Ibid.* 8.

during a short period of office, to promote the reign of righteousness. Their office must be short. The future of mankind is bound up with this cardinal political principle.[1]

For beyond the individual state lies the greater community of the human race. What should be the relation of state with state? What are the duties imposed upon us as moral agents by the love of our country? How should our duty to ourselves and our duty to others determine our choice in a conflict of loyalties? What should be the behaviour of the patriot, that is of the politically righteous citizen, in times of national sin? Once again in Price's work we encounter the phraseology of Locke without its substance.

It is true that states are independent separate entities, but they should stand to each other in the relation not of individuals in the condition of nature, but of individuals in a free state. Liberty is not a contradictory principle. "The freedom of a community or nation is the same among nations that the freedom of a citizen is among fellow citizens."[2] It is as essential for the State as for the individual that its will should be free to realize righteousness; nothing for instance could justify a union of states save their incorporation together by means of a just and adequate representation. For this reason all government of dependencies cannot but be despotic. If such government must exist, it is preferable that it should be frankly exercised by a tyrant rather than by a sovereign people: a tyrant may succumb to death or

[1] *Ibid.* 6–8.   [2] *Ibid.* 14.

deposition or any of the myriad illnesses of tyranny, but what can limit the undying tyranny exercised by a sovereign community? "No oppression is equal to that which one people are capable of practising towards another",[1] and there are no grounds upon which such oppression can be justified, least of all the grounds of victorious war, since war can only be just when it is defensive, and successful aggression gives no title to possession. Indeed, not the least drawback to 'provincial government' is the military force which it is obliged to retain in dispute of the clear truth that "to maintain by fire and sword dominion over the persons and property of a people not of the realm, who have no share in its legislature, contradicts every principle of liberty and humanity".[2] It is such sins against the eternal Law of Rectitude as these, which Providence, working slowly but surely in history, will unquestionably repay. It is no palliative for this unrighteousness to erect a provincial legislature only to make it the despised creature of a remote sovereign; even if the subjects of the province agreed to such an arrangement it would be an unlawful bargain, since it is not within the power of a people to barter away their own and their descendants' liberty.

Thus, the time may come when the politically righteous citizens of a state are summoned on their allegiance to participate in what they recognize to be a national sin; what at such a time is the duty of a patriot?

[1] *Ibid.* 38. [2] *Ibid.* ix.

What then is the love we owe our country? It was upon this theme that Price preached perhaps the most famous sermon of the century: the *Discourse on the Love of our Country* which inspired Edmund Burke to write the *Reflections on the French Revolution*.[1] That sermon forms an important chapter in the political writings of its author, since in it he endeavoured to set out his ideas upon the nature of human communities and of the duties of man in society. The formal purpose of the sermon was "to explain the duty we owe to our country and the nature, foundations and proper expressions of that love to it which we ought to cultivate".[2] Our duties perhaps become more readily apparent if we first of all determine in our minds certain things which the love of our country should not be. Love of our country should not be a blind, irrational conviction of our country's supreme value above all other countries; a conviction finding expression in "that spirit of rivalship and ambition which has been common among nations".[3] In much the same way that most evils in private life have their origin in that triumph of our private interest over public affection, which is the outcome, psychologically, of the exaltation of mere utility above the Law of Rectitude, so "most of the evils which have taken place

---

[1] *Discourse on the Love of Our Country* preached at the Old Jewry Meeting House 4 November 1789, before the Revolution Society; see *Proceedings of the Revolution Society*. The Discourse held on 4 November was a great institution at which Kippis, Towers, and Rees all officiated at various times. The text was Psalm cxxii, "Our feet shall stand within thy gates, O Jerusalem".

[2] *Love of Our Country*, 1–2.   [3] *Ibid.* 3–4.

among bodies of men, have been occasioned by their own interest overcoming the principle of universal benevolence".[1] True patriotism, that is, political righteousness, is not a blind obedience to nationalistic passion, but a just and rational principle of action arising from the perception of what is good and what is evil. For this reason, if no other, the lesson of the Good Samaritan is of all lessons the friendliest to the rights of mankind. True, we are sensible that our affections are drawn more strongly to some sections of mankind than to others (perhaps Providence is not without a hand in this), but such affections should always be rational affections. In the order of nature self-regard is primary and is followed by the regard we feel for our families, for our benefactors, for our friends and for our country. But if in the order of nature regard for mankind occupies the last place, because individually we have so few opportunities of exercising it, such regard is spiritually the first and highest. "The noblest principle in our nature is the regard for general justice; and that good will which embraces all the world."[2] Our love for our country then should not be exclusive because it is ardent, and we shall promote the best and most abiding interests of our country if we harmonize it with our love of general justice. The chief blessings enjoyed by men are truth, virtue, and liberty. We shall serve our country best by serving these with all our hearts; by striving to promote and strengthen them so that our country will become an example and an inspiration to other, less happy, peoples. It is the privilege of the patriot to educate his fatherland in righteousness. "Our first concern, as lovers of our country, must be to enlighten it...shew them they are men and they will act like men."[1] Especially blessed are those who enlighten their countrymen in the apprehension of their rights, the freedom of their religion, and the nature of civil government; those Miltons, Lockes, Sidneys, Hoadlys, Montesquieus, Marmontels, Turgots, who temper men's minds to the recovery of freedom, and the destruction of priestcraft and tyranny. For this reason it is the duty of all of us, within the measure of our ability, to seek virtue for ourselves and to propagate among others the "reformation of manners and virtuous practice". We can do great service to the cause of public liberty by our jealous scrutiny of each excess of power; a scrutiny conducted not in a spirit of faction (since obedience to our country's laws and magistrates is a necessary expression of our regard to the community, and, without such obedience, the purpose of government would be defeated),[2] but in the knowledge that power by a natural process of degeneration tends to despotism, an internal enemy more formidable than those external foes in defending our country against whom we express our love for it. But perhaps the most sacred duty of all arising from our love of our country consists in offering up "thanksgiving to God for every event favourable to it", for God is gratified by a nation's homage, just as He is alienated by its infidelity and licentiousness.[3] In-

[1] *Ibid.* 14.   [2] *Ibid.* 21.   [3] *Ibid.* 31.

deed, there are occasions when the security of a state may well depend upon the number of righteous men within it, although, in the last division of all, allegiance lies to a kingdom not of this world.[1]

Aggressive war must be utterly repugnant to a patriot, since warfare is an agglomeration of arbitrary will, force and licentiousness, the very negation of moral liberty and human dignity. War is an appalling evil and men should spare no effort to establish universal peace, to create some representative federation uniting in harmony sovereign independent states; a machinery by which all mankind will freely determine its own destiny and attain moral perfection. This idea lay very close to Price's heart, and belongs to the great revolt against war that captured men's imagination in the closing decades of the eighteenth century. He visualized this ultimate fusion of interests under two forms: the one a confederation of the British Empire; the other a confederation of Europe. The first of these two forms was an outcome of his reaction to the contest with the American colonies.

That contest afforded Price an opportunity of applying his principles to an historical situation. He applied them boldly and uniformly, and his creed survived the first great test of faith for the politically righteous in England. He died just as the second and severer trial of the French Wars was beginning to cloud over the dawn of liberty in

---

[1] For Price's view on the 'Heavenly City' which is entirely different from the most perfect upon Earth (since "all earthly governments have in them the seeds of decay and demolition"), see *Discourse*, 21 February 1781.

Europe. Apart from Tom Paine's *Common Sense* he wrote
the most influential pamphlet of the American controversy. His *Observations on Civil Liberty* was published
simultaneously in London and Philadelphia in 1776;
60,000 copies of it were sold, but the author was content
to sacrifice private emolument to a cheap edition.[1] He
brought an evangelical enthusiasm to his work, and
while the Burkes were crying 'retreat' and the Tuckers
'recant' Price was the first to reconcile himself to the
idea of complete independence for America. In upholding the cause of the colonies he felt himself to be an
advocate in the cause of God and moral progress and to
have apprehended the purpose for which Providence
was shaping contemporary history. "I am inclined", he
wrote in 1776, "to think that the hand of Providence is
in them, working to bring about some great ends"; and,
eight years later: "I see the hand of Providence in the
late war, working for the general good and can scarcely
avoid crying out 'It was the Lord's doing'."[2] Once the

[1] *Morgan*, 58, 62. A correspondent wrote to Price from Philadelphia: "A small Pamphlet addressed by you to the Congress
and the Legislature of each of the States would, I am sure, have
more weight with their rulers, than a hundred publications thrown
out by the Citizens of this country", 204.

[2] *Importance of the American Revolution*, 1784, 3; *Civil Liberty*, 55.
He contrasts the situation in America with that at home. "In this
hour of danger [1776] it would become us to turn our thoughts to
Heaven. This is what our brethren in the Colonies are doing.
From one end of North America to the other they are fasting and
praying. But what are we doing?—shocking thought—We are
running wild after pleasure and forgetting everything serious and
decent in Masquerades—We are gambling in gaming houses:
trafficking in boroughs; perjuring ourselves at elections; and selling
ourselves for places—which side is Providence likely to favour?"

Revolution was accomplished, he felt that an incomparable advance had been made in men's long ascent to moral perfection. "Perhaps I do not go too far when I say that next to the introduction of Christianity among mankind, the American Revolution may prove the most important step in the progressive course of human improvement."[1] He sensed himself as one of those privileged spectators to whom Clio appears undisguised. He knew that he was witnessing the birth of a new world, of a new and serene chapter in the annals of mankind in which one had only to turn a page to perceive "a revolution more important perhaps, than any that has happened in human affairs".[2] He was deeply sensible, too, that he was witnessing a supreme dispensation emanating from the goodness of God. The wages of what had been a great national sin had by the bounty of God proved to be the promise of a great new evangel of political salvation. The outcome of all these deep discontents had been that Liberty had reappeared on earth in answer to the prayers of the patriots, the politically righteous of the American colonies.

In the two series of *Observations* of 1776 and 1777 Price examined the ministerial case in the light of justice, the English Constitution, policy, humanity and honour; in his *Importance of the American Revolution* he sought to assess the value of the American achievement and its significance for less fortunate peoples. Against the stiffening imperialism of the ministry, he was able, on his principles, to decide without hesitation. The cause

[1] *Importance*, 1784, 5–6.   [2] *Additional Observations*, 88.

sustained by the ministry was the cause of naked power: that unrighteous sovereignty which holds that might is right and is the depraved principle resulting from excessive political licentiousness. Our simplest method, he says, of determining on which side justice lies, is to examine the nature of that power to maintain which the ministry are prepared to resort to arms. That power does not arise from the compulsive perception of rectitude, but from a tyrannous desire of a handful of men to impose their will upon a community which desires to determine its own destiny. Such an imposition is too great a price to be paid for imperial or any other unity. The language of the Declaratory Act is the language not only of political depravity but of political folly. The disasters arising from the attempt to enforce unity in religion have been abundantly illustrated and if, in the British Empire, "in order to preserve its unity one half of it must be enslaved to the other half, let it, in the name of God, want unity".[1] It is meaningless to plead at the bar of Right that we are the parent state—Germany might equally well profess the same title over us—or that we have run deeply into debt in order to defend our *interests* in America. We cannot claim that the colonists hold their land on our tenancy, since if that land ever belonged rightly to anyone it belonged to the native Indians who, of all who inhabited the continent, had most truly mixed their labour with it. If we are to hold our Empire together we must do so by some more abiding lien. We cannot retain it by force and remain true

[1] *Civil Liberty*, 22.

to the principles of our domestic constitution, the fundamental conception in which is the free consent of the
governed. The justification of 'policy' is a facile and
futile excuse, for there is a sort of intoxication arising
from over-government which may prove equally fatal to
the ruling and the ruled community. "There is a love of
power for its own sake inherent in human nature";[1]
this is an impure love akin to moral evil, and its predominance in a nation foreshadows disaster. Rulers
should have learned, too, by now, that power always
suffers from discussion. Clearly the English people have
been wandering in a wilderness of national sin; one
excess has followed another; after the Stamp Act
followed the Tea Act: "did ever Heaven punish the
vices of a people more severely by darkening their
counsels?"[2] We might, had we been more happily advised, have enlisted the aid of the colonies in the pressing
task of discharging our public financial burdens; instead
of which we have made imminent the *dies irae* inherent
in the national debt. Let the State in Britain once outlive
its credit and "the whole of Government would fall to
pieces: and a state of nature would take place—what a
dreadful situation!"[3] Our honour as a sovereign people
is not pledged in the American war: "Rectitude is
dignity, oppression only is meanness, and justice
honour", and both justice and prudence urge us to
retract.[4] We shall prevail in such a war no better
than did the Spaniards in the Netherlands, and the

[1] *Ibid.* 31.   [2] *Ibid.* 39.
[3] *Ibid.* 44.   [4] *Ibid.* 50.

Athenians in Syracuse. Our armaments are mighty, no doubt, but where on earth is to be found the might that can prevail over the will of God?

Price devised two solutions of the American problem —one by implication, the other expressly. The first solution was to unite ourselves to America in common submission to an imperial parliament built upon the principle of equal representation. This sovereign assembly was to shape the policy of the federation, but Price betrayed some doubt whether such an arrangement would suit the actual circumstances of the situation. In advancing this solution he had rather the thirteen colonies in mind than the wider empire.[1] His practical advice, though he formulated it on different premises, was very similar to that of Burke: "withdraw your armies", he said, "from your Colonies: offer your power to them as a protecting, not a destroying power. Grant the security they desire to their property and charters, and renounce those notions of dignity which lead you to prefer the exactions of force to the offerings of gratitude, and to hazard everything to gain nothing—by such wisdom and equity America may perhaps, be still preserved."[2] Britain may as well retain the sovereignty over trade since that has become a political palladium; indeed the Americans are better preserved from it.[3] But the foremost necessity of all is for the people of Britain to repent before their sins in India are revenged in America

[1] *Ibid.* 57 note.
[2] *Additional Observations,* 89.
[3] *Civil Liberty,* 60.

and before that mounting spirit of tyranny—already patent in the Quebec Act—returns repulsed from the shores of America, to rest in Britain itself.

That was written in 1776: by 1784 the success of the American Revolution had lifted it outside the realm of national debate, and enthroned it among the hopes of mankind. Price's *Observations on the Importance of the American Revolution* was a political testament to the proven land of liberty: a legacy to the new commonwealth which had so soon attained its majority and succeeded to its rights. The book was also an attempt to analyse and record the significance of this great example. To a greater degree, perhaps, even than Chatham, its writer had become the patron saint of the colonists: "I cannot tell you", wrote an American friend in August 1785, "how great the applause is, which its author receives throughout these States."[1] Price felt himself too old to undertake the task of organizing the finances of America, but he endowed the new state with all that was most precious in his political and philosophic treasury. The Revolution was primarily important, he felt, as a political precedent; as a great example of and stimulus to human progress. It was an experiment which must not be allowed to fail so long as the advice of righteous men could maintain and develop it. The first concern of the United States must be with their public debts; they must set an example of financial rectitude to the world. A national sinking fund working on the principles of compound interest must be established, and it will be suffi-

[1] Morgan, *Price*, 107.

cient to ensure the success of this fund if it is left to function untouched and unimpeded. "Could a sacredness be given it like that of the Ark of God among the Jews, it would do the same service."[1]

Peace must be established on an equally unassailable foundation so that America, happy in its geographical situation, may trace the first step towards universal peace. In order to accomplish these ends it will be necessary to invest Congress with power to enforce federal decrees: that power should be based, in the last issue, not on a standing army ("God forbid...") but upon a right to summon a quota of armed militia from each state of the Union, since, in troubled times, "free states ought to be bodies of armed citizens".[2] The choice, even so, is a choice of evils, but that was ever the cost of human imperfection. Congress, too, should have the power of imposing taxation and of making surveys and keeping registers. The greatest blessings which America may hope to enjoy will arise out of the establishment of full liberty of thought, since a country in which "truth and reason shall have free play" possesses a permanent guarantee of progress.[3] Complete liberty of discussion must be enjoyed. There must be no civil establishment of religion with its grudging concession of toleration, but complete freedom of con-

---

[1] *Observations on the Importance of the American Revolution and the means of making it a benefit to the World*, London, 1784, 12–13.

[2] *Importance*, 16.

[3] *Importance*, 21. It was the belief of the century. "Il est beau d'écrire", said Pococurante to Candide, "ce qu'on pense: c'est le privilège de l'homme."

science and discussion. Education, a supremely important qualification in the pursuit of virtue, must be advanced by every possible means short of the intervention of the State. The task ahead will not be easy, since America is exposed to many dangers; most notably those perils which arise from internal wars and the unequal distribution of property. Americans must keep especial guard against the establishment of hereditary honours, a nobility, and the unjust system of primogeniture. For Americans are supremely fortunate in one respect: in the stage in the evolution of society which they have attained. "The happiest state of man is the middle state between the savage and the refined or between the wild and the luxurious state", much in the same way that the most competent and worthy political material in a nation resides in the middle ranks of society; Americans should hug jealously this privileged midway.[1] Foreign trade is a menace. Such trade serves a useful purpose certainly in checking "one of the most destructive principles in human nature", excessive, unreasoning love of our country, and to this extent it is a force making for peace.[2] But it is also a potential force for public depravity, a huckstering in foreign corruptions. For this reason Price recommends the subordination and, if necessary, curtailment of foreign trade in the interests of

[1] *Importance*, 69. *Additional Observations*, 25. *Civil Liberty*, 41: "Our American Colonies, particularly the Northern ones, have been for some time in the very happiest state of society; or in the middle state of civilisation between the first rude and the last refined and corrupt state."

[2] *Importance*, 75.

public virtue. No gain is godly gain which brings with it "false refinement, luxury and impiety": before which "that simplicity of character, that manliness of spirit, that disdain of tinsel, in which true dignity consists, will disappear".[1] Another great evil, the slave trade, needs only to be mentioned to be condemned: it is "shocking to humanity, cruel, wicked and diabolical". These are the pitfalls which America must circumvent, or else "the fairest experiment ever tried in human affairs will miscarry".[2]

The contest with the American colonies was the only political crisis of the first order against which Price had to measure his political principles. He touched but lightly upon the British Constitution and then chiefly in the matter of representation. His writings upon finance and population, which placed him upon an uncertain eminence among the statisticians of his day, are perhaps best left unrecorded. The only works bearing directly upon domestic concerns which he composed were a sermon, in the worst spirit of mid-century complacency and national gratulation, which was preached in 1759 and published in 1791, and a party pamphlet of little theoretical interest, written in 1780 in collaboration with John Horne Tooke.[3]

[1] *Ibid.* 77.   [2] *Ibid.* 83–5.
[3] *Britain's happiness in full possession of Civil and Religious Liberty briefly stated and proved*, 1759. Posthumously published, 1791. Horne Tooke and Price, *Facts addressed to the landholders, stockholders, merchants, farmers, manufacturers, tradesmen...and generally to all the subjects of Great Britain and Ireland*, London, 1780. It contains a terrific chapter on the rum contract for the war. In 1775–8 a Mr Atkinson, a contractor of this commodity, received £1,780,000 of public money. It says: "if his Majesty should now choose to

To the arguments in favour of representational reform
he had little to offer which was not better said in James
Burgh's *Political Disquisitions*, save perhaps a profound
conviction of the moral dangers of representational
corruption. A government founded upon an imperfect
representation is, he felt, the very worst form of government, for it is sustained only by venality and spreads
profligacy throughout society.[1] Righteousness is not to
be attained by unrighteous means, and a parliament such
as England's, "a representation chosen principally by
the Treasury and a few thousands of the dregs of the
people, who are generally paid for their votes",[2] is but
a poor stimulus to national virtue. Price's sombre view
of the state of his country recalls the abiding pessimism of
Puritan thought. He saw it grown old in years and vice,
and sensed creeping upon it that death, the eutha-
nasia, of which Hume and Montesquieu had been the
prophets.

"Our circumstances", he wrote in 1777, "are singular
and give us reason to fear that we have before us a death

promote his postilion or (with the Roman Emperor) his Horse to
the office of first Lord of the Treasury, his neigh would be attended
by as great a majority as that which now follows the heels of the
present noble Lord in possession." 114.

[1] *Love of Our Country*, 39–40.

[2] *Ibid.* 40; cf. *Civil Liberty*, 8: "If a State is so sunk that the body
of its representatives are elected by a handful of the meanest
persons in it, whose votes are always paid for: and if, also,
there is a higher will on which even these mock representatives
depend and that directs their voices: In these circumstances
it will be an abuse of language to say that the State possesses
liberty."

which will not be easy or common."[1] Like Edmund
Burke he called for a return to the old, higher, healthier
ground, to our 'grand national security', but only
half-heartedly.[2] In these parts of his work there is that
sense of decay and growing isolation, that sadness
inherent in the optimistic thought of the eighteenth
century, invisible, like the little mists of a fen country,
in the bright sunlight, but always present and at evening
perceptible. He turned from despair of his own land to
hope in the New World. He was conscious of an omen
behind the strange dawn in the West. His intellectual
life after 1784 until his death in 1790, exemplifies the
swift generation among contemporary thinkers of that
millennium-psychology which was to hail the Revolution
in France with such amazing fervour; the growing
intensification of feeling, the feverish intermittency of
hopes and fears, the state of cataclysmic preparedness.
The second revolution he saw as a second revelation: it
confirmed him in the conviction that the hand of Providence had designed these great occurrences. He felt
that his work had been gloriously crowned by this
privilege of witnessing the commencement of something
for which so many generations had longed. "What an
eventful period is this! I am thankful that I have lived
to see it: and I could almost say 'Lord now lettest thou
thy servant depart in peace for mine eyes have seen thy
salvation'....Be encouraged all ye friends of freedom
and writers in its defence...tremble all ye oppressors of

---

[1] *Additional Observations*, 52.   [2] *Ibid.*

the world. Restore to mankind their rights; and consent to the correction of abuses before they and you are destroyed together."[1]

It is difficult to evaluate his work, since criticism from a modern viewpoint would be irrelevant and it cannot be judged by any contemporary standard. If in his optimism Price belonged to his age, philosophically the tide was flowing against him; flowing with Priestley and utilitarianism, and while Price certainly represents one major division of dissenting opinion, the division is slight enough compared with the numbers of those who based their claim to natural rights upon utilitarian foundations. In certain practical aspects his work was bad. It was notably weak in definition, and at no point did he attempt to distinguish adequately between the mass of mankind, a community, a state and a government. Perhaps for a twentieth-century reader, too, his system seems too bound up with the Newtonian theory of the rigid conformity of cause and effect; a dogma more favourable to materialism and necessitarianism than to philosophical liberty.[2] Again, while he made a

---

[1] *Love of Our Country*, 50-1. Burke was not the only one to be horrified by this passage. E.g. "What a picture have you drawn of expiring sedition! ruminating with horrid satisfaction on the confusion he has excited, yet casting back a longing, lingering look, anxious to see the completion of his mischief", *Observations on the Conduct of the Protestant Dissenters*, 1790, 4. "Depart, Incendiary, in civil, schismatic in religious rights", *Gentleman's Magazine*, December 1789, II, 1121-5. Priestley was "moved even to tears by it", *Letters*, 50.

[2] Cf. "the necessity of a cause for whatsoever events arise is an essential principle, a primary perception of the Understanding". *Morals*, 30.

creditable intellectual stand against the mechanistic ab-
surdities of the sensationalist and materialist thinkers:
that huge array of wheels, chains, springs and levers, all
functioning in the supreme irrelevance of analogy, his
belief in the existence of growing forces of decay inherent in every political society was itself something
very like determinism. In its components his system of
philosophic liberty owed much to Clarke, Beattie, Law,
Wollaston, Martin and Butler. Yet as a whole his philosophic system was perhaps unique and much of his
significance derives from his intellectual isolation. If he
could not convince his utilitarian opponents he at least
left the issue clearly stated.

His application of this system to politics, or rather,
his translation of his moral into a political philosophy
was both important and original. It was his political
conception of moral liberty which was least understood
by his opponents. Their attitude is typified in the *Essay
on the Origin, Progress and Establishment of National Society*
by the government pamphleteer J. Shebbeare, in which
is set out that psychology of sensation and hedonistic
motive, that utilitarian morality, that enslavement of the
will to material passion to confute which the *Review* was
written. In Price's dualism of soul and body Shebbeare
discovers only "a spiritual centaur, equally fabulous
with the corporeal";[1] in his free agency a principle only
of destruction. "Let us sing Te Deum and rejoice, that
Richard Price, D.D., F.R.S. was born, who has so

[1] J. Shebbeare, *Essay on the Origin, Progress and Establishment of
National Society*, 1776, 16.

graciously bestowed on man a new revelation of morality which, contrary to that of the Christian, comes not to fulfil the law but to destroy it."[1] At the same time, despite his high level of consistency there existed a friction between Price and the utilitarian strain of his times comparable with that friction which, many years after, was perceptible between the intellectual integrity of John Stuart Mill and his philosophic inheritance.[2] Indeed, in the moral atmosphere of their work, there is a resemblance between the two; Price preaching absolute right and wrong, often in the language of interest and utility; Mill stretching the hedonistic calculus out of all recognizable shape. But the lofty moral demands of Price's system rendered his political theory, whatever might be the value of his specific prescriptions, utterly and essentially remote from the political conditions of his time. He was confronted with the hopeless task of incorporating Fox, Wilkes and Sheridan into the universal Law of Rectitude. He felt the incongruity of such an attempt and he partly, though never wholly, realized that the political organization and temper of his country might well render impossible the reforms which he cherished. "Oh that I could see", he wrote, "in men who oppose tyranny in the state, a disdain for the tyranny of low passions in themselves";[3] in that

[1] *Ibid.* 20.

[2] As a coincidence, they both give the same solution of a problem: is a crime committed in drunkenness as heinous as one in sobriety? *Ans.* No, but the drunkenness itself thus becomes a crime.

[3] *Love of Our Country*, 42–3. "I can never", he wrote, "reconcile

one sentence is the sum of practicality in Price's system.

Yet many of the articles of his creed were significant. He was convinced that the actions and policy of the State could be judged adequately by individual moral standards. In revolt against the accepted ethic of *raison d'état* he erected each man who was capable of being a moral agent into a moral critic of his country. "En vain", wrote the Friends of the Constitutional Society at Aix to the Revolution Society, "les supports du Machiavélisme lancèrent sur lui leurs traits envenimés."[1] He boldly submitted the State to the moral law. He assessed the power of the State without reverence or mysticism; unlawful sovereignty, might unrestricted by right, 'political licentiousness' must, as the American Revolution so clearly showed, defeat itself. An individualist from his moral system, he nevertheless possessed a vivid sense of the community, an intuition of social complexity remarkable among the philosophers, which led him to the belief that the State could be a powerful instrument of progress in human morality and freedom. This deepening note is in all his work. He sought to find a profounder meaning for 'right' than a

myself to the idea of an immoral patriot." Hollis, too, felt the inadequacy of the patriots of his day. A poet of 1798 wrote of his hatred of those who

> "Amaze the Welkin with an empty cry
> Of 'Justice, Rights of Man and Liberty',
> As if the villain, whom no ties can bind
> In private life, can cherish all his kind."

[1] *Correspondence of the Revolution Society*, 27 June 1791, 213.

doubtful historical process or a controversial hypothesis. He was a political romantic, sensible to the intoxication of words and ideas.[1] In this respect he reached forward to the years to come, as he did in the moral and Divine sanction he gave to liberal nationalism in his conception of the Divinely ordained sacredness of self-determination. Historically his work reveals the extent to which the theories of Locke had become a technique, a political text capable of sustaining any gloss, and yet certain, from its familiarity, to excite attention. Historically, too, it is possible to trace in his work the Biblical and historical cast of thought amongst English political philosophers as opposed to the classical conceptions of the French thinkers—a momentous difference.

In himself Price was chiefly influential as an example; as the embodiment of the ideal of 'Candour'. As such he commanded a respect amongst his polemical enemies, comparable in its dimensions only to the hatred with which Priestley was regarded.[2] His personal disposition

[1] "Let us remember that we are men and not cattle: that the sovereignty in every country belongs to the people: and that a righteous man is the best member of every community and the best friend to his species, as being the most irreconcilable to slavery, the most sensible to every encroachment on the rights of mankind, the most jealous for equal and universal liberty and the most active in endeavouring to propagate just sentiments of religion and government." *Fast Sermon,* 1779, 21.

[2] Cf. Obituary Notice in the uniformly hostile *Gentleman's Magazine*, April 1791, 1, 389. "While his genius and his no less abstruse than valuable labours in calculation rank him with the first philosophers of every age, his political counsels and writings place him among the most distinguished patriots and benefactors of nations." Priestley never hoped to meet his equal in candour. Arthur Young, however, thought lowly of him, and Adam Smith despised his economics.

was purely that of the Enlightenment: he was no more a Hugh Peters than was Burke himself a Jeffries.[1] He wrote English of distinction without extravagance. It was his lifelong task to preserve an ordered liberality of mind. His openness to conviction was tinged with a romantic strain of wonder, a peculiarity which made him one of the few thinkers of his century who was in no sense a prig. To some he was too cold: too much the intellectual. "He understood the Laws of Nature", wrote Wakefield, "better than the spirit of the Code of Jesus; and, in an eager assertion of the rights of man, disregarded the privileges of Christians."[2] Others saw in him a deliberate incendiary.[3] The truth probably was that he was not dogmatic enough to satisfy the rationalism of his times. "And now", he wrote in 1784, "in the evening of a life devoted to enquiry and spent in endeavours (weak, indeed, and feeble) to serve the best interest, present and future, of mankind, I am waiting for the Great Teacher, convinced that the order of Nature is perfect; that infinite wisdom and goodness

[1] As Mackintosh suggested, *Vindiciae Gallicae*, 325. He compares Price to Sidney; cf. *Reflections on the French Revolution*, 71. Price always maintained his exultation was over the Fall of the Bastille alone.

[2] Wakefield, *Memoir*, 1, 377. He admits his "noble and amiable character". They disagreed at Hackney.

[3] E.g. John Stevenson, *Letters in Answer to Dr Price*, 1779, 17. "To see a reverend Doctor descend from the dignity of his important office, and, with the most determined resolution, scatter fire-brands, arrows and death amongst his fellow subjects, confessedly the most happy and free people now under heaven, is enough to fill every human heart with detestation." Stevenson himself was a Dissenter, prominent in the movement for abolishing slavery among the colliers and salters of Scotland.

Chapter V

JOSEPH PRIESTLEY

"I think it is not less honourable to be the hunted deer, shunned by his companions, than the leader of the peaceful herd."

PRIESTLEY

JOSEPH PRIESTLEY belongs to the category of those whose political greatness is thrust upon them. "The whole course of my studies", he declared in 1794 when, except perhaps for Tom Paine, he was the most maligned man in England, "from early life, shows how little politics of any kind have been my object."[1] If there was a guiding passion at all in a character which fulfilled so wholly the dispassionate ideal of his century, it was the pursuit of religious truth; a pursuit that led him not only through theology proper from Arminianism to Socinianism, but also carried him deeply into physical and chemical science, always and everywhere revealing to him the Divine purpose which he sought. This preoccupation with the works of Providence, manifest and secret, left little scope for a 'pure' approach to politics. Like Price, he acquired his political system as an extension of his general philosophical position, but there the resemblance abruptly ends, for Priestley belonged to the school of materialism and necessity: the school whose

---

[1] *Present State of Europe*, 1794, 524.

members ranged from Hobbes to Hume, Hutcheson and Hartley. Price's approach to politics was chiefly moral: Priestley's road lay through a theory of the nature of matter and of man's materiality. It was Price's desire to write the Universal Law of Rectitude upon the codes of states: Priestley was more concerned with the anatomy, especially the psychological composition, of political man. In place of Price's free agent, striving to realize his moral freedom to the utmost in obedience to an unchanging law, we are shown an agent 'free' only in a limited sense—in the sense that a magistrate is free under a fundamental constitution. For Priestley the will is not free. The will, like all mental and spiritual functions, is only an aspect of matter: only one of the thousand little processes which take place in the material world, none of which nevertheless can occur without the special will of God. For just as there can be but one will in a state, there can be only one ultimate will in the universe: the will of God willing the happiness of Man. God has plotted and allotted the course of the human race and it is the whole duty of the statesman to leave men free to follow that course unimpeded.

Thus, while his age busied itself with the dignity of man, Priestley upheld the dignity of matter with the affectionate ardour of a philosopher who was also a chemist. He declared his faith in his *Disquisitions Relating to Matter and Spirit* and applied it to the human race in his *Doctrine of Philosophical Necessity*. In a world which had grown so complex and corrupt, he saw in the philosophy of materialism and necessity a great force for simplification and regeneration, a creed to prepare men for the millennium which he never doubted was imminent, a testament to lighten the darkness preceding that glorious dawn. By no act of intellectual faith could he bring himself to believe in the existence of that strange creature for whom philosophical liberty was claimed: a creature half material, half spiritual, reconciling in himself two substances wholly irreconcilable save by some such absurd device as the 'pre-established harmony' of Leibniz or the 'vehicle of the soul' advanced by certain immaterialist thinkers. The immaterialists asserted that in human nature there are to be found two substances: matter and spirit. These two are utterly distinct. Matter possesses the properties of 'extension' or dimension and of solidity or 'impenetrability', but it is wholly destitute of 'powers' of any kind. Spirit, on the other hand, though destitute of all extension, of all dimensional relation to space, possesses certain 'powers', the powers of perception, intelligence, and self-motion. It is against the Cartesian dogma of the impenetrability of matter that Priestley directs his chief and most fundamental attack. He desires at the outset to prove the "uniform composition of man": to materialize the process of the human understanding.[1] His primary definition of matter is "a substance possessed of the property of extension and of powers of attraction or repulsion".[2] Matter seems to be solid or impenetrable not because it actually is so, but because of a certain power of repulsion which

---

[1] *Disquisitions Relating to Matter and Spirit*, 220.
[2] *Ibid.* 218.

always surrounds it. Thus, the powerless and inert mass of the immaterialist philosophy does possess a power: the power of repulsion. In addition it has the power of attraction, because every solid must possess a shape, must be 'figured', yet cannot do so unless it also possesses a power of attraction. Indeed, the very idea of solidity itself is at bottom a power-conception arising from the idea of resistance.[1]

Thus 'powers' are not the prerogative of some assumed spiritual substance in man: they can be and are possessed by matter, and, from this fundamental ground, Priestley goes on to prove the whole materiality of the human being. It is true that the powers claimed for the spiritual half of man are those of 'sense' or perception and 'thought', but Priestley concludes that these powers may also belong to those same substances which have the properties of attraction, repulsion and extension: may belong, that is to say, to matter. There is nothing, he declares, but a modern and absurd opinion of their incompatibility to prove the separation of matter and spirit. Perception and thought are found only in conjunction with a certain organized system of matter. Thus no man retains the faculty of thinking once the material of his brain is destroyed; indeed, even the material decay, let alone the total extinction of the body, is accompanied by decay of the mental faculties. Again, the mind holds not a single idea which cannot be proved to have been transmitted by the bodily senses or to have resulted from the perceptions of sense. How much more

[1] *Ibid.* 223.

rational it is, therefore, to believe that man, spiritually
no less than bodily, is wholly a material being, than to
distort our faith to embrace the curious and clumsy
hypothesis of dualism.

Once a materialist, and upon such grounds, Priestley
was automatically a mechanist and a necessarian. "The
Doctrine of Necessity", he writes, "is the immediate
result of the doctrine of the materiality of man, for
mechanism is the undoubted consequence of materialism."[1] The will is not free. It does not determine motive
but is determined by it. Human volition is conditioned
by the appearance presented by things in the material
world. Man, therefore, is necessarily determined in his
actions because the mind itself is constantly determined
by the motives presented to it. The epithet 'voluntary'
has philosophical significance only when it is opposed
to 'involuntary'; opposed to 'necessary' it must be
meaningless. For it follows from the nature of the
mental process that the will is unfree. All thought arises
from sense-perceptions: it is a vibration of the material
substance of the brain caused by the perception of
external objects.[2] All ideas are simple and particular;
and general ideas exist only as combinations of such
simple ideas. If we adhere to the Newtonian dialectic, it
is clear that everything must have a cause, and that the
will cannot enjoy an independent existence and function.
The will, it is true, has much freedom. It is especially
free as the distributing authority ruling over human
energy, but it is not a self-governing entity: it cannot

[1] *Ibid.* 220.   [2] *Ibid.* 247–50, 282.

escape from its own material environment. The process of willing is the effect of a cause and that cause is 'motive'. Our motives are determined by two factors: by the previous disposition of our minds and by our view of the object to which the motive is directed. Each of these determining factors is a mechanism. Within, the internal disposition of our mind is formed by a long chain of associated ideas; without, in the material world there revolves ceaselessly and change-lessly the wheel of cause and effect. The mind is a moral, just as the scientific balance is a physical, mechanism, and "if there be a real mechanism in both cases, so that there can be only one result from the same previous circumstances, there will be a real necessity enforcing an absolute certainty in the event".[1] The will is thus subject to the laws of nature. It serves as an intermediate, dynamic stage lying between motive and action. In their passage through it "automatic actions pass into volun-tary ones and then again into those which are secondary automatic"; all are equally mechanical and determined.[2]

Thus political man is not a separate, self-determined, moral entity: he is a small but essential part of that great mechanism in which God works out His purposes for the world. Necessity is not an indulgent doctrine of irresponsibility; indeed, its insistence upon the disposi-tion of the mind and on the motive alone as a cause, and upon action merely as an effect, makes it purely and peculiarly a doctrine of individual moral responsibility,

[1] *Doctrine of Philosophical Necessity Illustrated*, 467.
[2] *Ibid.* 480.

because although the chain of events is necessary, our own actions themselves are the necessary links in that chain. It is thus, in the strictest sense, a doctrine of philosophical self-help. Necessity is neither Spinozism nor fatalism nor predestination. It lifts a man out of the anarchy of free will and places him in the objective purpose of creation, teaching him that "the whole series of events from the beginning of the world to the consummation of all things makes one connected chain of causes and effects, originally established by the Deity".[1] It is also comfortable doctrine. It lights the dark and lonely depths of individual existence. It sees God's purpose in all that seems most purposeless, revealing "everything in a friendly and pleasing light".[2] Above all the doctrine of necessity brings with it a sure and universal optimism. It was a creed, Priestley felt, which must "tend to diffuse a joyful serenity over the mind, producing a conviction that, notwithstanding all present unfavourable appearances, *whatever is, is right*: that all evils respecting individuals or societies, any part or the whole of the human race, will terminate in good; and that the greatest sum of good could not, in the nature of things, be attained by any other means".[3] The great purpose for which God has built this huge philosophic apparatus called the world is to achieve the happiness of

---

[1] *Ibid.* 445; cf. Hobbes: "And therefore God, that seeth and disposeth all things, seeth also that the *liberty* of man in doing what he will is accompanied with the *necessity* of doing that which God will and no more nor lesse." *Leviathan*, II, 21. Cambridge, 1904, 148–9.

[2] *Ibid.* 508.   [3] *Ibid.* 507.

man, and Priestley transcends all utilitarianism, past and yet to come, in the magnificent formula of "the greatest good of the whole Universe".[1]

If political man is a mechanism destined to perfection, the State must be an apparatus for the achievement of liberty and the promotion of progress. If attainment of universal happiness is the goal of the Divine Sovereign, it must be a fundamental law for the earthly magistrate. Public good is the golden rule of right and wrong for states, the test of institutions, the foundation of individual moral obligation. When Priestley published his *Essay on the First Principles of Government* in 1771, he felt himself to be voicing a new and personal discovery: the discovery that 'good' or happiness are the great objects of government; objects hitherto unnoticed or rejected.[2] The enthusiasm of novelty pervaded the book. He felt confident that he had found the first axiom in a science of politics which, like the science of education, was still in its infancy. But however scientific his approach, Priestley was also profoundly sensitive to the historical setting of politics. History he regarded as a study doubly valuable to the political philosopher, partly as a lesson in cause and effect, but chiefly as constituting "anticipated experience" for the political thinker. "From this source only", he thought, "can be derived

---

[1] *Ibid.* 532. The utilitarianism is clear. "The connection between virtue and happiness and between vice and misery is upon no principles whatever so certain and demonstrable as on those of philosophical necessity", 539.

[2] *Essay on the First Principles of Government*, London, 1771, 3.

all future improvements in the science of government."[1] For history in addition to revealing the great progress of man in the past gives more than a hint of his future course.

In the *Essay* Priestley deals with 'first principles', and if at no time he gives us a definition of such principles it is because he considers them too axiomatic to require explanation. He is too eager to explore his new principle of happiness to be disconcerted by the occasionally jarring counterpoint of utilitarianism and natural rights. He imagines a hypothetical state of nature in which men live together, each by his unaided effort, each with his inalienable rights.[2] Psychological considerations intervene in this primeval state of society. From the superiority of his intellectual powers man derives two capital advantages. He can contemplate the past and the future as well as the present, so that his happiness, as he advances in intellect, becomes increasingly independent of temporary circumstances and sensations. From this prerogative arises the supreme advantage that "the human species itself is capable of a similar and unbounded improvement".[3] Men in the state of nature realize that many things can be better done in collaboration: they sense, too, the insecurity of their natural rights, which wear no legal dress. The State is generated from this new awareness. It is formed to facilitate a

---

[1] *Lectures on History and General Policy*, 34. History also cures us of a narrow love of our country, 33.
[2] *Essay*, 10.
[3] *Ibid*. 8–9. How men are aware of this is not clear.

social division of labour. But government, too, is primarily invoked as an instrument of progress. Men covenant together to realize the potentialities of progress of which they are conscious within themselves. Accordingly, any existing state is to be judged by the consistency of its adherence to the principles which gave birth to it. "Government being the chief instrument of progress towards this glorious end, that form of government will have a just claim to our approbation which favours this progress, and that must be condemned in which it is retarded."[1]

The State promotes progress, not positively by legislation but negatively by upholding liberty. Liberty is of two sorts: political liberty and civil liberty. Political liberty is epitomized in the *carrière ouverte aux talents*: it "consists in the power which the members of the State reserve to themselves of arriving at the public offices or, at least, of having votes in the nomination of those who fill them".[2] This is the 'right of magistracy': the exercise

---

[1] *Ibid.* 9–10. His system might be represented thus:

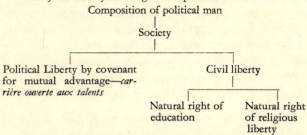

Composition of political man
|
Society
|

Political Liberty by covenant for mutual advantage—*carrière ouverte aux talents*   Civil liberty

Natural right of education   Natural right of religious liberty

[2] *Ibid.* 11. "In countries where every member of the society enjoys an equal power of arriving at the supreme offices, and

between these two spheres: to render to the State what is the State's, and to society the things that are society's. Priestley was a convinced individualist with little faith in the efficacy of the group-mind to forward intellectual progress, or in group-action by means of the State to forward material progress. *Pas trop gouverner* was his motto; better a dearth than a surfeit of government. In determining the province of the State we must distinguish between the 'form' of a government and the extent of its power. It is the power and not the form that demands attention. "It is comparatively of small consequence", he writes, "who or how many be our governors, or how long their office continues, provided their power be the same while they are in office and the administration be uniform and certain."[1] The end of government is simple enough: "a numerous, a secure and a happy society is the object of all human policy", but a government should beware of overzealousness, and of transcending its proper sphere in a laudable but dangerous attempt to promote progress.[2] The best rule is a reticent moderation; "it becomes the wisdom of civil magistracy to take as little upon its hands as possible, and never to interfere, without the greatest caution, in things that do not immediately affect the lives, liberty or property of the members of the community."[3] Its function is chiefly to ease the clash of natural powers outside the realm of civil liberty. Political liberty must be egalitarian but only because the people, bereft of an

[1] *Essay*, 29.　　　　　　　　　[2] *Lectures*, 220.
[3] *Essay*, 33.

active political function, would then have no constitutional security in the enjoyment of their retained natural
rights. It is desirable that political equality should prevail if only because "the more political liberty the people
have the safer is their civil liberty"; because it gives men
peace of mind in which progress can claim their un-
divided attention.[1]

But the real character of political liberty cannot be
appreciated unless we understand the social and political
function of property. To a conventional conviction of
the political weight which should be attached to property, Priestley added a remarkable belief in its limited
and essentially social character. The public good is the
consideration which should dominate all rank and
fortune. Private property is no less a trust than public
position. "There is", he writes, "in particular, a natural
connection between government and the ideas of property":[2] they arose together, and from a weak and
infantile state have grown to their present eminence and
importance. Both are fiduciary. "The very idea of
property or right of any kind is founded upon a regard
to the general good of the Society under whose protection it is enjoyed: and nothing is properly a man's own
but what general rules, which have for their object the
good of the whole, give him."[3] If the possession of large
property is an excellent qualification for public office, it
is because such possessions are a guarantee of security

[1] "Political Liberty, therefore, is the only sure guard of Civil
Liberty and it is chiefly valuable on that account." *Lectures*, 228.
[2] *Lectures*, 269–70.   [3] *Essay*, 26.

for the governed and of educated intelligence in the governor. Political liberty is not a thing absolute in itself, but a varying concept which must adapt itself to the actual state of mankind. A man with property is usually better educated than one without. Since it is just and politic that all classes of men should have some say in their government, a system of graduated franchise or graduated election is desirable. A minimum qualification of ability to read and write in the voter, too, would be an incitement to self-betterment, just as a graduated property qualification would be an incentive to acquire property. Priestley did not approve of universal suffrage, but believed that responsible electors should be permitted to vote by ballot.[1]

But the State is an expression of power: the power of a sovereign. This power of sovereignty is a separate entity, and although in actual fact the State is constituted of those in whose hands the power ultimately rests, they hold it only as a temporary trust, which is always revocable at the desire of the people. The power is always the same, whether it is expressed in a sovereign constitution or in ordinary legislation. But Priestley's conception of sovereignty, and indeed, the whole cast of his political thought, slowly changed with the experiences of his later life. Much that he had accepted under the rule of Candour he abandoned under the reign of rights. Before the times of trial he had been accustomed to speak of himself as a Unitarian in religion but a Trinitarian in politics. After 1787 his position was never as clear as it

[1] *Essay*, 13–14. *Lectures*, 244–5, 258.

had been in the *Essay* of 1771. Against the English Constitution he made two fundamental complaints. He distrusted its lack of definition and he disagreed with the dogma of the division of powers. He saw that political power, particularly in England, rarely resides where it ostensibly appears. The Constitution of England is kept from despotism only by the force of public opinion: by "the declared sense of the people at large".[1] The key reform must come in the system of representation. If only the Commons were made "a real representation of the people, every other reform would be made without any difficulty whatever".[2] As things are, the power of the Crown prevents this desirable fundamental amendment, but if ever foreign invasion or national bankruptcy were to destroy that power, the Lords and Commons might be free to unite to establish a better order. Perhaps a widespread system of committees of correspondence might achieve some degree of reform without these external aids. Priestley had no love for the old order as such; he was no political antiquarian. In the twilight of monarchy, he saw clearly the hopeless desolation of the old régime. For the Revolution Settlement he felt no reverence; it had accomplished a sufficient repair for the needs of its day, but had not graven a decalogue for all time. There was nothing done in 1688, that could not be better done in 1788. Constitutions have no divinity; "laws not coming down from Heaven but

[1] *A Political Dialogue on the General Principles of Government*, 1791, 102–3.
[2] *A Political Dialogue*, 107.

being made by men, may also be changed by them and what is a constitution of government, but the greater laws of the State?"[1] Indeed, it is wise to have a periodical revision of all established constitutions, the disposition of property not excluded.[2] He was impervious, too, to the fascination of old allegiances: "as a citizen the objects of my respect are the nation and the laws....I am proud of feeling myself a man among men."[3]

Even more strongly, he revolted from the three balanced powers in the State—the tritheism of political orthodoxy in England. There could, he felt, be but one will in a state, just as there can be but one will in the individual. "In every State—as in every single person, there ought to be but one will, and no important business should be prevented from proceeding, by any opposite will."[4] To erect more than one will in a state is to create, not a prudent check or balance, but another state. On this account, Priestley favoured a unicameral legislature of the French kind. If there must be a check, let the educated check the uneducated by means of a graduated franchise. Thus the State for Priestley is completely a power conception: it is a simple will working within a definite sphere. It is to be judged wholly by the extent to which it serves its purpose in promoting the public good. It can plead no special circumstances, no special morality or dispensation. Priestley will admit of no 'State-mind': no reason of state; no sacred shrine; no

---

[1] *Letters to Burke*, 1791, 173.　　　　　[2] *Lectures*, 223-4.
[3] *Letters to Burke*, 171.
[4] *A Political Dialogue*, 96. See *Lectures*, 30.

Arcana of mystery. Like Somers, he felt that *salus populi suprema lex* should be inscribed upon the cradle and the grave of government. Sovereignty, too, is sovereign only within the limited sphere of the State. He rejects emphatically "the preposterous and slavish maxim, that whatever is enacted by that body of men in whom the supreme power of the State is vested, must, in all cases, be implicitly obeyed".[1] That is the belief of political and religious tyranny. Nothing is clearer than that an oppressed people has the right and duty of resistance to the oppressor, and, if we consider how deeply oppression must sink in to the soul of a people before it touches the spring of action, it is equally clear that in all disputes between the governed and the governors, the governed have always had the monopoly of right. In the *Essay* of 1771 is to be found the resistance-calculus later adopted by Bentham and Paley. To decide his course of action, a man must weigh the evils of obedience against the evils of resistance, and strike the balance.[2] In Priestley, the half-medieval 'Appeal to Heaven' of Locke has become a quantitative formula of revolution graded in terms of the greatest public good.

The State, then, is strictly secular and limited. It is a sentinel pacing the walls, but never descending into the free city of civil liberty which it guards. Civil liberty belongs to men from their nature: it constitutes the

---

[1] *Essay*, 27.
[2] *Essay*, 18–19. He attributes this "great principle" to the Jesuits. Cf. Paley, *Principles*, 2nd ed. 424; and Bentham, *Fragment on Government*. See *Letters to Burke*, 174.

right of every man to be "exempt from the control of the society or its agents: that is, the power he has of providing for his own advantage and happiness".[1] It is a guarantee of unhampered self-improvement. All progress arises from the effort of individuals, and it is in the arena of individual effort that all which is most valuable in a man's life is won. Civil liberty is made up of two capital rights: the right of the parent to educate his child as he will, and the right to freedom of conscience without civil detriment in the profession of religion. A large part of the *Essay* of 1771 is devoted to an attack upon state education in the form of a polemic against the *Thoughts on Civil Liberty* of Dr John Brown. The civil magistrate has no right to interfere in education, for the decisive reason that "he cannot do so to any good purpose".[2] Any attempt of the State to regulate education could not, Priestley felt, but result in injustice and disaster. It would result in injustice, because every man has an inalienable right to educate his own children as he will, and every child an inalienable right to be so educated. State education is contrary to nature: it is a sin against natural diversity as well as natural rights. It is the glory of the human race to possess an infinite variety denied to brute creation. State education would destroy this variety. It would impose a dull uniformity upon a great time of beginnings in educational science. It would defeat progress, which can come only from unfettered individual effort. It would ruin the English Constitution.[3]

[1] *Essay*, 11–12.   [2] *Essay*, 41.   [3] *Essay*, 44.

the essence and inspiration of civil liberty, is freedom of conscience: the power of building the Kingdom of Heaven within us. Religion is a "constitutional property of man".[1] It conditions his personality: deprived of it, his individuality is gone, and an automaton incapable of progress is left. The portions of the *Essay* of 1771 which treat of the relations of Church and State were an attack on the undying adversary Warburton, delivered on Warburtonian grounds of public utility. "What", asks Priestley, "is the extent to which the civil magistrate should concern himself with religion? is interference to the public good?" He turns to fact and experience for his answers. The answer from experience is written everywhere in history, from Tamerlaine to Philip II. Whatever in religion the magistrate touches turns to ashes and corruption in his fingers. Fact shows religion to be a private, personal and not a political matter: "the business of religion and everything fairly connected with it is entirely a personal concern, and altogether foreign to the nature, object and use of civil magistracy."[2] The object of religion necessarily implies spiritual power in the individual, and responsibility arising from that power. If a magistrate deprives a man of spiritual power, he incapacitates him from the duties of religion. Like Price, Priestley believed that religious progress is inseparable from religious independency. His favourite analogy was the analogy of medicine. Had the State established thirty-nine articles for physicians, there would now be as many sick bodies as there were sick

[1] *Letters to Burke*, 187.   [2] *Essay*, 69–70.

souls.[1] In the interests of religion itself he demanded full toleration for all without negative or positive restraints. He did not, like Price, favour a minimum profession of theism: he would not, like Locke, exclude the atheist or the heathen. Complete freedom of conscience, without any loss of civil rights, should be accompanied by complete freedom of propaganda for both clergy and laity. Membership of a church is a voluntary adherence to a voluntary society. A man should enter it and leave it, a free and full citizen.

Thus, there is no justification in truth or utility for state control of the religion of the individual. Still less is there a justification for an establishment. Government exists in its own right, and an establishment is in no sense an indispensable adjunct. "I can see no reason to think that civil society could not have subsisted very well without the aid of any foreign sanctions."[2] All Warburton's talk of duties of imperfect obligation enforced by the Church only amounts to the doubtful belief that an ecclesiastical court can do more than a civil court.[3] Priestley, like Bentham after him, favoured free competition among religions as most likely to increase the store of human knowledge and public happiness.[4] He would have all religions impartially protected by the State, as they were in certain parts of North America. In 1771 he did not advocate immediate disestablishment. He would like a slow change, preceded by reforms among the Established clergy. In 1791 in his *Letters to Burke* all

[1] Cf. *Essay*, 82.   [2] *Essay*, 87–8.
[3] Warburton, *Alliance*, 17.   [4] *Essay*, 61–2.

is angrier and intenser. The Alliance which twenty years earlier had seemed only the legacy of an ignorant, unphilosophic age, Priestley saw in 1791 as the conspiracy of king and priest, the strong, real union of privilege against the rights of man: "nothing else than a league between two parties in the state against the common liberties of the country".[1] The time for gradual reform had gone by. "Let us", he urged, "come to a serious issue in this business."[2] The Alliance had shown itself firm enough in 1790, but if ever a disastrous war should add to the public burdens, if ever, indeed, the "growing light of the age" should reveal to the masses things as they actually were, then Burke and his Church must look to themselves. "The Alliance of any state with so weak and tottering a Church as yours must either be dissolved or both must fall together."[3]

In 1791, he felt that disruption was very near. Beside that of Priestley, the optimism of Price shrinks into human hope measured against scientific conviction. For Priestley the necessarian, the ultimate millennium on earth had all the certainty of the last term in a scientific series. It was to be the glorious culmination of that necessary sequence of events in which God realizes His will for men's happiness. "Whatever", wrote Priestley in 1771, "was the beginning of this world, the end will be glorious and paradisaical beyond what our imaginations can now conceive."[4] But his optimism was that of the Christian, as well as the philosopher. After the

---

[1] *Letters to Burke*, 208.   [2] *Ibid.* 235.
[3] *Letters to Burke*, 229.   [4] *Essay*, 1771, 9.

crowning mercy of the French Revolution, he lived in a
fever of expectation, and there was something dark and
apocryphal in his vigil. "As a believer in revelation",
he wrote, "and consequently in prophecy, I am led by
the present aspect of things to look forward to events of
the greatest magnitude and importance, leading to the
final happy state of the world."[1] Two thousand years
before, Isaiah had prophesied the French Revolution.
Now was the beginning of that stormy season which was
to herald the kingdom of political and religious righteousness. The Declaration of the Rights of Man in one hand,
and the Book of Revelation in the other, Priestley
awaited the imminent fall of the Papacy and of the
Ottoman Empire and the return of the Jews to Judaea.[2]
In the *Letters to Burke* the coming political millennium
is described in detail. "Now only", he writes, "can we
expect to see what men really are and what they can
do...how glorious then is the prospect, the reverse of
all the past, that is now opening upon us and upon the
world."[3] The social millennium will be brought about
by the influence of the commercial spirit aided by
Christianity and true philosophy. It will take the form,
politically, of an inexpensive, very limited and strictly
utilitarian state guaranteeing complete civil liberty.
Public money, no longer wasted, will be spent on public

[1] *Fast Sermon*, 1783.

[2] Cf. *Present State of Europe Compared with Ancient Prophecies*,
Fast Day Sermon, 1794.

[3] *Letters to Burke*, 237. Cf. The Divine Being sends conquests
and Revolutions as opportunities for mankind for reforming their
systems of government. *Essay*, 1771, 122.

works: "...what canals, bridges and noble roads", he reflects, "what public buildings, public libraries and public laboratories" might the expenditure on the American War have built?[1] These last days will see no American wars; no imperialism; no subjection of America, Africa or Asia to European powers. "The very idea of distant possessions will be for ever ridiculed."[2] For above all else "the Empire of Reason will ever be the reign of peace" and wars and the threat of wars will be unknown.[3] Like Price and many other dissenting thinkers, Priestley longed for the universal perpetual peace, that pleasantry of the Abbé Dubois which exercised such a fascination over a century of continual warfare. Priestley deplored the profession of a soldier.[4] He believed that the power of peace and war was safest in the popular part of a constitution, for, like Price, he was convinced that peoples would never make war upon one another.[5]

---

[1] *Letters to Burke*, 239. In his *Present State of Liberty in Great Britain and her Colonies* of 1769 Priestley summarized his attitude in the American dispute. His remedy was "to consult the good of the whole, as of one united empire, each part of which has the same natural right to liberty and happiness with the other; to encourage agriculture among them and manufactures among ourselves and by no means interfere in their interior government, so far as to lay any tax upon them either for the purpose of raising a revenue or for any other purpose whatever", 398.

[2] *Letters to Burke*, 238. "The expense of building one man of war would suffice to make a bridge over a river of considerable extent and (which ought to be a serious consideration) the morals of the labourers are much better preserved than those of seamen, and especially those of sailors". *Maxims*, 177.

[3] *Letters to Burke*, 240.

[4] *Miscellaneous Observations on Education*, 22.

[5] *Letters to Burke*, 159. *Letters to the Inhabitants of Northumberland*, 1801, 163. He strongly opposed 'commercial' wars.

Standing armies will come to be as unknown as religious establishments. "Together with the general prevalence of the true principles of civil government, we may expect to see the extinction of all national prejudice and enmity and the establishment of universal peace and goodwill among all nations."[1]

Beside this benevolent optimism of the necessarian, Priestley's sociology stands in brutal contrast. His social ideas lie scattered, haphazardly, through his works, but all unite into a harsh individualism of the kind which became dominant, when, in the nineteenth century, the industrial and commercial part of the Dissenting Interest came into its own. He considered sociology to be a branch of moral science, and the moral criterion he adopted was that of the middle class, whom, of all ranks of society, he esteemed the most. His economics were the economics of individual self-sufficiency. The best way to find what is economically good for the country is to consider the community in the light of the individual.[2] It has certain capital resources and from these it desires to gain the utmost advantage. State action of every kind is to be distrusted. "Individuals", he thought, "when left to themselves are, in general, sufficiently provident and will daily better their circumstances."[3] Despite his belief in the glorious destiny of the human race, Priestley had a low view of human nature. He saw men as creatures impelled by lust for power and wealth—excellent economic incentives were

[1] *Letters to Burke*, 238.
[2] *Maxims of Political Arithmetic*, 175.
[3] *Lectures*, 305.

they not frustrated by idleness and profligacy. He disapproved of state action in commerce and industry.
Commerce had always suffered from legislation in all
but the Navigation Act. He opposed great companies
such as the East India Company.[1] The power of a state
is greatly increased by the progress of manufacturers
within it, which creates a "fund of labour", but there is
little the State can do to forward that progress.[2] Priestley
was against all bounties, all apprentice laws, all regula-
tion of usury. "Interest", he wrote, "is the barometer
of a state."[3] He distinguished four classes in society:
labourers, agricultural and manufacturing; land and
money holders; traders and 'servants'; magistrates and
public officers.[4] He was a Lockian rather than a physio-
crat: all wealth is ultimately derived from labour, so that
the advantages of agriculture and manufactures are
reciprocal. The main thing is to keep bread at a reasonable
price, by a system of public granaries if need be, so that
"workmen's wages are kept lower and more fixed: a
thing of the utmost consequence in manufactures".[5] If
the State holds aloof and allows Necessity to work in
economic life, progress will be unlimited. Priestley had
a remarkable conviction of the great future before commerce and industry, especially in England since "the
Protestant religion is, on many accounts, more favourable to commerce than the Catholic".[6] Allied with
science, too, industry could achieve unbelievable things,

[1] *Lectures*, 322.   [2] *Ibid.* 308–11.
[3] *Ibid.* 333.   [4] *Ibid.* 303–4.
[5] *Ibid.* 302.   [6] *Ibid.* 323.

things no less desirable from the moral than the economic viewpoint. Material progress would mean a great increase of education; would bring with it all that moral betterment that goes with material prosperity. Abolish poverty, he preached, and depravity will hardly survive.

Applied to the English Poor Law, philosophical necessity amounted to "getting back to the plain path of Nature and Providence"—a grim and unrelenting *laisser-faire*.[1] In providing for the poor as it had done, the State had vastly exceeded its province, increasing, therefore, the evil it had sought to diminish. The whole psychology of the Poor Law is false: "our measures (proceeding from humanity but from weak and ill-directed policy) having in effect debased the very nature of man, have defeated the purpose of Providence with respect to him, and have reduced him to a condition below that of any of the brutes who, without having the capacity of man, never fail to provide for their real wants."[2] That was in 1787, before the Birmingham riots had finally taught Priestley the mischief of idle hands and undisciplined hearts. Men will never, he thought, cease to be idle so long as the Poor Law exists as an incitement to idleness: will never cease to shirk their allotted function in the Divine scheme of things. The Poor Law is a sin against self-help and philosophical necessity: a legalized affront to progress. But his opposition to it was moral as well as philosophical—an attack upon the ale-house and an

[1] *Some Considerations on the State of the Poor in General*, 1787, 316. *Lectures*, 226-7.
[2] *Some Considerations*, 315.

effort to better the morals of the poor. The State should care only for the disabled, especially those disabled in its service. The able-bodied paupers should be given, not doles, but education and other incitements to the conquest of property for themselves. Priestley's most practical scheme was borrowed from his friend, the Exchequer Baron Maseres: let a fund be started to which the industrious poor shall contribute. Such a fund would be a real help and a fine moral stimulant. Industrial areas should be given power to make by-laws to establish such funds.[1]

Still more ruthless was Priestley's conception of punishment. The game laws, certainly, he disapproved of, but that was a traditional grievance of the commercial against the landed interest. Apart from this customary concession, his attitude was savage. The end of punishment is the prevention of crime—an end that automatically excludes any consideration of the moral turpitude of the criminal. Punishment, therefore, should be designed to inspire "the greatest terror".[2] Perhaps slavery would be more efficacious in inspiring this than death, but for every slave there is always a chance of, or at least a hope to, escape, whereas "the loss to society by the destruction of criminals is soon made up by the production of better subjects".[3] Torture, however, he would reserve for atrocious crimes only. In imprisonment Priestley, like Howard, upheld solitary confinement and starvation diet. Unlike Bentham, he was sceptical of

[1] *Some Considerations*, 317–18.
[2] *Lectures*, 287–8.
[3] *Ibid.* 288–99.

the efficacy of shame as a punishment, but he believed the magistrate should retain a power of pardon. These sections on punishment were the only thing in his hero's life for which even his faithful biographer, J. T. Rutt, could not refrain a blush.

With such social ideas as these, it is difficult to believe that contemporaries regarded Priestley as the arch-leveller of England. His enormous unpopularity we have already seen. In a single paper of Cobbett's *Porcupine* he appears as "a hoary hypocrite, a malignant old Tartuffe, a lurking old illuminatus, a poor old wretch, a miserable perverse old man, a perverse old hypocrite and an unnatural monster". At the other end of the scale Edward Gibbon wondered how much longer Priestley's 'trumpet of sedition' would be tolerated.[1] It was his unhappy privilege to be the scapegoat of an age rendered bitter by the discovery of its own illiberality. His politics were made the excuse for a vituperation which was partly religious in quality. In a sense his was the last of England's religious martyrdoms.

His political system was not without its faults. He laboured some points overmuch to the absolute exclusion of others. He notably omitted giving any account what-

[1] Gibbon, *Memoirs*. Priestley was regularly burnt in effigy with Paine. At the time of the Birmingham Riots a mock epitaph was circulated which began:

"Near this place lies the Body of
JOSEPH FUNGUS LL.D. F.R.S.
And, strange as it may appear,
This FLAMING INCENDIARY
Owing to the clemency of a mild government
Died a natural death."

ever of the relationship between natural rights and
utility. Yet this particularization and this lack of clarity
are significant. The two primary rights of which Priestley's whole work was an elaboration, the right to freedom
of conscience and the right to the *carrière ouverte aux
talents*, were an epitome of dissenting political theory,
while the unexplained inconsistency of his combination
of natural rights and utility enabled his readers to
embrace the second without a jarring relinquishment of
the first. In this way he led men imperceptibly into new
paths, without their knowledge but with their goodwill.
He confirmed English Dissent in individualism; he con-
verted it to utilitarianism. He turned upon the State the
cold eye of the scientist and saw it in all its antique
unloveliness. He was constitutionally incapable of
understanding Burke: "by metaphysically true", he
wrote, "can only be meant strictly and properly true, and
how this can be in any sense false is to me incomprehen-
sible."[1] But he won the Dissenting Interest for philosophical radicalism and the future, by saving it from
what was most sentimental and pernicious in the romantic
revival. By his doctrine of necessity he justified to-day
and made to-morrow desirable. If he stripped the State
of splendour and left it most drab and matter of fact, he
at least insisted that it should be efficient. If in his
optimism he occasionally ran Pangloss a little too close,
he gave his system the tactical strength of a scientifically
certain millennium. At their highest, too, his ecstasies

[1] *Letters to Burke*, 168.

hardly equalled those of his great master David Hartley.[1]
To Hartley, Priestley owed much of his psychology,
while his philosophical debt to Collins, Joseph Bosco-
vitch and La Mettrie was considerable. But intellectually
he was a lonely man and, like Richard Price, unhappy in
the political company in which he unwillingly found
himself.

[1] Cf. David Hartley, *Argument on the French Revolution*, 1794.

Chapter VI

TOLERATION AND THE RIGHTS OF MEN, CITIZENS AND CHRISTIANS

"We are come out of Egypt but not yet arrived at the promised land." ROBERT ROBINSON

"Is this man going to make his peace with God and repent him of his sins?"

"No...he has lately received the appointment of first Lord of the Treasury." *Debate of* 1789

THE DISSENTING theory of toleration passed through a remarkable series of evolutions in the century and a half following the civil wars. Beginning as something purely Biblical and spiritual, it gradually changed its character, transforming itself from a Christian liberty into a natural right and, as such, into a political demand. This change illustrates more vividly, than any other single example, the great effort at reconciliation with the world: the ambition of English Dissent to secularize its relations with the community. In itself, the evolution was only one aspect of the vaster interaction of Church and State in society, but, in its widest historical significance, it marks the death of Calvinism as a social or political force: the disappearance of a specifically religious approach to civil government. Still a spiritual conception in Milton, the right of freedom of conscience developed in the writings of Locke a political character in which it was confirmed by Warburton's theory of the alliance of Church and State. As a natural right expressed in political terms, it appealed in 1772–3 to the spirit of the age for recognition. Its faith in 'Candour' shaken by the failures of these years, it was finally resolved into one of the rights of man and, as such, became identified with another article of that code: the right of the *carrière ouverte aux talents*. In this guise, it engrossed most of the language and all the significant history of the French Revolution in England. Indeed, it would hardly be an exaggeration to say that the agitation for repeal of the Test and Corporation Acts, disillusioned with the old régime and loudest in the cry of "give us back our rights", was really England's revolution in the eighteenth century, and its defeat, in 1790, marked the beginning of the European reaction. The movement gathered amazing political momentum after 1772. In its ideas, its technique of association and propaganda and the passions that it aroused, and in its demonstration of the shallowness of the widely professed enlightenment, it dominated domestic history from the last years of the American struggle to the beginning of the French Wars. As the foremost demand in a great claim for wider citizenship, it attracted to itself and gave a peculiar twist to all thinking about the State. But by one of those cynical coincidences with which history often avenges herself on philosophers, the theories of both friends and opponents of repeal coincided in their ultimate tendency, and led to a conclusion which neither party would have desired. The first contended for the things that were not Caesar's in an argument that greatly increased the power of Caesar; "let us", they said, "be

Ecclesiastical Causes lies less in its content than in the situation which produced it. Its whole tenour shows that men have ceased to hope for a 'comprehension', and, henceforth, can no longer expect to have Truth established in a national church, for the edification of the people and as a nation's homage to God, and when a pamphleteer of 1790 wrote "experience has proved that every hope of reconciling the Dissenters to the Church is vain and chimerical", he hardly realized the sociological revolution which his words implied.[1] Once comprehension was disposed of, and relative truths took the place of a single creed, the political evolution of the liberty-wherewith-Christ-has-made-us-free was inevitable. Toleration was the only remaining solution to the ensuing social deadlock. The civil magistrate has ceased to be *custos utriusque tabulae*, ceased to be concerned with the propagation of truth, and in his relations to the many different churches, he has begun to appear as an adjuster of civil interests, and no longer as the sword of the Lord.

The process of transformation from a religious to a juridical right, is already visible in Milton's *Treatise*.[2] The work itself is far from political in language or conception: "what I argue", he says, "shall be drawn from the scripture only: and therein from true, fundamental principles of the Gospel to all knowing Christians undeniable."[3] He is not concerned with the rights of the

---

[1] *Observations on the Conduct of Protestant Dissenters*, 1790, 11.
[2] *A Treatise of Civil Power in Ecclesiastical Causes*, 1658. The edition I have used is a reprint of 1790, dedicated to Richard Price "as the assertor and protector of the civil and religious rights of mankind".   [3] *Ibid.* 1.

individual against the State, but with the supremacy of
the Scriptures over all churches built upon tradition.
He advocates toleration not as a natural right or as a
private property, but as "the fundamental privilege of
the Gospel, the new birth-right of every true believer,
Christian libertie".[1] But this freedom, from the very
fact that it must bear some relation in the eyes of the
civil magistrate other than a relation of truth or error,
places its defender in a semipolitical position, nearer to
Locke than to the Puritans of the Great Rebellion. For
Milton the State is the guardian of the inviolability of
conscience; the guarantor not of a natural right but a
"Christian libertie". The State has placed its relationship to the Church upon a political basis; its duty is
more to guard conscience from violation than to force
it, and when, as states sometimes must, it uses force to
suppress "poperie and idolatrie", it is "for just reason
of State more than of religion".[2] In addition to this
entering hint of 'political' toleration, there are the
beginnings of another idea just perceptible in Milton:
an evolutionary doctrine of God's providence capable of
silencing any argument based upon history. Church and
State are separate societies. If, he contends, in the Jewish
race, they were identical, that is no argument for their
union nowadays: "if Church and State shall be made one
flesh again as under the law, let it be withal considered

[1] *A Treatise of Civil Power in Ecclesiastical Causes*, 1658, 31.

[2] *Ibid.* 20. Cf. Molesworth: "A real papist can neither be a true
governor of a Protestant Country nor a true subject", *Franco-
Gallia*, p. xi. In Locke, *Letters*, 45–6, we are given the impression
that Jesuits cannot be tolerated.

that God who then joined them hath now severed them".[1]

The thirty years which divide the *Treatise of Civil Power* from the *Letters on Toleration* might well be three hundred, so great is the contrast between the spirit of the two works. But in the second the two leading ideas of the first have continued to evolve logically and consistently. Considerations of 'Truth', of 'Comprehension', of 'Indulgence' are for ever put by; knowledge of the first is an impossible and undesirable attainment in the civil magistrate; the second and third are only palliatives for a fundamental evil: "absolute liberty, just and true liberty, equal and impartial liberty is the thing that we stand in need of."[2] For Locke, the issue has become purely political; there are in his work arguments drawn from "the Gospel of Jesus Christ", but the great bulk of them are from "the genuine reason of mankind". He appears in his habitual rôle of apologist. He wishes to show the reasonableness and practicability of a toleration in the necessity of which he more than half assumes every one to believe. With truth the State has no concern; no concern, that is, within certain limits, because Locke is always dealing with a Christian commonwealth in which toleration is conditioned by the possession of religion.[3]

[1] *A Treatise of Civil Power in Ecclesiastical Causes*, 1658, 27.
[2] *Letters on Toleration*, in *Works*, 1813, VI, 4.
[3] "The taking away of God, though but even in thought, dissolves all", *Letters*, 47. Rousseau upheld the same view in the *Contrat Social*. Cf. the doubting tone of the Declaration of 1789: Article X: "Nul ne doit être inquiété pour ses opinions, *même* religieuses", etc. My italics.

The State is an institution to defend property, and the treasures it guards are not to be spent upon atheists—vagabonds who have no property in religion. But the magistrate is not the defender of orthodoxy: "truth certainly would do well, if she were once made to shift for herself."[1] Even the most enlightened civil rulers are prone to error and if the faith of their realms were to depend upon their individual judgments, a man's precious salvation might well be lost or won by the accident of his birthplace. Again, if the State's desire to defend one exclusive religious creed were consistent, it would be obliged to extend its jurisdiction over the whole territory of moral delinquency—a clear impossibility. But such an exclusive defence would not only be impracticable in fact; it would be a violation of a natural right, and would betray a grave ignorance in the ruler of human psychology. A man enjoys his natural right to freedom of conscience both as a religious, Christian privilege and as a psychological prerogative, arising from 'human nature', from the composition of the human understanding. Toleration in any event is the mark of the true Church but, even if it were not, the human mind would of necessity reject an enforced creed, for conviction is born only from the union of 'light and evidence', of both of which the magistrate possesses no more than other men. "Nobody therefore, in fine, neither single persons nor Churches, nay, nor even commonwealths, have any just title to invade the civil rights or worldly goods of each other, upon pretence of

[1] *Letters on Toleration*, 40.

religion."[1] The truth is, that civil and religious societies are utterly distinct; neither can convey any rights to the other. A church is, in its essence, a voluntary institution; no man is born into it, but the faithful adhere of their own free will and nothing can alter this voluntary character, since it springs "from the fundamental and immutable right of a spontaneous society".[2] There can be no alliance between this voluntary society and the State, which is a secular apparatus designed to secure "the just possession of those things belonging to this life". "He jumbles heaven and earth together, the things most remote and opposite, who mixes these societies, which are, in their original, end, business and everything, perfectly distinct and infinitely different from each other."[3]

Thus, in Locke, the right to toleration is a direct outcome of his conception of the State, and is in some measure inseparable from it. It is a right which can be upheld against the State: a property conception, highly individualistic and personal. But in his work, too, there is a suggestion that toleration is more than merely negative. There is a duty of, as well as a right to, toleration, which arises from the Christian conception of fellowship: a duty which should be supplemented by charity, bounty and liberality in acknowledgment of the natural fellowship we are born in—another translation of a Christian idea into the language of natural jurisprudence.[4]

[1] *Letters on Toleration*, 20.   [2] *Ibid*. 18.   [3] *Ibid*. 21.
[4] *Ibid*. 21. Cf. Robinson, *Discourses*, XVII: "It is not enough not to persecute the enemies of Christ: we are bound by every solemn tie to perform every duty, yea, more, every kind of office of friendship towards them." 390, ed. 1805.

This positive doctrine of toleration became a powerful weapon, in the next century, in the hands of
writers like Price and Paine, while it tended more and
more to turn the natural right into a political claim. But
Locke must not be exclusively identified with the party
which fought against the Test and Corporation Acts:
in a sense, the opposition to repeal as well was founded
on his writings. After Locke and Milton, it was felt that
grounds of imperative political necessity alone could
justify state interference with religion or state intolerance; and this justification, this supreme right of state
preservation, was upheld by the Church party in their
conflict with the Dissenters, at the very time when the
latter were appealing to Locke's viewpoint as to an
axiom. It is clear that the matter had not been set and
fixed by Locke, and Warburton could still, like an
ecclesiastical Hobbes, draw completely different conclusions from his opponents' premises.

In the famous *Alliance of Church and State* of 1736, the
natural right to freedom of conscience received explicit
recognition, and after that date, the existence of such a
right was practically unquestioned by either the Dissenters or their opponents. "By the law of nature",
wrote Warburton, "every man has a right of worshipping
God according to his own conscience", and a toleration
is the natural complement to an establishment.[1] His
design was to build up an impregnable defensive system
against the "old battery of *imperium in imperio*", and the

[1] *The Alliance between Church and State*, 1736, ed. London,
1741, 46.

fortifying material which he used was purely political. But while such a method made for present strength, and set the tone of the long interval of religious peace which followed the Bangorian controversy, it was, nevertheless, a dangerous method. Quite apart from the mere indignity of regarding the established religion as a sort of subsidiary policeman venturing where the State cannot tread, it was unwise to strip the Church Established so completely of any Divine sanction: to base it wholly in utility and defend it in the language of Grotius, Pufendorf, and Locke.[1] Once the interpretation of political and philosophical phenomena should alter, the Establishment might well find itself outflanked on a political field. Even so, Warburton completed Locke's work, and the natural right to freedom of conscience became a secondary commandment beside that primary ordinance which ruled that "an established religion is, as we say, the universal voice of nature and not confined to certain ages, people or religion".[2] But while adopting this chief article of his opponents' creed, Warburton weighed it as he weighed establishments, in scales of utility. A test act is justified by its utility. Everything must be measured by the social intention: what may be

[1] All of whom he cites. As Blackburne asked, once the case is summoned before a "foreign judiciary...that is to say Holy Scripture...what becomes of the Alliance?" *Confessional*, 110.

[2] *The Alliance between Church and State*, 70. Warburton added the salvo: "1 always mean a legitimate government or civil policy founded on the principles of the Natural Rights and Liberties of Mankind", 153—an open door for an alliance of the Whig or Revolution State with the Church.

harmless in nature may well be eminently harmful in civil society, and to put opinions injurious to that society under restraint is no usurpation of 'natural' rights which have ceased to be 'natural' and have become civil. A test is no more than a restraint, and is justified on the principles of 'civil utility', for while men may have a right by nature to their own opinions, they have no such right to hold political offices, which are not a trust reposed in the magistrate from some external source, but a property *ex-officio*, a prerogative of the magistrate; an inherent right in the State, based on the State's right of self-preservation. By means of this contortion Warburton and the Establishment squeezed through the loophole left them by Locke and Milton. In *The Alliance between Church and State* the two fundamental contentions—the right of the individual against the right of the State—stand side by side.

Thus, by the turn of the eighteenth century, each party was armed with the sword of its forefathers. The situation did not remain static after Warburton, but all subsequent theorizing was in the nature of a glossary and amplification upon these two principles. It was felt clearly and surely that the grounds of disagreement had shifted: that it was no longer truth but a social principle that was being disputed, and the argument gradually drew away from Locke, becoming ever more political and particularized. Locke himself was widely read by the later controversialists: by Furneaux, by Robinson, by Towers. Fownes thought his own sentiments were wholly drawn from him; since Locke, wrote Israel Mauduit, no man has ventured to dispute the reasonableness of toleration, so that the invocation of abstract principles would be supererogatory.[1] Kippis, however, was inclined to think that Calamy's Introduction to the second volume of his *Defence of Moderate Non-Conformity* did more to enlighten dissenting opinion and to place the controversy on a new footing than even the *Letters on Toleration*.[2] But from whatever source conviction came, the belief in the natural right to freedom of conscience was universal among English Dissenters. Implicit in human nature, this right was held to be inalienable. "I am far from considering liberty of conscience as an indulgence of government", wrote Joseph Towers. "It is a right of nature which no government can deprive men of without being guilty of inhumanity and injustice."[3] "A christian not only cannot, but, if he could, ought not, to dispose of this right, because not only he cannot be a christian without its exercise, but all the purposes of civil government may be answered without it."[4] As late as 1808, when fashions of

[1] Fownes, *Enquiry*, 1772, VI. Mauduit, 1772, *Case*, 3.

[2] Kippis, *Vindication*, 1773, 42. He says that since the 'Clarendon' Code "a great, a just and important alteration has taken place in the sentiments of the Protestant Dissenters upon these subjects." 29.

[3] *Letters to Johnson*, 183. 'Photinus' in Lindsey's *Conversations on Idolatry* speaks of "the inalienable right of all men to judge for themselves in the things of God". To the Presbyterian Dissenters of the seventeenth century, liberty of conscience seemed something very different. "The Devil for some thousands of years", they felt, "had not found out this engine nor made use of it to support his kingdom." *Gangraena*, pt. III, 335.

[4] Robinson, *Arcana*, 49. "There is neither Jew nor Greek, bond nor free, prince nor subject: the right of one, argued from his nature, is the right of all." *Ibid.*

thought were tending to change, it was talked of as "one of the inalienable rights of human nature".[1] The great majority of the Established Church, from Dean Tucker to William Frend, believed in its existence.[2] Every member of Parliament prefaced his opposition to repeal by a declaration of faith in the principle of toleration.[3] The right came to be accepted as axiomatic, so that the language of repeal was largely an embroidery upon this essential theme. Accepted as a natural right, it was examined and defended in its social aspect. This is the attitude typified by Mauduit and Kippis.

But of those who did retraverse the old ground, the most explicit and revealing was Joseph Fownes, whose *Enquiry into the Principles of Toleration* was first published in 1772.[4] This work was important as being the fullest, as it was the last, exposition in the old idiom which the ideology of the French Revolution was about to supersede; the idiom of natural jurisprudence of Grotius, Pufendorf and Barbeyrac. It summarizes the theoretical position of the Appeal to Candour in 1772, and its purpose

---

[1] Bogue and Bennett, I, 202. Cf. *Case of the Protestant Dissenters*, 1787. "Every man hath an inalienable right, as it is now generally acknowledged, to judge for himself in matters of religion." 3.

[2] "That each religious persuasion ought to have a full toleration from the State to worship Almighty God according to the dictates of their own conscience, is to me so clear a case that I shall not attempt to make it clearer." Tucker, *True Interest of Britain*, 1776, 65. Frend thought there was no clearer proposition in Euclid. *Peace and Union*, 43.

[3] E.g. Hans Stanley, M.P. in 1772. Hansard, XVII, 260.

[4] The third edition reprinted in 1790 with an introduction by Kippis.

was to prove that toleration is the right of all good subjects. But Fownes did not ask for more than toleration and legal security. The demand of full citizenship had not yet been heard. For Fownes toleration is grounded not in 'Christian liberty' but in 'the original liberties of mankind'. The righteousness of its cause is to be determined in the light of political justice, and, before that tribunal, laws which sanctify oppression, penal laws directed against something which is not even legally a crime, laws which "incorporate incroachments upon the rights of men into the constitution", can hardly hope to stand uncondemned.[1] The nature of man and the nature of society both demonstrate the injustice of such laws and instruct us that the State should be not the enforcer but the patron of religion. That man has certain natural rights which he carries with him into civil society; that freedom of conscience is among these rights; that government is a creature of man designed to protect these rights; these are axioms and need not be discussed. The only question is: what social limitations can encroach upon this plenary right? How far can it be modified by the transition to the civil state? Rights, says Fownes, are of two kinds: primary and subsequent. The first are as unalterable as the composition of nature and as eternal as the human race: the second are social creations of an executive nature. The first can never be sacrificed to civil society which exists only as their protector, and foremost among these primary rights is the right of conscience, which "stands upon a founda-

[1] *Enquiry*, Preface, ix.

tion peculiar to itself and is distinguished from every other right, that it cannot be given up".[1] It is the most essential of "those higher rights which belong to men as such and which ought to be preserved under all States and Governments whatsoever".[2] It is more even than this: it is the root cause of civil society, for it is to secure the right of conscience that men form the State.[3] Thus the State itself is founded upon this supreme natural right, and, in Fownes, the Calvinistic hierarchical limitations of civil society have been transformed into juridical language, and reappeared as the basis and justification of the State in terms of pure natural right. The State has no choice but to repeal its iniquitous laws or belie its natal principle. "The matter indeed is reduced to this short and plain issue: either the just principles of toleration must be sacrificed or the laws, from which the Dissenters desire to be sheltered, must be allowed to be indefensible. The truth of the one and the justice of the other cannot stand together."[4] Such a claim could never have been made but for the aid of circumstances, and the events of the years 1760–72 combined to light a sort of *ignis fatuus* to the hopes of the Dissenters, leading them to an ever falser estimate of the spirit and 'candour' of their times. The decision in the Evans Case; the Petition movement in the Church itself; the sympathy and friendship of so many broad Churchmen of the type of Black-

---

[1] *Enquiry*, 17.   [2] *Ibid.* 21.

[3] *Ibid.* 15, and "no encroachments on the natural, original, rights of men to procure them a more extensive reception can be justified", 29.

[4] *Ibid.* 108.

burne, Lindsey, and Disney—all seemed to emphasize the fact that the time for repeal of the intolerant acts had come. So, too, did the character of the opposition to their claims encourage the Dissenters, couched as it was in legalistic or historical objections, but never in the language of bigotry. Many of these objections were no more than trivial excuses, such as the plea that the king would violate his coronation oath in giving his consent to a repeal bill; but this moving picture of a forsworn monarch in an age that was not solicitous for public reputations does show one thing: it shows the desperate tenacity with which each side clung to the rules of 'candour', afraid to admit, even to themselves, the real passions and prejudices which shaped their actions. But on the whole 'candour' favoured Dissent and the Church was the first to abandon it. In two particular fields, one legal, the other historical, the Church party lost the day. The first defeat was in the Case of Allan Evans, which was a judicial recognition of the Warburtonian principle that toleration is the complement of an establishment: that it is the negative aspect of a positive institution. The immediate influence of Mansfield's judgment that nonconformity is not a crime was not widespread. Blackstone in the *Commentaries* three years later spoke of the penalties as being 'suspended' only by the Toleration Act, implying that nonconformity was still a criminal offence.

Priestley's reply to this statement did not produce any considerable change. All this took place in 1769, when the repeal movement was gathering force. In 1771 appeared Furneaux's *Letters to Blackstone*, an able book pitched on a high moral note, which turned the decision of the Lords to the best account, and clarified all the implications of Lord Mansfield's judgment.[1] The book had a double importance: widely read, it strengthened English Dissenters in their resolve to secure an even broader legal basis for the existence of their churches, while, at the same time, it swelled the numbers of the repeal movement by bringing home to non-Trinitarians the danger in which they stood from unenforced laws. The only security for the many whose offences under the Test and Corporation Acts and whose non-compliance with the terms of the Toleration Act were connived at, for every Unitarian, Arian or Socinian minister or school-master, lay in the accepted spirit of the age in which all were soon to lose faith. If the repeal were to fail, the widespread advertisement which it had given to the actual situation of Dissent would have done the greatest harm. The times might well change; already many, with the example of the American dispute before them, were revising their opinions of their enlightened government and model constitution.

The second victory of Dissent was in a matter of historical interpretation. The Union with Scotland, it was argued, had guaranteed a religious *status quo* in both countries, and, with the disappearance of the Scottish Parliament, the Union had passed into the Constitution

---

[1] Philip Furneaux, D.D., *Letters to the Hon. Mr Justice Blackstone*, London, 1771, 2nd ed., Letter 1.

of Britain; had become part of the fundamental law[1] of the realm. In this Act of Union, religious legislation was, by implication, included and could not be repealed without a dangerous violation of the Constitution itself. The argument was a weak one, but popular with the pamphleteers and in Parliament; demolished though it had been in 1771-2, Henry Beaufoy still felt himself constrained to refute it fifteen years later.[2] The Dissenters' reply to this argument was threefold: interpretation of the Union in its political principles; actual examples proving that such laws were not included in the Act of Union; and the tenet of State sovereignty. In the sphere of theory, Furneaux's reply was the most philosophical and the most interesting. As a practical argument he felt the contention was absurd, but, in its wider aspect, worthy of attention, and best judged in the light of the fiduciary character of the State. The Union was not a contract of incorporation between two parliaments, but the bond of two nations, acting in a corporate capacity through the agency of their Parliaments. One of these agencies has ceased to exist, but the nation still remains, and can still express itself as a contractor, so in theoretical

---

[1] Cf. Newdigate in the Debate on the Clerical Petition: "The Union as well as Magna Carta, I hold an irrevocable decree, binding at all times, and in all circumstances, like the law of the Medes and the Persians", Hansard, xvii, 256.

[2] In 1787 he told the Commons that such an argument "supposes that, if my agreement with him gives me a right of common on his manor, I violate my compact if I afterwards voluntarily offer him a right of common upon mine". Published Debate of 1787, 38. Beaufoy was educated at the Warrington Academy.

terms the Union offers no obstacle to repeal.[1] But the
bulk of dissenting opinion chose to rely upon practical
examples, the most pertinent of which was the failure
of the Commons in 1706 to incorporate the Test and
Corporation Acts in the Act of Union. The argument of
sovereignty, too, came easily if not altogether consistently. Furneaux employed it, and so did Priestley: "the
bare idea of a state", he wrote, "without a power, some-
where vested, to alter every part of its laws, is the height
of political absurdity."[2] This was hardly the language in
which to sustain a claim to natural rights. But these two
controversies, one legal, one historical, were important
chronologically, for they ceased to command much belief
after 1773. The opposition to repeal was forced more
and more on to grounds of political expediency, descending from the theory of politics to the language and
judgment of party.

Thus the stage was set for repeal and the Dissenting
Interest only needed an encouraging prologue. They had
not long to wait for one. Dissatisfaction with the
Alliance was breaking out in the Establishment itself and
a group of rebels, ultra-liberal Churchmen like Lindsey,
Blackburne, Wyvill, Jebb, Law, Disney and Chambers,
made that dissatisfaction articulate. The Clerical Petition
movement is important, not so much as the inspiration of,
but as the prelude to, the great repeal agitation. It contained two elements: the one clerical and doctrinal,

[1] Furneaux, *op. cit.* Letter v, 153–61.
[2] *Remarks on Blackstone's Commentaries*, 1769, 308, a deferential
chiding.

which opposed subscription from principle and from actual disagreement with the contents of the Thirty-nine Articles;[1] the other lay and educational, which protested against the restriction which subscription to the Articles laid upon learning. Francis Blackburne, Archdeacon of Cleveland, gave the movement a creed; Theophilus Lindsey became its martyr. The official beginning of the movement dated from the publication of Blackburne's *The Confessional* in 1766, but it had its broader inspiration in the religious and social history of the times. The left-wing Churchmen had for long had some affinities with the Rational Dissenters, whose theological opinions they embraced, and whose friendship they enjoyed. There was a group in Cambridge consisting of men of the stamp of Tyrwhitt, William Frend and John Jebb. These men knew Wakefield and Robinson and were to become the guiding spirits of the movement. There was another little coterie, consisting of William Turner the prominent Presbyterian, Joseph Priestley, and Theophilus Lindsey, who used to meet regularly in 1769 at Francis Blackburne's house in Richmond; it represented those who were already confirmed anti-Trinitarians and those who were in the way of becoming so.[2] But the soul of the movement was embodied in Theophilus Lindsey,

---

[1] Wakefield felt subscription was "the most disingenuous action of my whole life". *Memoir*, 1, 120. He says, "to think of the abominable wickedness of requiring an unfeigned assent and consent to such a medley of propositions, some of which are unutterably stupid, beyond the sottishness of even Hottentot divinity!", 121.

[2] Belsham, *Memoirs of Lindsey*, 34.

who was overtaken by Unitarianism in the middle of a brilliant career in the Establishment, and gave up his all, which was considerable, to follow it. A Fellow of St John's College, Cambridge, and a son-in-law of Blackburne, he was appointed Vicar of Catterick in 1763, just at the genesis of the movement in which he was to distinguish himself.[1] When his doubts began, two courses were open to him: to follow the precedent of the Reverend William Robertson, who in 1760 had left the Establishment for Unitarianism, or, before taking action, to await the issue of the Clerical Petition. He chose the latter course and abided by its decision.

The Clerical Petition was essentially an appeal to 'candour' but not wholly so. Blackburne, its theorist, was a fanatical anti-Papist, like his friend Thomas Hollis, and the obverse side of the movement he instructed was an attack upon the ever-present menace of Popery.[2] The *Confessional* was widely read and recognized as the manifesto of the Petitioners: "the *Confessional*", Fitzmaurice told the Commons, "I hold to be their creed."[3] The book itself was a philosophically worded incitement to action. Much of it was an historical examination of the Articles reaching back to Burnet and beyond, into the days of Episcopius and the Remonstrants. Subscription to the Articles, he argues, is useless as a test of opinion and unfair to the prospective Churchman, since all confessions of faith are "a bridle upon the tongue and

---

[1] Belsham, *Memoirs of Lindsey*, 7, 11, 25.
[2] *The Confessional, Works*, Cambridge, 1804, V, 113.
[3] Hansard XVII, 262. He opposed the Petition.

a shackle upon the pen hand".[1] But worse than that, such confessions infringe a natural right, and are in direct opposition to the cardinal principle of Protestant-ism. "There is indeed nothing more evident than that every Christian hath a right to search the Scripture: a right which he cannot transfer either to any Church or to any single person, because it is his indispensable duty to exercise it personally for himself."[2] It is not a matter of establishing truth but of recognizing a principle. A Scriptural test would be quite adequate for purposes of State, since truths which are merely speculative can have no effect upon the foundations of government.[3] Black-burne's publication was preceded by the *Free and Candid Disquisitions* of 1749, an anaemic work, soon forgotten, but influential in its time. Both announced the season propitious for some attempt at legislative amelioration. From this belief arose the Feathers Tavern Association.

At a meeting of liberal clergy and laity, the 'Anti-Articularians' as they were named,[4] at the Feathers Tavern in London, on 17 July 1771, a Petition, drawn up by Blackburne, was drafted.[5] It declared the belief of the petitioners in a natural right to the free exercise of their judgment in matters of religion: a natural right upon which the Reformation was founded and incom-patible with the existence of the Thirty-nine Articles as a subscriptive creed. It opposed the Articles, too, as a cause of disunion between Protestants, while the laity

---

[1] Hansard, xvii, 194, 208. [2] *Ibid.* 173.
[3] *Ibid.* 361, 480–1. [4] Cf. Shebbeare.
[5] Hansard, xvii, 246.

among the petitioners complained of the University Test.[1] A separate petition was also drawn up by the laity.[2] The petitioners were not numerous, being less than two hundred and fifty, but numbering among them men of the calibre of Lindsey, Blackburne, Jebb, Wyvill and Disney.[3] David Williams was one of those who met at the Feathers Tavern: true to his tradition, he disapproved of everything: the matter, the manner, the people, the time and, above all, the *Confessional*.[4] Lindsey travelled two thousand miles and more on Petition business.[5] Parallel with this metropolitan movement was a gradually rising tide of dissatisfaction in the universities. In December, 1771, the undergraduates petitioned the Vice-Chancellor of Cambridge for relief from subscription to the Articles on taking their degrees, but without success.[6] Robert Tyrwhitt, a friend of Lindsey and Fellow of Jesus, failed to carry a grace embodying a similar reform.[7] Another Fellow of that college, William Frend, was already laying up evil for himself in years to

[1] Hansard, XVII, 246.

[2] They are both printed in the *Gentleman's Magazine*, 1772, I, 61, 218. The Clerical Petition is given in Frend's *Proceedings*, 258 and Belsham's *History of Great Britain*, V, 527, Appendix.

[3] Belsham, *Memoirs of Lindsey*, 50–1.

[4] David Williams, *Essays on Public Worship*, etc. London, 1774, 43. He was as trying a person as Wakefield himself and no lover of his fellow Dissenters. "I was educated among the Saints; and now I live, thank God, among sinners...I declare on the word of a man of honour, and one who knows the world, that of all the sinners I ever met with, the Saints are by far the greatest", 25. From being a dissenting minister he became a deist of the Paine type.

[5] Belsham, *Memoirs of Lindsey*.

[6] *Gentleman's Magazine*, 1772, 41.

[7] Dyer, *Life of Robinson*, 79. *Memoirs of Lindsey*, 103.

come by his activities[1] in the cause of repeal. Blackburne's son, Thomas, at Peterhouse, was refused a degree
because he could not take the bona fide oath.[2] Shortly
before the debate on the Petition in the Commons, Jebb
preached a powerful sermon against subscription at
St Mary's Church.[3] "It appears to me a melancholy
thought", Lord George Germain told the Commons,
"and indeed a crying grievance, that my son at 16 must
subscribe, upon entering the University, what I cannot
understand, much less explain to him at sixty."[4]

The presentation of the Petition was fixed for 6
February 1772: Sir William Meredith was to introduce it,
Cavendish and Savile not feeling themselves competent
to do so. The times seemed hardly propitious: the press
was hostile:[5] the Dissenters indifferent. John Lee doubted
if it would collect forty votes.[6] Indeed, it had been Lord

[1] *Proceedings.* He left a copy of Hoadly upon all the Heads of
Houses.

[2] *Gentleman's Magazine*, 1772, 219. He was a contemporary of Capel
Lofft at that College. Walker, *Admissions to Peterhouse*, 1912, 330–1.

[3] Belsham, *History*, v, 370.

[4] Hansard, XVII, 266. This was at Oxford, where subscription was
exacted on matriculation. Cambridge postponed it until the degree.

[5] Cf. *Gentleman's Magazine*, 1772, 225. A savage fable addressed to
the petitioners of the Feathers Tavern about rats who managed to
get into an old house and then wanted the door taken off its hinges
"that animals of all kinds might have free access". For the attempt,
see also Aikin's *Annals of George III*, i, 34. A Bedfordshire vicar
spoke of the scheme as "A diabolical, mischievous, machination...
by the enemies of religion, to serve some jesuitical, methodistical,
schismatical, atrocious purpose". Towers, *Dialogue*, 305. For
Jesuit complicity see *Gentleman's Magazine*, 1772, 276.

[6] Hansard, XVII, 248. He agreed with Lindsey that it would be
good propaganda.

North's intention to let the Petition die a natural death from neglect upon the table of the House, but this serene course reckoned without Sir William Newdigate, member for Oxford.

Sir William Meredith presented the Petition and Thomas Pitt seconded it. The ensuing debate was chiefly interesting for the controversial precedents it set. Meredith appealed to common sense against the retention of the errors of a less enlightened generation.[1] But it was the fate of the Clerical Petition, and of the philanthropists of the Feathers Tavern, to be completely misunderstood. Public opinion professed itself shocked that men, so uncertain in their faith, could permit themselves to continue to receive the bounty of the Establishment, and agreed with Newdigate that they were a "slippery protean race".[2] Newdigate made the most of the political aspect of the case: "if you remove this institution", he said, "I cannot see how the State can for a moment subsist. Civil and Religious establishments are so linked and incorporated together that, when the latter falls, the former cannot stand. They seem to me to be as inseparably connected as soul and body. And indeed what is religion but the soul that animates the body politic?"[3] He felt the Coronation Oath and the Act of Union were grave obstacles in the

[1] Hansard, xvii, 248. Meredith had distinguished himself by attacking the validity of general warrants in the Wilkes case. Aikin, *op. cit.*   [2] *Ibid.* 255.

[3] *Ibid.* An example of what Robert Robinson called "a midnight tale, fit for the tenth century, but not to be repeated now". *Sacramental Tests,* Sermon. Cambridge, 1788, iv, 123-4.

path of any alteration of the existing laws. Stanley extended the civil side of the case, which to Newdigate was little more than the 'Church in danger' translated into political terms, into a matter of the purest expediency. Toleration had no greater friend than himself, but he subscribed to a fortieth article which was public peace. He hinted that any alteration in the law might bring back the days of Sacheverell. The precedents of the previous century were not forgotten: "stir not the plague", urged Charles Jenkinson, "from the pit in which it is buried."[1] Against such a tradition, it was hopeless to appeal to Newton, Locke, Clarke and Hoadly; to confront Blackstone with Blackburne.[2]

It was Lord North himself who made the most influential speech of the debate. He found the Act of Union a fundamental obstacle, but there was a stronger case against the Petition than the existence of legal difficulties. Neither the State nor the rights of conscience had been prejudiced by the Establishment. "Every person is allowed to go to Heaven his own way. The only restraint laid upon us is that we create no public disturbance."[3] A visible church cannot subsist without a rule of faith. Like Fitzmaurice, Shelburne's son, he hinted that the Petition was the manifesto of an anti-Trinitarian cabal: an innuendo which Germain denied but without much conviction.[4] It remained to Burke to make the most remarkable speech of the day: a speech which foreshadowed his attitude in 1790. Act of Union,

[1] Hansard, xvii, 261, 269–70.   [2] *Ibid.* 264, 266.
[3] *Ibid.* 273.   [4] *Ibid.* 264, 265, 274.

coronation oaths, these are all things with which temporal sovereignty can deal. But men cannot legislate
away their own nature upon abstract principles, and a
man must be prepared to sacrifice something to society.
In society there must be "a general standard which
obtains throughout the whole community".[1] Religion
must be institutionalized so that it will escape the fatal
attraction of metaphysical systems. "In short I would
have a system of religious laws that would remain fixed
and permanent, like our civil constitution, and that
would preserve the body ecclesiastical from tyranny and
despotism, as much at least as our code of common and
statute law does the people in general: for I am convinced that the liberty of conscience, contended for by
the petitioners, would be the forerunner of religious
slavery."[2] Liberty for the candidate for Ordination in
the Establishment means that the electors, the people (for
the nation is in a sense a huge corporation electing its
ministers), will be deprived of theirs. "Dissent not satisfied with toleration is not conscience but ambition."[3]

The Petition was rejected by 217 votes to 71. It had
failed because it was untimely and little understood. Its
supporters felt, however, that the attempt had not been
without value. Lindsey wrote to a friend that the debate
was one "which entered gloriously into the whole merits
of our cause; and which was well worth going two

---

[1] Hansard, XVII, 288.   [2] Ibid.
[3] Ibid. 281. Lindsey wrote to Turner: "Burke declaimed most
violently against us in a long speech but entirely like a Jesuit, full
of popish ideas."

vain. The rumoured resignation of Lindsey had made a profound impression upon public opinion, and had more than half condoned the imprudence and untimeliness of the Clerical Petition. The arguments, too, employed against that measure did not, it was thought, apply to Dissenters, while if the temper of the Establishment could be gathered from the writings of Dean Tucker, it seemed supremely unlikely that any one Churchman would be found to oppose the extension of toleration: to refuse a legal existence to a situation which had already grown old in fact.[1] It was felt, also, that the Lord had been at work in history, shifting the once immutable foundations, fusing elements that had seemed irreconcilable, and so completely transforming situations and ideas, that the passions and extravagances of former days lay buried among the years which had begotten them. In their place was to be seen what Andrew Kippis saw: "a generous prince of the Brunswick line: a seemingly equitable administration: moderate and wise members of both houses: candid bishops: a liberal spirit in all ranks of men and Toleration lifting her voice loudly in Europe."[2] It would have seemed almost an affront to Providence, to neglect so favourable an opportunity of making one decisive appeal to the spirit of the times: not to confront history and prejudice once again with all-conquering *candour*. For strongest of all the many incitements to action, was a universal self-esteem that translated itself, as in a writer like Joshua Toulmin, into a faith in the 'genius of the age' and the prevailing

[1] Kippis, *Vindication*, 11. [2] *Ibid.* 15, 51–2.

fashions of thought. "Never", he wrote, "were the grounds of liberty, civil and religious, better understood: never was the spirit of liberty more universally diffused."[1] Every man in Britain had grown acquainted with the simple principles of enlightened politics and would willingly translate them into practice.

But the Dissenting Application to Parliament in the years 1772–3 was not unaffected by less enlightened considerations. Not a few advocates of toleration would not have loved it half so well, had they not been convinced that Popery loved it far less, while the dwindling congregations of the Dissenters, abandoned by those who could not afford to pay both tithe and the dissenting minister's stipend, added an economic impetus to the convictions of philosophy. The movement, however, as a whole, was sincerely what it professed to be: an appeal to 'candour', and it differed as much in the spirit in which it was conducted from the Applications of 1787–90, as it differed in object from those of later years. The cry in 1790 was "give us back our rights which your government has usurped", but in 1772–3 it was no more than a plea for co-operation in erecting a common monument to Justice: "let us", it was urged, "recognize our common rights which were lost in an age of barbarity and extravagance—rights which the common sense of every man teaches him to recognize." There was also a strain of educational grievance. Where the Petitioner

---

[1] Toulmin, *Two Letters*, 39. Cf. David Williams in the same year: "the weapons only of persecution remain: its legions are wasted and gone." *Essays*, 2.

had felt himself aggrieved over matters of University subscription, the Dissenter felt that the penal statutes infringed the sacred right of instructing his own children in such a way as he might wish. For the lay Dissenters this was a matter of deep concern, leading them to unite with their clergy in a common cause, as Priestley always urged them to do.[1]

The Applications of 1772–3 had a double object: one immediate and one ultimate. The immediate object was to obtain legal security for those dissenting ministers whom the Toleration Act did not cover, and whose security depended upon public opinion alone. "In the present situation of things", wrote Toulmin, "the Toleration is not complete and we are not in possession of our full natural rights", and his design, and that of his colleagues, was to gain as much new ground as was possible within the rather narrow limits of the Act of Toleration.[2] But anticipation did not end there: this immediate object was to be the first step towards a greater, which amounted to a review of the whole situation of religious liberty in England, and to effecting a complete reformation upon the best model known to philosophy. In these designs, it was the desire of the Applicants to appear quite uninfluenced by any doctrinal motives. The Application was to deal with discipline and not with doctrine: it was designed to solve a problem of

[1] Kippis, *Vindication*, 93. Priestley, *Letter of Advice*. The attempt of 1772 produced much correspondence in the newspapers— *St James' Chronicle, London Chronicle*, etc.—from 'Hubert Languet', 'Locke', 'Hoadly', 'Tillotson', and so on.

[2] *Two Letters*, 10.

organization and not to set up truth.[1] By thus professing to deal with discipline only, the Applicants hoped to silence all irrelevant arguments drawn from history: to be able truthfully to claim with Joseph Fownes that "in a word, the question is not what was formerly determined, but what the rights of conscience make it equitable for men to request and for the legislature to grant": that a new situation had arisen which could only be dealt with in a new way.

Briefly, that new situation was this. The benefits of the Toleration Act could be enjoyed only under certain restrictions, the most notable being a compulsory subscription to all save three of the Thirty-nine Articles and certain portions of two others.[2] Similar restrictions hampered dissenting schoolmasters and educationalists. At the time of the passing of the Toleration Act, the Dissenters had been, for the most part, strictly Calvinist, with few objections of conscience to the Articles themselves—so few that their dissent was represented by opponents as nothing but a contumacious obstinacy over 'things indifferent'. So complete had been the revolution in beliefs of English Dissent in the century after 1689, that few of the Applicants of 1772–3 could

---

[1] Wilton, *Apology*, 27. "It was not as Arians or Athanasians, as Calvinists or Arminians but Protestants and Protestant Dissenters, that we...engaged in this application." 33. Robinson, *Arcana, or the Principles of the late Petitioners*, 1774, 127.

[2] I William and Mary, c. 18. The Articles were 34, 35, 36, half of 20, and 7. Priestley, omitting the ten articles against heresy, could only agree with one and that was "a dictate of common sense". *Letter of Advice*, 471.

comply with the subscription required.[1] Deprived of the protection of the Act, the position of the advanced Dissenters was, on paper at least, full of peril—a peril likely to become a very real one, should the intolerant enthusiasm of the Methodists ever penetrate to the Establishment. Thus, they existed only by connivance, criminals in the shadow of laws *in terrorem* at the very time when the Evans Judgment had declared nonconformity to be no crime. It was with the iniquity of such laws *in terrorem*, with the inadequacy of a security by connivance alone, that the Application was concerned, and when Burke, in 1773, told the Commons that "connivance is a relaxation from slavery, not a definition of liberty", he was only repeating what Fownes, Toulmin and their like knew and feared.[2] To bring the Toleration Act up to date, and gain an explicit constitutional acknowledgment of Mansfield's Judgment were urgent needs beside which the existence of the Test and Corporation Acts seemed a grievance easily borne. Toleration was the sum of dissenting hopes in the years 1772–3, and with confidence they appealed to their fellow Christians to join in placing it "on a more enlarged basis and procuring for those, who request it, that extensive legal security which the spirit of the Gospel requires they should enjoy and to which Natural Justice gives them an unquestionable title". But this simple programme involved all the great and fundamental issues which it

[1] Mauduit, *Case*, 5. Kippis, *Vindication*, 30.
[2] Hansard, xvii, 7778. Toulmin, *Two Letters*, 43–4. "It is the glory of a state to exercise no connivance", 72.

appeared to avoid. The nature of the complaint necessarily provoked doctrinal considerations, while any attempt to alter the Toleration Act would challenge the prevailing interpretation of the constitutional position of the Revolution Settlement. A public airing of their largely anti-Trinitarian beliefs, too, was the last eventuality which the Applicants desired, while against the sanctity of 1688 they could produce only an argument of state sovereignty which seemed queer company for natural justice and rights.

But beyond the immediate object of amending the Toleration Act, lay the ultimate design of "petitioning for rational liberty", and the pamphleteers of 1772-3 were not insensitive to this. Two schools of thought divided the dissenting apologists of the Appeal to Candour. The first was the traditional school of English Whigs, drawing its principles from Locke and Edmund Calamy, and arguing freely from history. To this school belonged writers like Fownes and Mauduit, Kippis, Toulmin and Towers. Their work was chiefly an embroidery of the natural right to toleration, re-enforced by appeals to Scripture, reason and experience. But besides this group, which represented the majority of Dissenters, was a smaller body, largely inspired by French thought, and essentially romantic in temper, men like Robert Robinson and David Williams. They built their case more upon nature, upon the function of the understanding and the character of truth. These two divisions were by no means hard and fast. Rather they resembled two different poles, towards one of which most writers consistently gravitated. Priestley steered a middle course. He felt that the grounds of controversy had certainly shifted since the days of Locke, yet he was eager to warn his readers against adopting too 'political' a view of the movement—the view of those "who might have learned the principles of Toleration from Voltaire or Rousseau".[1] Of the two schools, the efficiency of the first as a political force was certainly diminished by the historical incumbrances of whiggism, and the second, though more effective as a political creed, could not command the same immediate sympathy as 'the good old cause'.[2] Both schools, from different approaches, found themselves confronted with problems of the province of the State and the nature of religious establishments.

With the essential principles of those who fought under the banner of natural justice and natural and Christian rights, we are already conversant. In 1772-3, however, the natural right to freedom of conscience had not attained its full stature; the Dissenters were asking only for the rational fulfilment of a process which had been begun in 1689. In asking this, they felt themselves to be "acting in conformity to the first law of God and of Nature, and under the regular influence of that principle of self-preservation which the common Father of all mankind hath implanted in every heart".[3] The claim to the *carrière ouverte aux talents*, to an active function in the State itself, had not yet been voiced. "The Test Act", wrote Kippis, "only excludes those who cannot comply

---

[1] *Free Address*, 1771, 272.   [2] *Ibid.*
[3] Wilton, *Apology*, London, 1773, 20-1.

with it from civil honours, whereas the penal statutes deprive us of the common rights of human nature and Christianity", and all Christians know that the concern of the true Church is not with this world.[1] But an application to the State for mitigation of the rigour of the law was necessary for several reasons. The Church, though not of it, is nevertheless in this world, and the existence of a social and public function of religion was an axiom accepted among the most heretical of the Dissenters.[2] Thus some public relationships with the State there must be. Again, it was felt that toleration was, and must be, the work of the State, because no established exclusive church, unless forced to do so by the sovereign civil power, could willingly admit of anything so contrary to its own natal principle. The lesson behind the rebuff received by Blackburne and the Clerical Petitioners seemed to be chiefly this: that Dissenters should turn from recriminating the Church to supplicating the State. Establishment was the sin of the State and toleration its repentance.[3] The stimulus to political thinking derived from this change of sphere is obvious, but even without it the Dissenters, from the widespread conviction among them that the rights of

[1] *Vindication*, 16. Cf. Mauduit, *Case*: "the exempting of their preachers from penalties and the entitling of their laity to honours are very different things", 13.

[2] Cf. Priestley, *Letter of Advice*, 1773, "Christianity expressly requires a public profession of important truths", 447. "Real religion is undoubtedly calculated to promote the happiness of society", etc. Towers, *Letter to Nowell*, 1772, 206.

[3] "It was", as Priestley wrote later, "the liberality of the State in spite of the Church." *Familiar Letters*, 176.

second dissenting failure in 1773, which made 'Nature' the first ally of English Dissent. Both as a piece of literature and as a controversial work, it ranks with Furneaux's *Letters to Blackstone* as one of the two ablest performances in the literature of Repeal. It surrounds the events of 1772–3 with an atmosphere that can only be described as political romanticism.

In *Arcana*, the whole movement and its apologetics are summarized in a single sentence of Aristotle: "that only can please which accords with Nature." But Robinson's interpretation of the key-word was hardly Aristotelian. Nature, he felt, when applied to religious belief, was valuable chiefly as an embodiment of the works and will of God: a pattern and measure for the truth of men's theories and the righteousness of their acts. As such, Nature carries an authority even more primary than revelation itself, for it is in the light of Nature, Nature as created not Nature as corrupted, that we should interpret revelation. "In everything", writes Robinson, "Nature is the standard, Nature is the critic, Nature is the comment after all."[1] Religion is a matter of primary principles; it is woven into that elemental creed of the 'dictates of Nature' to which all men subscribe. Christianity is an address to these primary principles: it is at its truest and best when most in accordance with them. If we particularize, it is at once apparent why those who appeal for religious liberty cite 'Nature' as their justification, seeing that "jurisprudence is perfect as it fits the nature of man, and universal toleration in

[1] *Arcana*, 78.

matters of conscience is a tendency towards that per-fection".[1]

Thus, in the particular case of subscription to certain Articles under the compulsion of civil penalties, the law of England is clearly at fault, since it does not satisfy the essential demands of human nature and personality. Nature glories in diversity. Among men are to be found a thousand differences of character and circumstance, of desire, of understanding, of material and spiritual wealth, yet upon them all the law attempts to enforce a code of beliefs, although the magistrate must be fully aware that human invention is incapable of producing any thirty-nine Articles upon which any thirty-nine men could exactly agree. It is not contumacy, but necessity, that makes this so. Uniformity of belief among men is no more possible than physical uniformity, and the only result of attempting to enforce it is to transform what is a physical impossibility into a moral injustice. Revela-tion affords no better justification. "The idea of uni-formity is neither the idea of a philosopher nor of a Christian",[2] because Christianity, more than anything, is founded upon the right of private judgment, a right which no state, whatever its origin, can violate: a right too essential to personality to alienate, too precious to barter for any other advantage. The magistrate, having no claim in nature to control conscience, has no claim to do so as a magistrate, because civil society, in so far as it forms a human association at all, is a moral and not a sentimental union.

[1] *Arcana*, 9.   [2] *Ibid.* 32.

Even if the diversity in Nature did not defeat an act of uniformity, the composition of the human understanding would render its enforcement impossible. In the *Arcana*, as in Furneaux's *Letters*, there is a detailed and extended argument, drawn from the psychology of mental conviction. Conviction can be produced only by the submission of evidence, because "religion is seated in the heart of man and conversant with the inward principles and temper of the mind",[1] a region far remote from temporal commandments. Robinson is more explicit. Belief has three constituents: an object, a proposition representing it, and "an operation of an intelligent being assenting to that representation"—assenting not on the precept of the magistrate, but because he sees the agreement of the proposition with its object. "Belief or assent is an after operation of the mind, fixed by the God of Nature as immutably as the parts of the body are", and no human legislation can enforce what the Supreme Legislator has written in the code of Nature.[2]

No man has an appointed mission as defender of truth; that was the contention of the Applicants of 1772–3. They agreed with Locke that truth would do well enough if left to shift for herself. Truth was, they thought, a developing content: it thrived best when most

[1] *Letters to Blackstone*, 36–7, 42.
[2] *Arcana*, 96–8. His psychological "doctrine of proportion", which "would unroost every human creed in the world" and under which "all like the celestial bodies, will roll on in the quiet majority of simple proportion, each in his proper sphere, shining to the glory of God the creator", is to be found in his *Reflections on Christian Liberty*.

challenged and once found could never be lost. "Truth has claims", wrote Priestley, "that require only to be seen and known, in order to recommend itself to the acceptance of all mankind."[1] "I rather think", wrote Furneaux, "the free exercise of the human understanding, without any bias from interest, would tend very much to promote both the purity and progress of religion."[2] A man's beliefs, too, lie outside the province of the State. The dissenting publicists were never tired of insisting upon the supremacy of the State within its own sphere, a political dogma to which they had recourse more and more in the controversies after 1773. They employed it, at first, against Warburton's free alliance, to show that the Church was, after all, only a privileged slave and not an equal partner. In later years state-absolutism was upheld as the only means of destroying religious privilege and civil disability. In dissenting political theory the State appears, though not always consistently, in all the scarlet and splendour of earthly sovereignty, and dissenting religion professed itself to be "so far from setting up an *imperium in imperio*, that it leaves no *imperium*, no supremacy, indeed no power at all in society, but that of the civil magistrate".[3]

But the sovereign's power is limited to behaviour: it does not extend over opinion. Human law is concerned with overt acts: it does not concern itself with principles. Neither in religion, nor in morals, can the magistrate hope to assess tendencies; his legitimate province is

[1] *Free Address*, 1771, 237.
[2] *Letters to Blackstone*, 46.   [3] *Ibid.* 175–6, 212.

confined to their effects.[1] If he tries to control religious conviction, it is but a second circle of error into which he has been cast by the original error of an establishment. An establishment can be justified only as a provision made by the governor of a state for advancing the knowledge and practice of religion and virtue, but even then, the utmost means allowed by natural justice is peaceful persuasion. Stronger measure once permitted, an establishment becomes "a powerful corporation, full of such sentiments and passions as usually distinguish these bodies: a dread of innovation, an attachment to abuses; a propensity to tyranny and oppression". An act of uniformity consecrates a reign of religious privilege. Who, asked the Applicants, can regard the system of religious liberty prevailing in some parts of North America, without admiring it: can see Presbyterianism established in Scotland and still believe that truth reigns in Anglican England: can see the minority Church established in Ireland, and still maintain, with Warburton, that the Establishment exists as an expression of the rights of the majority?

For in the ultimate analysis, the Dissenters felt, it was, as Furneaux wrote, an issue between right and expediency. The right was all on their side, and who, in so candid an age, could question the expediency of mitigating such ungenerous and outmoded laws, or could oppose such 'innovation' in negation of the principle of the Reformation itself?[2] Encouraged in the possession

[1] *Letters to Blackstone*, 59.
[2] Towers, *Dialogue on Subscription*, 1772, 278.

of so extended and cogent a body of theory, they approached the legislature in a spirit of fantastic confidence. To this overblown optimism was added that fatal preoccupation with 'mankind' which blighted so many of the schemes of that fruitful century. "The right of all parties of Christians to a full toleration being seen, owned and legally settled", wrote Joshua Toulmin, "that of Jews, Deists and Mahomedans will, of course, be the next object of enquiry."[1] The established powers had yet to discover the heresy called Jacobinism.

Thus the Dissenting Application to Parliament of 1772 was born in haste and hope. Immediately after the rejection of the Clerical Petition, those dissenting ministers who had heard the debate, and who had interested themselves in the closing scenes of that movement, resolved that so favourable a time should not be lost. A meeting was called of the recognized London ministers of the three denominations. They numbered, in all, ninety-five, and of these ninety-five, seventy obeyed the summons. The movement was essentially metropolitan, originating with and conducted by the ministers of the London congregations; an unfortunate peculiarity in that it stressed, once again, the distinction between the town and the country Dissenter. It was announced that time was too short to consult the views of the country brethren, in that every moment lost would diminish the effectiveness of the appeal, but behind this official haste lay a dread of revealing the doctrinal feuds in the Interest itself: a dread which the events of

[1] *Two Letters*, 82.

1773 fully justified.[1] A number of provincial ministers do, however, seem to have been privately sounded. Certainly, the London meeting never doubted its representative character.[2] Its numbers were small but respectable, and it was thought that to appeal to the legislature on quantity rather than on quality would leave a prejudicial savour of intimidation. With one dissentient voice, the seventy passed a resolution, "that the taking off the subscription required of Protestant Dissenting ministers and the obtaining relief of tutors and schoolmasters are very desirable and important objects: that application should be made to Parliament for these purposes: and that a committee should be chosen to manage the affair, with power to summon the general body, as they should see occasion."[3] A distinguished committee of fifteen was chosen which contained, among others, Israel Mauduit, Andrew Kippis and Samuel Wilton. It was decided to ask the legislature for a revision of the laws relating to subscription, and a declaration of faith in the Scriptures, as the word of God, was composed and submitted as a substitute.[4]

[1] Mauduit, *Case*; postscript, 54–8. Serious charges against the London Committee together with the whole case of the Calvinist opposition are in *Remarks on the Postscript to the Case of the Dissenting Ministers*. Anon. London, 1772.

[2] Kippis, *Vindication*, 91–2.   [3] Mauduit, *Case*, 57.

[4] "I A.B. declare, as in the presence of Almighty God, that I believe that the Holy Scriptures and the Old and New Testaments contain a revelation of the Mind and Will of God, and that I receive them as the rule of my faith and practice." Mauduit, *Case*, 37. The idea of such a declaration owed something to Blackburne; cf. *Confessional*, 361.

The Application, following swiftly and unexpectedly upon the Clerical Petition, caused something of a panic among the Established clergy, but they were taken too much by surprise to offer much public opposition. The debate, like the movement behind the bill itself, was "very warm though short". On 3 April it was introduced by Sir Harry Houghton, one of the firmest friends of English Dissent, and once again Newdigate headed the opposition, describing Presbyterianism as the resolute foe of monarchy. But the House showed itself disinclined to listen to his historical forebodings, or to those of his solitary ally, Sir William Dolben. Many who had voted against Blackburne and Lindsey, distinguished themselves in the cause of the Dissenters.[1] Constantine Phipps thought that "the Dissenters had always proved themselves a free, loyal and dutiful body and their request was very different from that of the Clerical petitioners".[2] Burke could find no danger to either Church or State in the measure, and heartily supported it. The first reading passed with only two dissentient votes. Sir William Dolben opposed the second reading in April, but to no better purpose. The House professed itself, with Montagu, overjoyed that the Dissenters "proceeded upon the large and comprehensive plan of Mr Locke", and voted the second reading by 70 votes to 9.[3] 'Candour' could have hardly dared hope as much.

By now the Establishment had awakened to the urgency of the moment, and in the Lords the measure

---

[1] Belsham, *History*, v, 374.
[2] Hansard, vii, for the debate.   [3] *Ibid.* vii, 438.

met with a very different reception. A month of precious time was consumed in the passage between the two Houses. Chatham introduced the bill on 19 May 1772, with an effective speech, which Richmond aptly seconded.[1] Shelburne and Lyttelton supported the bill. But the Establishment had had time to prepare its case, and the Bishop of Llandaff made the most influential speech in the Upper House. Despite their irrelevancy, he quoted, with terrible effect, passages from the works of Dr Priestley: a recital which Chatham himself punctuated with exclamations of "monstrous, horrible, shocking".[2] In the interval, too, in the bill's passage, opposition to it had become sufficiently articulate for the Bishop of London to claim that the majority of the Dissenting Interest itself opposed the measure. The bill was rejected by 102 votes to 29. "On the one side", wrote Kippis, "were truth, reason, justice, eloquence and religion; on the other—*pudet haec opprobria dici potuisse*—most of the temporal peers and all the bishops."[3]

Thus, an unhoped-for beginning had given place to an unlooked-for end, and all that the attempt of 1772 had brought to English Dissent was the discovery of a weakness in its defences and an active enemy within its gates. The weakness lay in the willingness shown by the Committee to offer a Scriptural test to the State. To offer any test was felt, by many friends of toleration, to be a sort of pandering to political unrighteousness. These

----

[1] Hansard, VII, 440. Chatham "showed as much oratory and fire as perhaps he ever did in his life".
[2] *Ibid.* VII, 441.   [3] *Vindication*, 54–5.

held, with David Williams, that "to offer a declaration of faith to the magistrate as a condition of liberty was giving up their first principle"—a view to which Priestley came round in later years.[1] The immediate excuse offered by the Applicants for this apparent inconsistency, was Priestley's own: that the application did not ask the magistrate for more than was his province to grant, because what was sought was simply relief from certain civil penalties. "It is only applying to the temporal powers for a temporal privilege."[2] This contention was extended by Joshua Toulmin into a remarkable piece of dissenting casuistry. "I do not see", he wrote, "that a submission to the requisites of a superior who has us in his power, is always an acknowledgment of human authority in matters of religion."[3] If the Dissenters publicly and in the form of an oath declare their belief in the Scriptures, they do so on an authority and evidence independent of, and distinct from, those of the magistrate; a *confessio fidei* very different from subscription to a human creed. Again, prudence and necessity require such a course, and, next to the dictates of conscience, the commands of prudence should be sovereign. This argument was ingenious, but tended more to underline than to conceal a suspicion which the proposed declaration had already aroused.

That suspicion was of its doctrinal implications, for it was in the doctrinal sphere that the whole movement was beginning to encounter its most serious challenge:

[1] Williams, *Essays*, 52-3.   [2] *Letter of Advice*, 474.
[3] Toulmin, *Two Letters*, 56-78.

a challenge from within. The challengers were aided by external allies in the shape of the Calvinistic Methodists, zealots of the Articles and enemies to all toleration of unorthodoxy, who opposed the application with a bitter enthusiasm.[1] Within the Interest itself opposition came from the same Calvinistic source: from those who were able faithfully to subscribe to the Articles, and were most unwilling that the immunity which they enjoyed under the Toleration Act should be extended to anti-Trinitarian heretics.[2] They loudly professed their dissatisfaction with the manner and matter of the application, and with the personnel of the applicants. They disliked the exclusively metropolitan character of the assembly, the composition of the committee, and the shock tactics employed.[3] To their activities, more than to any other single cause, is the failure of 1773 to be ascribed. The *regium donum*, too, the traditional Achan's wedge, was at its habitual work of division, creating the equivalent of a body of *King's friends* in the Dissenting Interest; swiftly widening the breach already opened by those who "trembled for the ark of God".

The vote of the House of Commons, however, still remained as an incentive to a second application and, before the year 1772 was out, the London Dissenters had determined to renew their attempt. Perhaps, it was

[1] Mauduit, *Case*, 11. Priestley, *Letter of Advice*, 480. Kippis, *Vindication*, 6.

[2] Aikin, *Annals*, 1, 130. Wakefield, *Memoirs*, 339. Priestley, *Letter of Advice*, 478.

[3] Wilton, *Apology*, 15. William Frend himself did not approve of the conduct of the London Assembly. *Peace and Union*, 110.

thought, some formula might yet be found upon which toleration could be extended; perhaps the infectious spirit of 'Candour' which seemed to reign in the Commons might yet penetrate to the Upper House. But whereas the attempt of 1772 had only to contend with vague alarms, the Application of 1773 was faced with an organized opposition of Calvinist Dissenters, well equipped with pamphlet and counter-petition. The result was remarkable, if hardly edifying. A general meeting of the London ministers took place in the Library at Red Cross Street on 23 December 1772: a meeting summoned to decide upon a fresh formula and, if possible, a better and more comprehensive one. "As your last bill", Priestley had advised them, "was an improvement on the former, let your next bill be an improvement on the last."[1] After a discussion of some hours, it was resolved that "an application to Parliament for the removal of the subscription required of Protestant dissenting ministers, and of obtaining relief for tutors and schoolmasters, be renewed on *the common principle of liberty*, should friends advise, and if it be judged proper by a majority of the members of this body".[2] Four days later, a representative of the Calvinist opposition was allowed to state his case against renewal of the Application, but no change was made in the resolution. In the meantime, the situation of the Applicants was becoming embarrassing. There had been no substantial change of personnel either in Assembly or in Committee, and this

[1] *Letter of Advice*, 1773, 442.
[2] Wilton, *Apology*, 10.

second omission to consult the country Dissenters was excused on the grounds of previous mandate and the superiority of quality over quantity in such affairs; an excuse even less convincing than the plea of pressure of time had been in 1772.[1] These difficulties grew. No sooner was the resolution of 23 January made public, than the Calvinist opposition printed a sheet of reasons against renewal of the Application, signed by thirteen of its most prominent members. The sheet attracted much attention. When Houghton asked leave of the Commons to bring in a bill for the relief of Protestant Dissenters, a member announced that he would oppose it, because at the door of the House he had been handed a printed paper containing objections to the bill on the part of the Dissenters themselves.[2]

On 22 February 1773 leave was given to introduce the bill. The month was hardly propitious, for on the following day the House refused by a large majority to consider the abolition of university subscription.[3] The first reading, which Newdigate allowed to go unopposed, was carried on 2 March, and 10 March was fixed as the date for the second reading.[4] On 3 March, the counter-petition of the Calvinist Dissenters, signed by both clergy and laity, was received and read to the House. It declared the counter-petitioners "well satisfied with the

---

[1] Toulmin, *Two Letters*, 64.

[2] Hansard, XVII, 759. Wilton, *Apology*, 3. The sheet declared "we are neither afraid nor ashamed to declare, that we believe the doctrines of the Articles to be both true and important", 22–3.

[3] Hansard, XVII, 742 *et seq.*

[4] *Ibid.* XVII, 759 *et seq.*

present mode of qualification, prescribed in the Act of Toleration", and begged to be heard by counsel before the second reading.[1] By 10 March, however, no counsel had appeared, and the second reading passed by 87 votes to 34. But the counter-petitioners had found a spokesman in Sir William Bagot, who, on the motion on 17 March that the House go into Committee upon the bill, delivered a long and sounding warning upon the perils to Christianity implicit in it. He compared it with the Clerical Petition: however much they might differ in appearance both were similar at bottom and both "detrimental to the doctrinal parts of Christianity".[2] But if the counter-petitioners had found an advocate in Bagot they had, by repercussion, given one to the Applicants. The romantic sensibility of Edmund Burke revolted against such a spectacle of ungenerous bigotry. To the Calvinist petitioners he could say only "arrangez-vous, canaille". Fragmentary as it is, his speech towers in its solid magnificence over the dreariness of Newdigate and the paltriness of the petitioners. "I would have Christians united: I would have them join in every attempt to crush the powers of darkness and trample under foot the foe of God and Man. Like a mother tender to her children, I would have the Church, with wide extended arms, clasp to her bosom her believing sons, not by unnatural austerity, repudiate her offspring and tempt them to seek ease in the harlot lap of infidelity." The issue before the House did not embroil

[1] Hansard, xvii. Disney, *Catalogue*, 7.
[2] Hansard, xvii, 767.

Establishment with toleration but concerned the justice of their cause who, tolerated themselves, refuse toleration to others. "I may be mistaken but I take toleration to be a part of religion."[1]

The third reading took place on 25 March. In the interval, several petitions against the bill had been received.[2] Before the final reading, the counsel for the counter-petitioners, Robert Chambers, LL.B., Vinerian Professor of Law at Oxford,[3] was heard. His brief, chiefly a diatribe against anti-Trinitarians, had no great effect. But his appearance had. Ninety years after the death of Locke, in a century in which no one doubted that philosophers should be kings, the most enlightened government in the world found itself treated to the strange spectacle of one party of Protestant Dissenters employing the Vinerian Professor at Anglican Oxford, to oppose the extension of toleration to another party of their co-religionists. It is difficult to say whether the amazement or the disillusionment was the greater. The bill passed by 65 votes to 14, but 'Candour' was dead.

On 2 April, despite the efforts of Richmond, Mansfield, Camden, Shelburne and Lyttelton, the Lords rejected the bill by 86 votes to 28; a rejection which surprised no one. In the Church of Tucker, Toplady, and Francis Wollaston, one alone of the bishops, Green of Lincoln,

---

[1] Hansard, XVII, 778 *et seq.*

[2] From ministers and congregations in Liverpool, Bolton, Exeter, and Gloucester.

[3] Toulmin, *Two Letters*, 104. Hansard, XVII, 787. He complained that one effect of the bill would be to deprive the petitioners of £500 a year under the great Coward Charity.

had been found to support the measure.[1] The whole business of the Application had failed decisively and spectacularly, and its failure coincided with the growing alienation of the Dissenting Interest from the Crown, to leave the 'spirit of the age' at a discount. Various explanations of the disaster were given by its subsequent apologists. Some hinted that opposition came "from the very summit of power": others said that all the show of liberality had only been an election trick on the part of the administration. But the central cause of failure was, undoubtedly, the undreamed-of divisions and animosities within the Dissenting Interest; a state of disunion which rendered a suspicious precipitancy in the Application imperative. The best that could be said for English Dissent was that it had twice secured the vote of the House of Commons in its favour, but it had done so at the heavy price of a complete surrender of its hopes in 'Candour'. One lesson was palpable: without unity in the Interest, it was hopeless to expect any substantial achievement. "Our unanimity", wrote Toulmin in 1774, "is our bulwark",[2] and in order to secure that unanimity any fresh application would have to be based on an even wider and more comprehensive principle than "the common principle of liberty"; would have to sound some universal chord in harmony with all mankind. That necessity once grasped, the drift towards the

[1] "Green, Green", said George III, "he shall never be translated", and he never was. Tucker did not approve of the bill. *Letters to Kippis*, Gloucester, 1773, 51.
[2] *Two Letters*, 84.

rights of man had begun and England's Revolution was envisaged.

For the time being the cause had to wait for fresh principles and a new confidence. The immediate reaction was a disgusted apathy. "Let the great and filthy streams take their course", wrote David Williams, "let us withdraw into some retired corner and cultivate some deserted spot in the manner we best approve",[1] and, though few followed this romantic counsel of despair, the years after 1774 heard little of dissenting ambitions. But once again events were combining to deceive observers. The great happenings of these years: liberty triumphant in America, liberty soon to dawn in France, played the same deceptive part which 'Candour' and the Clerical Petition had done, and if they seemed incentives on a far vaster scale than those of 1772, the character of the dissenting claims could show a corresponding amplification. A wider basis, a more universal appeal: some transcendent principle which could carry all before it; this and this only, it was felt, was the condition of success. "Cancel therefore", Priestley had written in 1773, "the obnoxious name of Christian and ask for the common rights of humanity",[2] and so swift since that date had been the drift towards the Rights of Man that when, in 1779, the Toleration Act was amended in a fashion which satisfied many of the grievances of the Applicants of 1772–3, it passed hardly noticed and barely welcomed. Already the publicists of the Interest were

[1] *Essays*, 47.   [2] *Letter of Advice*, 1773, 442.

committed to a greater quest.[1] What in Joshua Toulmin's *Letters* had been a simple plea for unity within the Interest had become, by 1789, a plan for a vast organization of the unprivileged of every kind: of Jews, Protestant Dissenters and Catholics, united upon the common ground of the rights of man and citizen, and the animation of 'Candour' had been swept away before the surging optimism of the French Revolution.[2]

Had such a combination of the unprivileged ever come into being in the critical times of 1790 and after, the history of England might have been very different. The attempt to realize the scheme failed, not from lack of advertisement, but because the Catholic 'leaders', men like Geddes, Englefield, Petre and Joseph Berrington, were in much the same position as the Rational Dissenters: prominent at the head of a body which by no means acknowledged their leadership. "Bigotry still lives", wrote Joseph Berrington in 1787, "prejudices flourish and the constitution of intolerance seems almost as vigorous as ever",[3] and nowhere was this observation more clearly confirmed than within the Dissenting Interest. The pamphleteers' charge of responsibility for the Gordon Riots was not without a symbolic truth. Blackburne and Hollis had been one in their belief that Popery was spreading, and many an advertisement in the press warned England of this menace to civil liberty

[1] Belsham, *Memoirs of Lindsey*, 67.
[2] MSS. *Letters* (D.W.L.), Millar to Lindsey. Capel Lofft, *History of the Test Act*, 42. Disney, *Catalogue*, 21.
[3] *Address to the Protestant Dissenters*, 46.

and the Protestant religion.[1] The tone of Kippis, Towers and Furneaux becomes uniformly harsh at the mere mention of the word 'Popery'.[2] Dr Lardner trembled to see the growth of the Church of Rome. Dissenters were prominent critics of the Quebec Act of 1774, as establishing Popery and arbitrary government within the Empire.[3] Savile's Act of 1778, which freed Catholics from some of the more shameful penal laws of 10 and 11 William III, was denounced from more than one dissenting pulpit, a dissatisfaction which the city mobs echoed in more practical fashion.[4] During the applications of 1787–9 it was contended by many dissenters that a removal of the sacramental test would always leave the declaration against Transubstantiation to exclude the Papists. "They knew", wrote a Catholic pamphleteer in 1789, "how the prejudices of many stood against them, and fancied their own tawny complexion might seem blanched in proportion to the additional smut they could lay on ours."[5] It was only a minority among the Protestant Dissenters; only men of the widest sympathies, ministers such as Priestley, laymen such as Percival, who were able to see the milk-white hind without the horns

[1] Cf. *St James' Chronicle*, 1 January 1766. Blackburne, *Hollis*, 1, 297; 11, 707.

[2] Cf. Kippis, *Example of Jesus Recommended*, 23: "so superstitious, so idolatrous, so wicked and so monstrous a system...."

[3] Cf. Towers, *Letter to Johnson*, 180, 188.

[4] "Associations were formed to oppose popery by mechanics and manufacturers in Glasgow, Edinburgh and other towns: the weavers of Renfrew and Paisley displayed a peculiar zeal against the doctrines of Anti-Christ." Bisset, *Burke*, 11, 32.

[5] Berrington, *Rights of Dissenters*, 1789, 22.

and hoofs of the arch-enemy. Priestley, though personally convinced that Popery was on the point of an apocalyptic and picturesque eclipse, never tired of asking in his publications for toleration for Catholics, as for all men, especially in their natural right to educate their children as they would. Dissenters, he thought, cannot consistently claim for themselves what they would deny to Papists, and clamour for justice while they violate that golden rule of the Gospel "do as you would be done by". The indignity of such inconsistency disgusted him. "It is cowardly to kick an old and dying lion."[1] In an interesting letter to Berrington, Priestley voices his hope of a nationwide combination of Dissenters to demand the repeal of the Test and Corporation Acts. But Priestley was always an exception.

In asking the repeal of the Test and Corporation Acts, the Dissenting Interest had abandoned the limits which the movement of 1772–3 had specifically set upon its activities. In 1779, the Toleration Act, that "imperfect Magna Carta of the Dissenters", had been modernized and made more comprehensive, but forgetful of all its previous declarations, a general meeting of deputies of the three denominations at Red Cross Street on 5 January 1787, with Edward Jeffries in the chair, decided unani-

[1] Cf. *Free Address*, 1780. *Reply to Blackstone*, 222. Priestley wrote to Lindsey in 1770: "As far as I can recollect I was singular in my opinion concerning the Toleration of Popery. Mr Aikin, I know, was against me." *Memoirs*, 113. Percival wrote in 1787: "an Englishman ought to blush at the severity of the Penal Statutes against the Papists." *Memoirs*, cxxvi. Berrington, *Address*, 1787, 44, 59.

mously to apply to the legislature for repeal of the Test and Corporation Acts.[1] The language of this new demand was far more political and universalist than the phraseology of the 'Appeal to Candour' had been. "The grievance from which the Dissenters seek relief", wrote a pamphleteer of 1789, "is a *civil* and not an *ecclesiastical* oppression: they complain of being injured as *citizens*, of being wronged as *Englishmen*, and all they ask is a restoration of their civil rights."[2] The efforts of opposition interests to deflect the question once more on to doctrinal ground were, this time, unsuccessful. The issue remained political, and grew more so with the increasing urgency of the demand. When the cry of heresy was at last raised, it was against political heresy: against, not Arians and Socinians, but Jacobins. The character of the controversy also changed. The publications of 1787–90 have less philosophical interest, becoming more intensely partisan in tone, dictated in a feverish enthusiasm which in 1772 would have been despised as extravagance.

In a word the new demand was for a full and free citizenship: for an equal status for all in the organization of the State: for the abolition of the reign of privilege. It was the same demand, in another guise, which the Dissenting Interest was everywhere putting forward in the movement for representational reform, for the abolition of the slave trade, for rational commercial life. The Test and Corporation Acts, as Dissenters saw them,

[1] *Rights of the Protestant Dissenters.* Priestley, *Works*, XXII, Appendix.
[2] *Half an Hour's Conversation...on the Test Laws*, 1789, 2.

perpetrated a double iniquity in imposing not only a
test on holders of office, but a sacramental test, in blas-
phemous combination against rational justice and
Christian revelation. "If it be thought requisite to
break through the eternal law of Justice, by depriving
the Dissenters of their rights as citizens, why must the
awful institution of the sacrament be made the instrument of the wrong?"[1] It is the sacred and rational duty
of all Christian assertors of the Rights of Man to destroy
such injustice and such unrighteousness.

The situation of English Dissent under the Test and
Corporation Acts was complex and full of inconsistencies.
Before the Evans judgment, it had been impossible to
plead nonconformity, still held to be a crime, against a
civic election: a disability easily exploited by an un-
scrupulous corporation. After Lord Mansfield's judgment, the position was this. Under the Corporation Act
if a man was elected to a corporate office and did not take
the sacrament within twelve months of his election, his
office became voidable, provided he was prosecuted
within six months of this period. If no prosecution took
place after six months he was left in peace. The Test Act
was infinitely more formidable. There was no limit of
time to its enforcement. It extended to all offices, civil
and military,[2] and the penalties incurred under it were
heavy: deprivation of office, a fine of five hundred

---

[1] *Half an Hour's Conversation...*, 1789, 5. George Walker com-
plains of the use of the sacrament as "a key to unlock the temple
of Plutus" in words reminiscent of Cowper's lines, *Plea*, 31.

[2] "Not even a bug", wrote a pamphleteer of 1787, "can be
destroyed within the purlieus of the royal household but by the

the *laisser faire* of men like Priestley, arose from the
extension of the Test Act to cover all positions in the
Bank of England and in the Russia, South-Sea and East
India Companies. Prominent as they were in the commercial life of the country, the sacramental test debarred
the Dissenters from any active part in these enterprises.[1]

There was a widespread conviction among the Dissenters of the futility as well as the iniquity of these
laws. Not only were they a violation of the supreme
right to freedom of conscience and an impious degrada-
tion of a holy rite, but in addition they completely
failed to achieve their object. Their only effect was to
exclude the conscientious in favour of the most depraved
characters, a debasement which the clergyman officiating
at the sacramental test was practically helpless to prevent.
In no other country was such a test exacted, and its
repeal could have no ill effect upon the Established
Church. So long as it continued, Dissenters would be
marked with a badge of infamy, deprived of their natural
rights and denied the rich and full life which every
citizen expects to enjoy in the State. And all this injustice, the Dissenters contended, was due to an accident
of history. The Test and Corporation Acts had originally
been directed not against Protestant Dissenters but
against Roman Catholics, and it was to preserve the
liberties of England that the Dissenting Interest had
submitted to the sacrifice. Now was the time; this

---

[1] *Case of the Protestant Dissenters*, 1787, 5. This was the official
'case' published by the Jeffries Committee. The Test Act was
thought by some to cover the Censors of the College of Physicians.

was the generation to repay a debt of so long standing.[1]

But co-ordination was still lacking in the dissenting forces. There was no active opposition, certainly, as there had been in 1773, but the Committee of 1787 was no more a representative body than its predecessors had been, and the country Dissenters showed all their habitual apathy to this unsolicited metropolitan leadership. Such internal criticism as there was came from those who, while not denying the rightness of the cause, doubted if the times were propitious, or whether civil gain might not be religion's loss.[2] But for eyes straining after them, there were many signs of the fitness of the times for the attempt. In America, the new republic guaranteed complete toleration. A pamphleteer of 1787 felt that the Declaration of the State of Virginia respecting religious liberty was worthy to be written in letters of gold. At home, too, the election of 1784, in which the Dissenters stood solidly by Pitt and the King to the discomfiture of Fox and North, had shown how fraternal their relations with the Establishment might be.[3] Besides, the Applicants had been endowed with a golden

---

[1] Priestley, *Sermon on Conduct of Dissenters*, Birmingham, 1789, 394.

[2] *Letter to the Deputies*, London, 1787, 15–16, 20, 23. Cf. *Dissenting Gentleman's Answer to the Reverend Mr White*, 1748, on the Test Act: "tho' I think this law to be a most unrighteous restraint upon us and an undoubted violation of our natural Rights, yet I am far from being persuaded that its Repeal would be of the least service to our Interest as Dissenters."

[3] In the 1784 election "the Dissenters, catching the Contagion, shook hands with Jacobites and high-churchmen." *Right of Protestant Dissenters*, 204.

phrase from oracle Paley, who had professed himself in favour of 'complete toleration'. Not all the Dissenters were so confident as their leaders,[1] but if misgivings persisted, they were quietened in an optimism which felt a quickening in the rhythm of the world and a new hope, not in kings or bishops or ministers, but in the goodwill of fellow citizens.[2] The attempt, it was believed, was certain to succeed because "the Dissenters are invited to it, by as opportune a concurrence of circumstances as could reasonably be expected ever to occur in the dispensation of Providence".[3] It mattered little if the old cry had again been raised against republicans and levellers; indeed the liberal sentiments of dissenting politics would profit by having public attention drawn to them. "Delightful spectacle", exclaimed Wakefield, "to see Christianity and Liberty such inseparable companions."[4] "I would exhort ye then, my countrymen", urged Samuel Catlow, "to rouse your native spirit, to assert the rights of men and Britons, and to exhibit in the face of the world that it is your determined resolution to attempt by every means, the recovery of your ancient privileges and to place yourself in a respectable situation among your fellow citizens."[5] The faith of 1787 was expressed less in 'Candour' than in propaganda.

---

[1] Cf. Percival, *Memoirs*, col. 11.

[2] Cf. "Let not the Protestant Dissenters put their trust in Kings, ministers or prelates; but let them confide in the justice of their cause and the generosity of their fellow citizens." *Right of Protestant Dissenters*, 207.

[3] *Ibid.* 201, 207.   [4] *Address*, 7.

[5] *Address to the Dissenters*, 1788, 13–14. Could all Britons be

It was decided that the attempt to secure repeal of the Test and Corporation Acts should be by motion and not by petition. On 28 March 1787, Henry Beaufoy, himself a member of the Establishment, brought in the bill, in a speech which illustrated the strength of his declared conviction that he was "addressing the most enlightened men of the most enlightened age".[1] He was an advocate not in an ecclesiastical but a civil cause; indeed, the only possible justification for retaining such legislation as the Test Act was that it involved the security of the State itself. That security and that of the Church were in no way imperilled by the proposed repeal. The wealth of the Dissenters, their stake in the country, the nature of their application all combined to prove that there was nothing anti-monarchical or levelling, 'nothing of disestablishment' about the motion. The Dissenters were only asking for rights which, self-evidently, should be theirs. "Every man has a right to the common privileges of the society in which he lives, and among these common privileges a capacity in law of serving his sovereign, is undoubtedly one of the most valuable." Their claim was not the right to be chosen, but the right to be eligible. Reason of state is a limited extenuation. "Considerations of general good can never justify any invasion of civil rights that is not essential to that good", and clearly *general good* is for the Dissenters' cause, not against it. Upon these

sufficiently animated even the "sons of the Establishment...should clasp us to their bosoms as the Friends of Mankind and the Assertors of Nature's equal rights." 17.

[1] Published Debate of 1787. London, Stockdale, 6. Also Hansard, xxvi, 780–832.

grounds he moved that the House should go into committee upon the bill; Sir Harry Houghton seconded.[1]

The opposition was led by Pitt and North. North
defended the Test and Corporation Acts as part of the
fundamental law of the realm, as "the corner-stone of the
constitution which should have every preservation". To
repeal these acts would be a piece of iconoclastic
temerity, contrary to the happy experience of a century.[2]
From North such sentiments were to be expected, but
many a Dissenter regretted his vote of three years earlier
when Pitt rose to defend the established order on the
grounds of expediency. It was inexpedient, he thought,
to deprive the Legislature of the exercise of a discretion-
ary power so long invested in it, and impossible to
separate the ecclesiastical and political liberties of the
country.[3] The argument was a century old, but new in
that it represented the first use against the dissenting
cause of 'reason of state' in avowed opposition to
admitted right. The division showed that the motion
had been rejected in its first stage by 178 votes to 100.[4]

That rejection in itself should have been forewarning

[1] Debate, 1–39.

[2] Debate, 45, 48. Sir James Johnstone, on the other hand, said:
"that he should vote for repeal because he thought that religion
which was the cheapest, was the best, and he, for his part, wished to
go the cheapest road to Heaven which was, he said, by the road of
the Church of Scotland", 52.

[3] Debate, 53. Priestley speaks of the horror of the Dissenters at
Pitt's attitude. The Establishment dedicated an edition of Sherlock's
works to him—a grim reward. Heywood, *High Church Politics*, 1792,
13.

[4] In the debate Dolben quoted Priestley's famous gunpowder
analogy. In December 1787 a grace to remove degree-subscription

enough. Even more significant, perhaps, was the absten-
tion of Burke, both from participating in the debate and
from voting.[1] The *damnosa hereditas* of the Great Rebellion was beginning to revenge itself on a century-distant
posterity. But the Applicants seemed rather stimulated
than discouraged by failure. Their faith in the goodwill
of the country at large grew stronger during the year
which followed. "I am truly concerned", wrote Percival
to the Bishop of Llandaff in September 1787, "that
religious liberty has still so many opponents both in our
Universities and in Parliament"; but he was solitary in
his fears.[2] On 8 December 1787, three hundred and
three Dissenters dined together at the London Tavern,
and heard Price preach an excellent sermon on repeal.[3]
A new application was decided upon and again its
conduct was entrusted to the Jeffries Committee. On
8 May 1789, the month in which the States-General met
in Paris, Beaufoy repeated his motion of two years
earlier. The debate on this occasion was far more impassioned, a fitting prelude to the great agitation of 1790.
Beaufoy was insistent upon the natural rights of the Dissenters. "They complain", he said, "of being injured as
Citizens: of being wronged as Englishmen."[4] The merits
of the Applicants were not to be judged from the conduct
of a few individuals but from the settled political tenor

was brought in, William Frend playing a prominent part, but it was
defeated. Dyer, *Life of Robinson*.
   [1] Bisset, *Burke*, II, 231.   [2] *Memoirs*, CXXVII.
   [3] MSS. Letters, Fysche Palmer.
   [4] Published Debate of 1789, Johnson, London, 1789, 5. Also
Hansard, XXVIII, 1-41.

of the Dissenting Interest. The spirit of their general conduct was admirable, and yet Dissenters were still excluded "from rights which they hold by a higher title and claim by a superior authority than any which civil government bestows".[1] For the Test Act he could not express condemnation strongly enough. "If in the records of human extravagance or of human guilt, there can be found a law more completely destructive of all respect for the Church and all reverence for religion, I will give up the cause."[2]

Lord North replied with an equally animated reiteration of his previous opposition. If the motion were renewed again and again, he declared, he would always hope to reject it again and again.[3] He agreed that it was not a religious but a civil issue: not a matter of persecution, but of the rights of self-defence, since it was evident from history that the cause of the Church was the cause of the State.[4] Wyndham also opposed the motion: he thought that religious legislation should become "part of the constitution of the country".[5] William Smith, Member for Norwich, restated the Dissenters' case: redress was asked "as a matter not of favour but of justice".[6] Fox, unable to resist the attraction of natural rights, made a powerful speech in favour of repeal. "No human government", he was sure, "has a right to enquire into men's public opinions, to presume that it knew them or

---

[1] Debate, 12.　　　　　[2] Debate, 31.
[3] Debate, 37.　　　　　[4] Debate, 46.
[5] Debate, 94.
[6] Debate, 53. A Dissenter prominent in the Dissenters' cause. His portrait is in the St Andrew's Hall, Norwich.

to act upon the presumption."[1] The motion failed, but by the small majority of 122 votes against 102, and the failure was quickly forgotten before the happenings upon the Continent; before the miracle of the Lord raising up liberty out of the land of despotism and Popery. A new confidence, sudden and deep as a quickly drawn breath, filled the Applicants. Repeal now seemed a certainty; a matter of days or weeks. "The period", wrote Berrington, "cannot be distant: France has set the example."[2] The parable of the third estate acting in unison was not wasted. "Babylon", wrote Fysche Palmer to a friend, "is surely hastening every day to her overthrow. The wily, timorous, episcopal minister Pitt will not be able, I trust, to withstand the united force of the Kirk, the Catholics and the Dissenters."[3] In an atmosphere of fierce excitement, among men convinced that they were midway through the eve of a political and social millennium, England's Revolution began its brief existence.

Controversially the issue was reduced to its simplest terms: the rights of man against the rights of the State: natural justice against social convention. In a publication which Gilbert Wakefield and Fox considered the most able work on the subject, George Walker enumerated

[1] Debate, 70. Among the Supporters of the Bill were Barré, Philip Francis, Sir Watkin Lewes, John Sawbridge and Sheridan.

[2] Berrington, *Rights of Dissenters*, 1789, 66. He thought, as a Catholic, "that all dissenters from the National Church are entitled to every civil right which that Church enjoys", 61.

[3] To Millar. MSS. Letters [D.W.L. Folio 46]. "God", wrote Wakefield, "created men to be free and happy and will soon make them so." Wakefield, *Cursory Reflections*, 1790, 24.

the principles of Dissent as chiefly two: a belief "that political society is for the good of all, that protection and accessibility to all the advantages and privileges of a citizen, are the rights of a citizen, and that responsibility for civil allegiance is the only condition of this right", and a conviction "that Religion is not within the juris- diction of the magistrate; that it is the unalienated property of every individual, for which he is answerable to God alone; and that no difference of religious faith and worship, ought to exclude a citizen from one of those rights or privileges which he claims on the grounds of the preceding principle."[1]

The first is the claim to the *carrière ouverte aux talents* in its fullest expression, a claim to be found on the lips of all dissenting publicists in 1790. They repeated it with the affectionate wonder of men who have come suddenly upon a great discovery. For them this right is not only a negative article of natural justice; it possesses in addition a positive function in the organization of government, and a moral function as a constituent of political obliga- tion. "It is a natural, inherent right of the subject", wrote a pamphleteer of 1790, "to expect appointment to an office under government, when qualified by abilities and inclination to serve the state, and ministers of state betray their trust when they do not, according to the

---

[1] *The Dissenter's Plea.* Birmingham, 1790, 3. The British Govern- ment should not represent the Church but "all free sons of Britain", 10. Cf. "...tous les citoyens étant égaux à ses yeux, sont également admissibles à toutes dignités, places et emplois, selon leurs capacités, et sans autre distinction que celle de leurs vertus et de leurs talents." *Droits de l'homme et du citoyen*, 1789, Article VI.

best of their judgment, employ such men", for when they do not "the link that mutually binds the state and the subject, is broken asunder."[1] Against this right of the individual, the Establishment opposed a rival right: the right of the State to select its own instruments in obedience to the dictates of self-preservation. This right of the State was the constant theme of the resolutions passed by the numerous meetings of the Established clergy and of other bodies that preceded the debate of 1790. "That every society has a perfect right, inherent in itself, to prescribe the terms on which its members can be admitted to places of trust and power and, consequently, that no individual can have a right inconsistent with that public right" was the unanimous resolution of the clergy who met at Sion College, London, on 13 February 1790.[2] The State's supreme right is founded in self-preservation. The Rights of Man, for which the Dissenters contend, have no real existence. The only existing rights are the rights of citizens, that is to say, social rights created by the State, and conditioned by its sovereign will. But the controversy was not only a pitting of right against right: it was also the clash of two property conceptions. The right which the Dissenters upheld, they represented as an 'unalienable property' of human nature; a 'property' inseparably bound up with human personality, deprived of which no man can be truly called either spiritually or materially free. Thus government is an 'estate' held by the magistrate, not in

[1] *Letter to a Friend on the Test Act*, London, 1790, 9.
[2] *Resolutions of the Clergy*, 4.

freehold but in 'trust' for the governed. The 'estate' and its properties are "committed to the governor by all, to be returned to all, in the way of equal protection and equal favour, whose equal services and equal merits support an equal claim".[1] To this contention, as to the major one, the Establishment replied with a different inference from the same premises: the sovereign magistrate holds the 'estate' in the free-est of freeholds, dispensing it with the advice of his ally the Church.

Against the second principle in the Dissenters' claim, the principle which would separate Church and State in province and in kind, the Establishment produced, with monotonous regularity, the Alliance of Church and State, the alliance of equals for common utilitarian ends. But the old story was fast wearing thin. It had outlived its day, and Warburton's reckless squandering of political coin had brought his posterity into a poverty difficult to disguise. The Alliance remained, however, as a useful platitude, fit for a clerical meeting and even for the House of Commons. George Walker thought that the whole theory was founded on a confusion of two very different things; a confusion of the Anglican Church with religion in the abstract.[2] That there is a natural alliance between human nature and religion he was the last to deny, but only the wildest misuse of analogy could transform this bond into a justification of the existence of the Establishment, and still less of laws which violated a man's natural rights. The Church reinforced

---

[1] Walker, *Plea*, 18.   [2] *Ibid.* 9.

its case by identifying itself with the Constitution, and placing the Test Laws in a safe refuge amidst the unchanged and unchangeable Revolution Settlement. A writer of 1790 brought the statute forth as fundamental law: "the Test Act is part of the Constitution and that in the higher and stricter sense of the term and, consequently the repeal of it will be a material change in the Constitution."[1] A meeting of Anglican clergy in 1790 resolved by a large majority "that the Corporation and Test Acts give strength and permanency to our excellent constitution, and ought to be transmitted unimpaired to the latest posterity".[2] To destroy these monuments of departed wisdom, it was urged, would be to upset the sacred balance by increasing the power of the 'popular part' of the Constitution, seeing that all Dissenters are notoriously republicans.[3] To this the Dissenters replied in kind that the Church was a disreputable relic of sixteenth-century despotism, reproducing all the slavish principles of the Tudors. The Test Act was a "tool of arbitrary power".[4] One of Priestley's foremost objections to both the Establishment and the Test Act was the parliamentary corruption which they made possible.[5]

But although the cry of 'the Church in danger' echoed through England in newspapers, in pamphlets, in corporation and county meetings in the early months of 1790, disestablishment never really became a general

[1] *Political Observations on the Test Act*, 1790, 5.
[2] *Resolutions of the Clergy*, 29.
[3] *Political Observations*, 49.
[4] Wakefield, *Cursory Reflections*, 9. Capel Lofft, *Test Act*, 8.
[5] *Familiar Letters*, 194.

demand, still less a practical issue.[1] The French Revolution infected the established order in England with a certain fear of social, and a real terror of ecclesiastical levelling, but to English Dissent it came more as a stimulant than an inspiration. As Fox claimed, and claimed truly in the debate of 1790, the situation in France had not produced the agitation in England.[2] There was nothing in the attempt of 1790 which was not implicit in those of 1787–9. However enthusiastic their references to events in France might be, however much they might reprint and quote the speeches of Rabaut-Saint-Étienne and Clermont-Tonnerre, a large number of Dissenters believed in the necessity of some established church or churches in every nation; a belief inseparable from their conception of the social function of Christianity. What was new was their far wider conception of the nature of toleration; a conception which the Establishment could not but regard as a new-fangled and menacing innovation. This novel conception arose from a logical development of that positive duty of toleration, first articulated by Locke, but so grown by 1790 that it had come to reject the very name of 'toleration' as too narrow and cringing a description.[3] This wider interpretation called for complete liberty, not as a state-

[1] "Our very faith", wrote Walker of the Church, "forbids us even to wish her own downfall but with her own will." *Plea*, 18.

[2] Fox's Speech, Debrett, 1790, 34.

[3] Cf. *Address to the Opposers*, 13. "Complete convalescence is no longer convalescence but Health, and complete Toleration is no longer toleration but Liberty." In Johnson's *Dictionary*, Toleration was defined as "an allowance given to that which is not approved"

created privilege, but as a right to be demanded. "Toleration", wrote George Walker, "is but an invidious term and springs out of abuses which do no credit to human nature or to religion. It is a mistaken idea that toleration is a grace and favour: it is the restoration of a right which ought never to have been violated: it is, on the part of the State, the concession of a wrong that ought never to have been committed."[1] This was also a view common to Price and Paine.

New, too, in its intensity was the desire of the Applicants to abolish all wills in the State save one. Never before, perhaps, have sincere members of a church shown such willingness to submit themselves to Caesar. They demanded the proud submission of citizenship. "We would be considered", they wrote, "as children of the State though we are not so of the Church."[2] "It is not a contest for power between Churchmen and Dissenters, nor is it as Dissenters we wish to enter the lists: we wish to bury every name of distinction in the common appellation of citizen."[3] They desired the complete secularization of political man; free voluntary churches in a free sovereign state; a clean sweep of all privilege, of all rule of saints or saintly corporations. They were sure that righteously exercised sovereignty could be a tremendous force for righteous

[1] Walker, Plea, 21.
[2] Address to the Opposers, 9.
[3] Ibid. 16. "We look forward to the period when the name Dissenter shall no more be heard of than that of Romanist or Episcopalian, when nothing shall be venerable but truth and nothing valued but utility." 41.

reform, and in the sovereignty of the people, directed by justice, they saw a Divine blessing, a sort of political testament and salvation: "the pole star", as Robert Hall termed it, "that will conduct us safe over the ocean of political debate and speculation: the law of laws: the legislator of legislators".[1]

The Church, despairing of philosophy, fell back upon the mob, and the practical opposition to repeal it succeeded in arousing, easily redressed a balance which was beginning to swing against the apologetics of Sherlock and Warburton. The English mob had always shown itself peculiarly susceptible to the warnings of history, and in 1790 the old story of 1649 was enlivened by the comparatively new story of dissenting activity in the American Rebellion.[2] Bishop Horsley declared, in a much-quoted opinion, that "the principles of a Nonconformist in religion and a republican in politics are inseparably united", and no amount of demonstration to the contrary could diminish the popularity of this pronouncement. The Church had called them 'republicans', the mob had agreed and 'republicans' the Dissenters remained until the progress of events made 'Jacobins' a more modish form of vituperation. Much of the bitterness and hatred

---

[1] *Freedom of the Press*, 1793, 131.
[2] Cf. *Jack and Martin*, 1790:

> "Yet when our transatlantic friends
> Contrived for great and glorious ends
> Their Independence to assert,
> We backed their cause with hand and heart,
> Nor left it till their parent's yoke
> From off their neck they piecemeal broke."

in English politics during the last ten years of the eighteenth century had their origins in the agitation for and against repeal. The party alignment of 1790, however, had other aspects than that of the Church against the sectaries. In one sense, it was the struggle between those who believed in the Rights of Man, Fox and Capel Lofft no less than Priestley and Paine, and those who did not. In another, it was the old feud of the Commercial Interest allied with the Dissenters, against the Landed Interest and the Establishment.[1] There was much talk, too, of emigration to France, where religious liberty prevailed, should the application of 1790 fail, and England was warned of the peril to her commerce of a widespread dissenting secession.[2]

Once again the Dissenters decided to join battle with the Test and Corporation Acts; once again they acted and wrote like men who have absolute surety of victory. This continued optimism in the face of continual defeat can only be understood or explained in one way: by an appreciation of the wholly exceptional character of the early years of the French Revolution: by remembering

[1] See especially *Observations on the Conduct of the Protestant Dissenters*, for this aspect. Cf. 23–4.

[2] *Case*, 1787, 8, for America. A pamphleteer of 1790 writes: "the distance from France is short, the climate desirable, the necessaries of life reasonable, the expense of removing trifling and the consequence of it might, perhaps, prove fatal to the prosperity of England." *Observations on the Origin of the Test Act...by a Dissenter*, London, 1790. Tom Paine says: "soon after the rejecting of the Bill for repealing the Test Law [1790], one of the richest manufacturers in England said in my hearing 'England, Sir, is not a country for a dissenter to live in—we must go to France'." *Rights of Man*, 69 note.

the innumerable hopes which rose and fell with it, the thousand frustrations which it consoled. "The minds of men", wrote a pamphleteer, "are in movement from the Borysthenes to the Atlantic...Liberty, here with a lifted cross in her hand and the crucifix conspicuous on her breast: there led by philosophy and crowned with the civic wreath, animates men to assert their long forgotten rights."[1] Certainly, in 1790 the dissenting cause commanded a unanimity and an attention it had never aroused before. In addition, however, to an optimism almost mystical in its intensity, the Dissenters had at least one concrete incitement to action. On 21 October 1789, the 'Junior Council' of Nottingham sent a public letter to the Mayor, William Smith, pointing out, professedly without malice, that he had not yet publicly received the sacrament and that, if he did not do so, they would feel themselves "obliged to enforce a law which they think founded in wisdom".[2] A prosecution against him was entered at the King's Bench in the following January.[3] The affair attracted considerable attention, and almost simultaneously the

[1] *Address to the Opposers*, 1790, 31–3. *Observations on the Origin and Effects of the Test Act*, London, 1790, 32–3. See also 21: "every principle therefore, of duty, a regard for the Constitution, the example of other nations, the conduct of our government respecting Ireland, sound policy, the principle of Christianity of doing as we would be done by, public justice and the inalienable rights of man, all conspire to establish the propriety and necessity of restoring to the Dissenters their civil rights." The same optimism is in Wakefield, e.g. *Cursory Reflections*, 2.

[2] Wakefield, *Address to the Inhabitants of Nottingham*, London, 1789.

[3] *Country Curate's Observations*, 14.

pamphlet war broke out afresh with unprecedented volume and virulence.[1] From thence the controversy overflowed into the public newspapers, a sphere in which the prominence of dissenting journalism gave their cause a distinct advantage. "The public prints", wrote a hostile observer, "are crowded with their advertisements, complaining of grievances which do not exist and demanding privileges to which they have no pretensions."[2] The Dissenters' cause had become the focus of political attention, second hardly even to the progress of the Revolution, because it was felt that the success or failure of repeal would be the first official intimation of the attitude of established England to the new France. "The consideration of the repeal of the Test and Corporation Acts", declared a speaker in the Guildhall debate of February 1790, "engrosses at this present time the serious thoughts of almost every denomination of people throughout the kingdom."[3]

Even more remarkable than this controversial prominence, was the movement towards association and counter-association. For the first and only time in the eighteenth century, the country Dissenters followed with equal enthusiasm the lead of the London Committee. There was a much discussed plan for a huge National Convention of Dissenters in London, a bogey

---

[1] Capel Lofft, *History*, 20. *Observations on the Origin*, 41. The *Gentleman's Magazine* (1790, II) says that in 1790 already nearly a hundred publications had appeared, whereas the attempt of 1772 produced only forty-two in all.

[2] *Observations on the Conduct of the Protestant Dissenters*, 15.

[3] *Gentleman's Magazine*, 1790, I, 267.

which, though it came to nothing, haunted the Establishment long after 1790. All over the country, large
meetings of Dissenters voted fervent resolutions which
were printed in the newspapers. Foremost among these
was a great meeting at Leicester of representatives of the
three dissenting denominations in the Midlands: in
Derby, Nottingham, Lincoln, Warwick, Worcester,
Salop, Stafford, Leicestershire and Rutland. William
Russell, a prominent Dissenter in Birmingham and
friend of Priestley, was treasurer and secretary.[1] The
meeting resolved that religious opinions lie without the
jurisdiction of the magistrate, and that "all subjects of a
state have a right to eligibility to civil honours". The
plan of a National Convention appealed strongly to the
meeting, which in its eleventh article resolved "that a
permanent mode of collecting the sense and uniting the
efforts of the whole body of dissenters of every denomination, so that they may have their representatives to
meet in London or elsewhere, and make proper application to the Legislature as circumstances may require,
appears to be a measure well calculated to promote the
desirable end above mentioned". A committee was
established for this purpose.[2] These meetings of Dis-

[1] Priestley (*Familiar Letters*, 212) notes the wide use made of the
Leicester Resolutions by enemies of repeal.

[2] *Principal Claims of the Dissenters considered*, Birmingham, 1790.
The idea persisted, cf.:

> "While thus we unite, our toast let it be,
> May every fashion of worship be free,
> And Catholic, Jew and Dissenter all yoke
> The Palm of Religion to Liberty's oak."
>
> *Cambridge Intelligencer*, August, 1793.

senters turned to good account the valuable technique learned in Wyvill's County Association Movement. Profiting by the proximity of a general election, they did their best to influence Members of Parliament in their favour; a practice which the Establishment roundly condemned and speedily followed.[1]

But the meeting of Dissenters of the West Riding of Yorkshire at Wakefield on 30 December 1789 had been rash enough to claim that the sympathy of many of the Established clergy lay with their cause, and the Church rose up in indignant repudiation of any such misplaced liberality. A counter-association movement was launched, led by the clergy of Leeds. Widely attended meetings followed among the clergy at Sion College, London, and of the archdeaconries of York, Chester and Cleveland.[2] All agreed to the existence of a right inherent in the State to lay a test upon its servants, and of a living alliance between the Church and the State in England. The Society for Promoting Christian Knowledge met at Bartlett's Buildings in London, on 1 February 1790. In its published resolutions, the Society trembled for the safety of Church and State should the Test Act

---

[1] *Country Curate's Observations*, 1790, 12. *Letter to Parliament*, 1790, 5. Fox's published speech of 1790, Debrett, 66. Bishop Horsley of St Davids sent a circular letter to his clergy (August 1789) telling them not to vote for the candidate who had supported the Attempt of 1787. "I hope I shall not have the mortification to find a single clergyman in my diocese who will be so false to his own character and his Duty to the Established Church as to give his vote to any man who has discovered such principles."

[2] *A Collection of the Resolutions passed at the Meetings of the Clergy, etc.* London, 1790.

be repealed, and returned "its warmest thanks to those upright members of the House of Commons, who, however divided in their general politics, have twice successfully united their virtuous efforts to resist the attempted innovation in the Constitution of the United Kingdoms"; a resolution which provoked a good deal of uncharitable comment from the pamphleteers.[1] The laity hastened to follow the example of the clergy in widely attended county meetings. "It is marvellous indeed", wrote Gilbert Wakefield, "if a numerous pack did not run together, helter-skelter when the lord-lieutenant blows his horn: a noisy rabble-rout, barking and yelping: 'the Church and the Constitution for ever': great is Diana of the Ephesians."[2] The Duke of Newcastle was particularly zealous. So was the Earl of Aylesford, who presided over a numerous meeting of the nobility, gentry and clergy of the county at Warwick on 2 February 1790.[3] This assembly declared the Established Church to be "an essential part of the British Constitution". Copies of its resolutions were to

[1] Nash, *Reply to Burke*, 82. *Resolutions of the Clergy*, 1790, 43. Coetlogon, *Test of Truth*, 1790, 26. Heywood, *High Church Politics*, 1792, 13. Heywood suspects the Society's association with the King of Denmark.

[2] *Cursory Reflections*, 10. In all there were twenty large meetings against repeal. Nash says: "You will judge then my surprise and indignation, when I discovered the Union of Priests with Corporations, of courtiers with 'country clowns' and of some turn-coat whigs with tories, to traduce Dissenters, decry philosophy, light, liberality, the rights of men and to embrace the Test Act with universal ardour as the main pillar of the Church." *Letter to Burke*, 15.

[3] *Resolutions of the Clergy*, 16.

be sent to Sir Robert Lawley and Sir George Shuckburgh, the county representatives in Parliament, and to be published in the London, Birmingham and country papers.[1] The resolutions of the Suffolk county meeting, later in the month, were signed by "upward of 1200 Gentlemen, Clergy and Freeholders".[2] Other county meetings took place in Nottinghamshire and Yorkshire. In addition many city corporations assembled for the same purpose. At the Maidstone meeting on 19 February 1790, the Mayor and principal inhabitants resolved "that we consider religious toleration and civil liberty to be equally the Rights of Man, but, at the same time, it is our decided opinion that the welfare of the State necessarily depends on the preservation of the Church, as it is at present by law established".[3] The meetings at Barnstaple, Southampton, Coventry, Bolton le Moors, Leicester, Gloucester and Tewkesbury were of much the same mind. On 11 February 1790, the Rev. C. E. de Coetlogon, Chaplain to the Lord Mayor, preached an alarmist sermon before the Lord Mayor, Aldermen and Sheriffs of the City of London against the proposed repeal.[4] On 25 February the Common Council in the Guildhall, despite the efforts of Joshua Toulmin, resolved "that a full free and perfect toleration in the exercise of religious

[1] *Resolutions of the Clergy.* The most popular newspapers for this purpose were *St James' Chronicle*, the *General Evening Post*, Woodfull's *Diary* and the *Morning Herald*.

[2] *Ibid.* 23.

[3] *Ibid.* 41.

[4] *The Test of Truth, Piety and Allegiance*, London, 1790, printed by order of the Common Council: he wanted to extend the Test Act to Members of Parliament.

duties, must be the wish and glory of every liberal mind; but to remove the bulwarks of our sacred constitution in Church and State by the repeal of the Corporation and Test Acts, would tend to produce that civil anarchy which at first pointed out to the Legislature the necessity of making such wise and salutary laws". The preceding debate was an admirable forecast of the greater debate which was to follow.[1]

One week later, on 2 March, Charles James Fox introduced the bill for the repeal of the Corporation and Test Acts.[2] The debate was a faint but unmistakeable echo of the furious uproar in the country. Fox's speech lasted nearly three hours. A believer in establishments, a communicant of the Church of England, he felt sincerely that he was speaking, not on behalf of a religious sect, but in the cause of all his fellow-believers in the rights of mankind. Religious and political tests are all absurd. The only reliable test, indeed the only test admissible to civilization, is the test of human actions. That test, it is true, had been applied, but unfairly in an attempt to collect a high-church party in England, and the Dissenting Interest as a whole was not to be judged from Dr Priestley's writings. In the theory of the Alliance he could discover only religious corruption and political slavery. "The Christian Religion is neither dictated by politicians, nor addressed to politicians nor cherished by

[1] *Resolutions of the Clergy*, 36. The best account of the Debate is in the *Gentleman's Magazine*, 1790, I, 267–364.

[2] Published Debate, London, 1790. Hansard, xxviii, 387–452. Published speech of Fox, Debrett, 1790. Published speech of Pitt, Stuart, 1790.

politicians."[1] He founded his case on right and right alone. Sir Harry Houghton seconded the bill, appealing not to the generosity of Parliament but demanding from it "the restoration of a right unjustly withheld". Fox's speech, like the debate which followed, was essentially a party speech of little philosophical interest, a tribute to the real and pressing nature of the question.

Pitt replied for the Establishment. Once again he upheld the interest of the State as the ultimate justification for the statesman. It was not toleration in itself which he opposed in the face of the Dissenters' demands. "I flatter myself that it is needless to assure them, that I should blush at resisting the claims of the Protestant Dissenters, if what they considered as *right* and *justice* were not at variance with the *public welfare*."[2] He complained of the attempt to influence members. It remained for Burke to lift the debate momentarily upon a higher level, though he soon fell back on to personal grounds and examples of individual conduct. Ten years ago he would have voted for repeal: to-day, confronted with the principles professed by the Dissenters, he could only oppose it. His speech was a synopsis of his *Reflections* published in the following November. As a boy he had always hated abstract principles and his silver

[1] Speech, 56. He had embraced the dissenting cause because he had discovered that its principles were perfectly consonant with those of 'Whiggism', 51.

[2] Speech, 17. In a footnote is inserted a scheme for welding the dissenting convention proposed by the Jeffries Committee into "one great and powerful phalanx for rescuing the rights of private judgment from violation", 28.

hairs had not taught him to love them better, "but of all abstract principles, abstract principles of natural right, which the Dissenters relied on as their stronghold, were the most idle because the most useless and dangerous to resort to".[1] More easily appreciated by the Commons was his denunciation of Samuel Palmer, Robert Robinson and Richard Price.[2] Amongst others, William Wilberforce was "decidedly against the bill".[3] Parliament had declared its opinion of the French Revolution: declared it in limited and unworthy language, but clearly and unmistakeably. When Fox, at the end of a long and hard debate, rose to reply to the House, the cause was irrevocably lost.[4]

The bill was defeated by 294 votes to 105: by a majority of 189. Throughout the country was heard a hymn of exultation and thanksgiving for deliverance from

---

[1] Hansard, xxviii, 434–5.

[2] Priestley wrote to Lindsey, 2 March 1790: "Mr Burke's conduct, I think, best accounted for by his leaning towards the Court and not to Popery." *Memoirs*, ii, 57.

[3] Hansard, xxviii, 445. Wakefield made much of this alliance personified of "politician Pitt and Rabbi Wilberforce". *Letter to Wilberforce*, 1792.

[4] Debate. A comparative table of votes in the Test Act debates is interesting:

Motion	Votes for repeal	Votes against
1736	123	251
1739	89	188
1787	100	178
1789	102	122
1790	105	294

Thus 1790 was the largest majority ever noted against repeal. Percival thought both repeal and abolition of the slave trade failed from "the spirit of the times". *Memoirs*, xxxvi.

French principles and Puritan levellers. "The great senate of the Nation", declared the *Gentleman's Magazine*, "unawed by any considerations held out to them, have asserted that Independence worthy of the representatives of a free people."[1] Amidst this triumph the indignant protests of the Jeffries Committee passed unheeded and unheard, while the clamour of the Church-and-King mob grew everyday more audible.[2] "Test Act 189" was chalked generously all over the houses of known Dissenters. The bells were rung in many Anglican steeples to the confusion of the Rights of Man. "A friend of mine", wrote Nash, "happening to pass through one of these ringing towns, asked a man on the road what the bells were ringing for? who answered 'that the Church and Dissenters had been to law and the Church had got the day'."[3]

But the passions which had been so deliberately aroused could not be calmed by the simple sedative of a parliamentary victory. The storm that had been gathering broke over Priestley's head. The Birmingham riots were a direct result of the counter-propaganda of the Repeal movement, and few Dissenters failed to realize their significance.[4] It was the beginning of a persecution that

[1] "For the glorious and decisive termination of this question", wrote the Rev. William Keate, "all the Established Church have great reason to be thankful." *Free Examination*, 1790, vi.

[2] The manifesto of the Committee of 19 May 1790 repels the accusation of republicanism and disloyalty: "We spurn with indignation at this charge." It is printed in the *Gentleman's Magazine*, May 1790, and Disney's *Catalogue*, 27.

[3] *Letter to Burke*, 65.

[4] "Although", wrote the Deputies in London to the Birming-

was to extend from the great Socinian himself down to every pitiful little ale-house blasphemer against the divinity of Church and State Established. Jerusalem had turned against the prophets. The Dissenters awoke from the shock of their defeat to realize how remote Repeal had always been. Some still remained who urged that the cause should not die down now that the Rights of Man had been so publicly defined, but the great majority of the Dissenters counselled patience and dignified acceptance.[1] The glorious optimism that had united all denominations was on the wane. "Be ye", a pamphleteer of 1790 had commanded, "the chariots of the British Israel and the horsemen thereof",[2] but there was a rising and guilty conviction that the Lord had turned away his face from Israel, offended at this obsession with worldly dignities, with states and the affairs of state. Henceforth the leaders among the Rational Dissenters would turn to the French Revolution for political salvation and be separated once again from the mass of the Interest. The Rights of Men, Citizens and Christians remained unacknowledged. In 1792 Fox failed to repeal the Act of William III against blasphemy. "Now", wrote a pamphleteer of 1797, "the Dissenters are farther from their point than ever and Mr Fox is not much nearer the Ministry." But by 1797 the Dissenting Interest had

ham Dissenters in February 1792, "in this instance the storm has fallen on you, we feel ourselves to have been equally within the aim of the spirit which directed it." *Gentleman's Magazine*, 1792, i, 566.

[1] *Address to the Dissenters of England*, 1790, 80. Wyvill, *Defence of Price*, 18.

[2] *Hint of Advice to the Protestant Dissenters*, 1790, 22.

fallen into its old state of atomistic schism, and the Prices, Priestleys and Wakefields of 1789 were scattered in prison, in exile and in the grave.

But in such measure as historical change is born of disillusionment, England's Revolution had not failed in vain. Like the Great Rebellion, it had created definition out of disaster. It had helped to sum up the forces of a hundred years into that crescendo of developing conflicts in which the eighteenth century ended. It left the Alliance of Church and State in detailed delineation to the critical eyes of a new age. It was a vital movement in the history of political philosophy because it revealed the process by which Christian liberties could be transformed into the Rights of Man. The process was psychological. The philosophy of Natural Right has been widely and rather unfairly criticized upon historical grounds, but its historical backing was always purely academic and secondary. "The Rights of Man" is not an historical but a psychological generalization, and is better expressed in its alternative formula "the rights of human nature". Such rights imply the requirements of human personality. Once men have taken the short step of investigation from the spiritual privileges of the Christian to the spiritual composition of the understanding, the transformation into Natural Rights is achieved.

In its concrete form England's revolution was an opening realization of the desirability of citizenship and for the established order victory did not bring peace. The Repeal movement had destroyed all institutional quietude. In England after 1790 there was the same sense of insecurity which haunted restored Europe after 1815. The brigands, as de Maistre called them, had all been hanged, but the road refused to regain its old comfortable safety. The Dissenters had traced a new campaign on the ground of their defeat and ahead of the Alliance lay, not Priestley and the Rights of Man, but Newman and the Oxford Movement. But above all and in direct negation of its purpose, England's Revolution had dethroned the philosophers. It was as though an unsuspected door had suddenly opened into the mansion of urbanity, diffusing everywhere an autumn sense of decay and disturbing sounds of change. In the strange new light the company within no longer recognized each other as "the most enlightened men of the most enlightened age".

significant and important. Their philosophy was an active preparation for a new age. The Dissenters had hardened their hearts against a State that had rejected them. Deeply and firmly established in the society of England, they formed a great, permanent undercurrent of dissatisfied criticism of the State of England. Their political philosophy demanded secularization and extension. They desired that the State should speak one language and one only: pure political language, without so much as an intonation of religion or romanticism. This mission of purification they engaged in with an almost religious zeal. Lay apostles of the secular State, they yearned to propagate the testament of citizenship in the broad, uncivic spaces of the old régime. Alongside this passion for secularization, went an individualism equally overgrown, but full of social potentialities for the nineteenth century. While the confirmed Alliance still held them without the civic pale, the Dissenters were busy preparing for a new heaven on earth, as remote philosophically from Rousseau as from Burke, in which men were to live, neither free in a common purpose of self-realization nor equal in the eternity of history, but as unfettered adventurers in a gray, predatory world of political and social *laisser faire*; the industrial state of nature. The Rational Dissenters did not live to see that day, but the changes consummated in their generation had perhaps been even profounder. "We have learned", wrote George Walker in 1790, "the liberality of these better times; perhaps it might be proved that we have greatly contributed to teach it." In his words can be heard the funeral oration over the grave of the Christian Commonwealth, and the sum of the social and political ideas of English Dissent between 1763 and 1800. If our subject holds another lesson besides this it is, perhaps, only the reiteration of what we already know: how much of what we call Political Philosophy is a camp-child born on the battlefield of Church and State.

BIBLIOGRAPHY

ABBEY and OVERTON. *English Church in the Eighteenth Century.*
AIKIN, JOHN. *Annals of George III.* 2 vols. 1816.
   Letters of a Father to his Son. 2 vols. 1796.
   Life of Howard. 1792.
AIKIN, LUCY. *Memoirs of John Aikin.* 1823.
Anti-Jacobin Review. Vol. I, 1798; vol. II, 1798–9.

BELSHAM, THOMAS. *Memoirs of Theophilus Lindsey.* 1812.
BELSHAM, WILLIAM. *Essays Philosophical and Literary.* 2 vols. 1791.
   History of Great Britain. Vol. V. Edition of 1805.
   Nature and Necessity of a Parliamentary Reform. 1793.
BISSET, ROBERT. *Sketch of Democracy.* 1796.
   Life of Burke. 2 vols. Edition of 1800.
BLACKBURNE, FRANCIS. *Memoirs of Thomas Hollis.* 2 vols. 1780.
   The Confessional. Edition of 1804.
BOGUE and BENNETT. *History of the Dissenters.* 4 vols. 1808.
BRIGHT, H. A. *Warrington Academy.*
BURGH, JAMES. *Political Disquisitions.* 3 vols. 1772–3.

Cambridge Intelligencer. 1793.
'CANDIDUS.' *Plain Truth.* 1776.
CHANDLER, SAMUEL. *Funeral Sermon for George II.* 1760.
CLAYDEN, P. W. *Early Life of Samuel Rogers.* 1882.

DALE, R. W. *History of Congregationalism.* 1902.
DAVIS, V. A. *History of Manchester College.* 1932.
DODDRIDGE, PHILIP. *Correspondence and Diary.*

DODDRIDGE, PHILIP. *Memoirs of,* by Job Orton.
DYER, GEORGE. *Memoirs of Robert Robinson.* 1796.
   Poems. 1802.

EDEN, WILLIAM. *Four Letters to the Earl of Carlisle.*
   1779.
ENFIELD, WILLIAM. *History of Philosophy.* 1791.

FLOWER, BENJAMIN. *Life of Robert Robinson.* 1806.
FOWNES, JOSEPH. *Inquiry into the Principles of Toleration.*
   1772. Edition of 1790.
FREND, WILLIAM. *Peace and Union.* 1793.
   Proceedings against. 1793.
FURNEAUX, PHILIP. *Letters to Blackstone.* 1771.
   Sermon on the Importance of Education. 1775.

Gentleman's Magazine. 1772; 1789–93.
GODWIN, WILLIAM. *Memoirs of Mary Wollstonecraft.*
   Edition by Clark Durant.
GREGOR, FRANCIS. *Works.* 1816.

HALL, ROBERT. *Apology for the Freedom of the Press.* 1793.
   Christianity Consistent with Love of Freedom. 1791.
HALLEY, ROBERT. *Lancashire, its Puritanism and Non-
   conformity.* Vol. II.
HANSARD. Debates, 1772–3, 1787, 1789, 1790. Vols.
   XVII, XXVIII.
HARTLEY, DAVID. *Argument on the French Revolution.*
   1794.
HORSLEY, SAMUEL. *Charges to his Diocese.* Edition of
   1830.

KENRICK, W. B. *A Nonconformist Family.* 1932.
KIPPIS, ANDREW. *Considerations on the Provisional Treaty
   with America.* 1783.
   Example of Jesus Recommended. Sermons. 1782.

KIPPIS, ANDREW. *Excellency of the Gospel as suited to the Poor.* 1777.
   Ordination Sermon. 1782.
   Sermon before the Revolution Society. 1788.
   Vindication of the Dissenting Ministers. 1773.
KNOX, VICESIMUS. *Essays Moral and Literary.* 1782.

LINDSEY, JAMES. *Funeral Sermon for Towers.* 1799.
LLANDAFF, WATSON OF. *Address to the People of Great Britain.* 1798.
LOCKE, JOHN. *Letters on Toleration.* Edition of 1813.
LUCAS, E. V. *David Williams and the Royal Literary Society Pamphlet.* 1920.

MARTIN, BENJAMIN. *Young Gentlemen's and Ladies' Philosophy.* 1758.
MAUDUIT, ISRAEL. *Case of the Dissenting Ministers.* 1772. Reply to Above. (Anon.)
M'CLAUCHLAN, H. *English Education under the Test Acts.* 1931.
MEDLEY, SAMUEL. *Life.* 1800.
MILTON, JOHN. *Of Education.*
MOLESWORTH, LORD. *Preface to Franco-Gallia.* 1721.
MORGAN, WILLIAM. *Life of Richard Price.* 1815.
MORRIS, J. W. *Biographical Recollections of the Rev. Robert Hall.* 1833.
MSS. (All MSS. in Dr Williams Library, London.)
   Account of Dissenting Academies.
   Catalogue of Books in the Caermarthen Academy.
   Inaugural Lecture of John Horsey at Northampton Academy. 1790.
   Letters of Blackburne, Toulmin and Wakefield.
   Letters of Fysche Palmer and Millar.
   Magazine. The Academical Repository.
   Minute Book of the Northampton Literary Society.
   Minutes of Hackney College. 1791.

Occasional Essays. 1809. (Newspaper Extracts, etc.)
ORTON, JOB. *Memoirs of Doddridge.*

Pamphlets, etc.
    Ambition and Conquests of France.
    The Conspiracy of Kings, by Joel Barlow. 1792.
    A Controversial Letter to Dr Price.
    A Dissenting Gentleman's Answer to the Rev. Mr White.
       1748.
    The Fall of British Tyranny. 1776.
    Letter to the Deputies of the Protestant Dissenting Congregations.
    Letter to Charles James Fox. 1793.
    Letter to Edmund Burke, by Lord Stanhope. 1790.
    Letter to John Bull from Thomas Bull. 1793.
    Letter to the People of England, by William Playfair. 1792.
    '*Look at the Last Century.*' 1790.
    Observations upon the Conduct of Protestant Dissenters.
       1790.
    Observations on Dr Price's Sermons. 1790.
    Pursuits of Literature, by T. J. Mathias. 1794.
    A Scourge for the Dissenters. 1790.
    Sermon before the House of Lords, by William Markham.
       1774.
    Sermon before the University of Dublin, by Thomas Leland. 1776.
    Sermon before the University of Oxford, by Miles Cooper. 1776.
    Thoughts on Government, by George Rous. 1791. (A reply to Burke.)
    Three Letters to the People of Great Britain, by 'Alfred'. 1785.
PARKER, IRENE. *Dissenting Academies in England.* 1914.
PERCIVAL, EDWARD. *Memoirs of Thomas Percival.*
PERCIVAL, THOMAS. *Moral and Literary Disquisitions.* 1789.
    Works. 4 vols. 1807.

PRICE, RICHARD. *Additional Observations.* 1777.
  Britain's Happiness in Full Possession of Civil and Religious Liberty. 1791.
  Discourse at Hackney. 1781.
  Essay on Population. 1780.
  Fast Sermon. 1779.
  General Introduction. 1778.
  Love of Our Country. 1789.
  Nature and Dignity of the Human Soul. 1766.
  Observations on the Importance of the American Revolution. 1784.
  Observations on the Nature of Civil Liberty. 1776.
  Review of the Principal Questions in Morals. Edition of 1787.
PRICE, RICHARD and JOHN HORNE TOOKE. *Facts.* 1780.
PRIESTLEY, JOSEPH. *Address to Protestant Dissenters.* 1774.
  Appeal to the Public on the Riots. 1792.
  Conduct of Dissenters. 1789.
  Considerations on the State of the Poor. 1787.
  Discourse on Death of Price. 1791.
  Disquisitions Relating to Matter and Spirit. 1777.
  Doctrine of Philosophical Necessity. 1777.
  Duty of Forgiveness. 1791.
  Essay on the First Principles of Government. 1771.
  Familiar Letters to the Inhabitants of Birmingham.
  Fast Sermon. 1793.
  Free Address. 1780.
  Free Address to Protestant Dissenters. 1771.
  Funeral Sermon for Robinson. 1790.
  General Appendix, vol. XXII.
  Heads of Lectures. 1784. Dedication.
  Lectures on History and General Policy.
  Letters.
  Letter of Advice to the Dissenters. 1773.
  Letter to the Author of Remarks. 1770.

PRIESTLEY, JOSEPH. *Letters to Burke*. 1791.
  Letters to the Inhabitants of Northumberland. 1801.
  Maxims of Political Arithmetic. 1798.
  Memoirs. Vols. I, II.
  Miscellaneous Observations on Education. 1784.
  Political Dialogue on General Principles of Government. 1791.
  Preface to the History of Electricity. 1767.
  Present State of Europe. 1794.
  Present State of Liberty in Great Britain and her Colonies.
    1769.
  Proper Objects of Education. 1791.
  Remarks on Blackstone's Commentaries. 1769.
  Sermon on the Slave Trade. 1788.
  *View of the Principles and Conduct of Protestant Dis-
    senters*. 1767.
      (N.B. For Priestley, J. T. Rutt's great edition of
    the Works, 25 vols. 1821, has been used.)
Protestant Dissenters' Magazine. Vols. I, II. 1794–6.

RAMSAY, DAVID. *American Revolution*. 1790.
REES, ABRAHAM. *Funeral Sermon for Kippis*. 1795.
Revolution Society, Correspondence of. 1792.
Revolution Society, Proceedings of. 1789.
ROBERTS, SAMUEL. *Love of Our Country*. 1745.
ROBINSON, CRABB. *Diary and Memoirs*. Edition of 1869.
ROBINSON, ROBERT. *Arcana*. 1773.
  Christian Submission to Civil Government.
  Christianity as a System of Humanity. 1779.
  Circular of the Eastern Association. 1776.
  Discourses. Edition of 1805.
  Essay on Liberality of Sentiment. 1784.
  General Doctrine of Toleration. 1781.
  History of Baptism.
  Lectures on the Principles of Nonconformity.
  Letters.
  Political Catechism. 1782.

ROBINSON, ROBERT. *Reflections on Christian Liberty.*
   Sermon on Becoming Behaviour. 1773.
   Sermon on Sacramental Tests. 1788.
   Slavery Inconsistent with Christianity. 1788.
        (N.B. For some of Robinson's Works, the col-
   lected edition of 1806 has been used.)
RUDKIN, OLIVE. *Thomas Spence.* 1927.

SACHEVERELL, HENRY. *Nature and Mischief of Prejudice.*
   Sermon. 1703.
SHEBBEARE, JOHN. *Answer to Queries.*
   Reply to Price. 1776.
SOMERS, LORD. *Judgements of Whole Kingdoms.* Edition of
   1710.
SOUTH, ROBERT. *Sermon on Education.*
SOUTHEY, ROBERT. *Essays.* 1832.
STEVENSON, JOHN. *Letters in Answer to Dr Price.* 1779.
STOKES, ANTHONY. *Desultory Observations on Great Britain.*

TOULMIN, JOSHUA. *Historical View.* Edition of 1814.
TOWERS, JOSEPH. *Dialogue between an Associator and a Well
      Informed Englishman.* 1793.
   Dialogue Concerning the Late Application to Parliament.
      1772.
   Letter to Rev. Dr Nowell. 1772.
   Letter to Samuel Johnson. 1775.
   Observations on Hume's History. 1778.
   Observations on the Rights and Duties of Juries. 1784.
   Oration at the London Tavern. 1788.
   Remarks on The Association of the Crown and Anchor.
      1782.
   Review of the Genuine Doctrines of Christianity. 1783.
   Thoughts on a New Parliament. 1790.
   Vindication of the Political Principles of Mr Locke. 1782.
        (N.B. For some of Towers' Works, the collected
   edition of 1796 has been used.)

TROELTSCH. *Social Teaching of the Christian Church.* Vol. II.
TUCKER, JOSEPH. *Four Letters on Important National Subjects.*
True Interest of Great Britain.

WAKEFIELD, GILBERT. *Address to Dr Samuel.* 1790.
    Address to the Inhabitants of Nottingham. 1789.
    Address to the Judges. 1799.
    Age of Reason. 1794–5.
    Cursory Reflections. 1790.
    Four Marks of Anti-Christ. 1788. (Against Warburton.)
    Letter to Wilberforce. 1792.
    Letters with Fox. Edition of 1813.
    Memoirs, vol. I, 1792, by himself.
    Memoirs, vol. II, 1804, by J. T. Rutt and others.
    Remarks on the General Orders of the Duke of York. 1794.
    Reply to Burke's Letter to a Noble Lord. 1796.
    Reply to a Letter. 1794.
    Reply to Llandaff. 1798.
    Sermon on the Peace. 1784.
    Short Strictures on Dr Priestley's Letters. 1792.
    Social Worship. 1792.
    Spirit of Christianity Compared with Present Times. 1794.
WARBURTON, WILLIAM. *The Alliance between Church and State.* Edition of 1741.
WHITE, JOHN. *Letters to a Gentleman Dissenting.* 1746.
WILLIAMS, DAVID. *Essays on Public Worship.* 1774.
    Lectures on Political Principles. 1789.
    Lessons to a Young Prince. 1791.
WILLIAMS, JOHN. *Life of Thomas Belsham.* 1833.
WYVILL, CHRISTOPHER. *Defence of Dr Price.* 1792.
    Political Papers. 6 vols. 1800.

YOUNG, ARTHUR. *Example of France, a Warning to Great Britain.* 1793.

SUPPLEMENTARY BIBLIOGRAPHY OF THE LITERATURE
OF TOLERATION, 1772–1790

1772–3

Bill for the Relief of Protestant Dissenters. Hansard,
XVII.

Debate on the Clerical Petition. Hansard, XVII, 246.

Debates, 1773: (*a*) On Subscription. Hansard, XVII, 742.
(*b*) Bill for Relief of Protestant Dissenters. Hansard,
XVII, 759.

TOULMIN, JOSHUA. *Two Letters on the Late Application
to Parliament*. London, 1774.

TUCKER, JOSEPH. *Letters to Kippis*. Gloucester, 1773.

WILTON, SAMUEL. *Apology For the Renewal of the Application*. London, 1773.

1787–9

BERRINGTON, REV. JOSEPH. *Address to Protestant Dissenters*. 1787.

Rights of Dissenters from an Established Church. Birmingham, 1789.

The Case of the Protestant Dissenters. 1787.

CATLOW, SAMUEL. *An Address to Protestant Dissenters*.
London, 1788.

Debate in Hansard, XXVI, 786–832.

Published Debate of 1787. Stockdale, London, 1787.

*Half an Hour's Conversation Between a Clergyman and a
Dissenter*. 1789.

*The Right of Protestant Dissenters to a Complete Toleration
Asserted*. London, 1787.

1790

An Address to the Dissidents of England on Their Late Defeat. London, 1790.

An Address to the Opposers of the Repeal. London, 1790. (By Anna Barbauld.)

COETLOGON, C. E. DE. *The Test of Truth.* Sermon. London, 1790.

A Collection of the Resolutions passed by the Meetings of the Clergy, etc. London, 1790.

A Country Curate's Observations. London, 1790.

Debate in Hansard, XXVIII, 387–452.

DISNEY, Dr JOHN. *An Arranged Catalogue of the Several Publications...Relating to...Repeal of the Test and Corporation Acts.* London, 1790.

Fox's Published Speech. Debrett, London, 1790.

HEYWOOD, SAMUEL. *High Church Politics.* 1792.

A Hint of Advice to the Protestant Dissenters. London, 1790.

HOBSON, Rev. JOHN. *Remarks on a Sermon by George Croft.* 1790.

Jack and Martin. A Political Diary. 1790.

KEATE, Rev. W. *Free Examination of Dr Price's and Dr Priestley's Sermons.* 1790.

A Letter to the Right Hon. Edmund Burke from a Dissenting Country Attorney. Birmingham, 1790. (By Nash.)

A Letter to a Friend on the Test Act. London, 1790.

A Letter to the Parliament of Great Britain, by a Member of the University of Cambridge. London, 1790.

A Letter to the Rev. John Martin, by No Reverent Dissenter. London, 1790.

LOFFT, CAPEL. *History of the Corporation and Test Acts.* London, 1790.

Observations on the Origin and Effects of the Test Act, by a Dissenter. London, 1790.

PALMER, SAMUEL. *A Vindication of the Modern Dissenters*. 1790.

Pitt's Published Speech. Stuart, London, 1790.

Political Observations on the Test Act. 1790.

The Principal Claims of the Dissenters Considered. Birmingham, 1790. (By Madan.)

Published Debate of 1790. London, 1790.

A Serious Address..., by a Layman. Birmingham, 1790.

The Spirit of the Constitution and that of the Church of England Compared. London, 1790.

WALKER, GEORGE. *A Dissenter's Plea*. Birmingham, 1790.

INDEX